Ecocentrism for Knowledge Management and Sustainability

Through theoretical-practical studies, this book explains the foundational concepts of ecocentrism, knowledge management, and sustainability and advances the understanding of how ecocentric paradigms can be leveraged for the process of knowledge management and knowledge creation, showcasing various applications of this practice and illustrating advantages and disadvantages of adopting an eco-centric approach. With a focus on the three themes of sustainability, knowledge management, and ecocentrism, this edited volume presents practical case studies from various organizational contexts, illustrating how sustainability-related practices make use of knowledge management to meet their business objectives from an ecocentric perspective and highlighting the transversal application of this approach to various types of contexts. The book also addresses cases of how post-industrial organizations of the 21st century are using knowledge management in advancing the Sustainable Development Goals with reflections on ecocentrism. There is practical, theoretical, and methodological content, making this valuable to researchers, academics, and advanced students in the fields of knowledge management, sustainability, organizational studies and strategic management.

David Israel Contreras-Medina is Research Professor at Universidad de Guanajuato, Mexico, and Member of the Mexican National System of Researchers.

Elia Socorro Díaz Nieto is Research Professor at Autonomous University of Queretaro, Mexico, and Member of the Mexican National System of Researchers.

Sergio Ernesto Medina-Cuéllar is Research Professor at Universidad de Guanajuato, Mexico, and Member of the Mexican National System of Researchers.

Noé Aguilar-Rivera is Research Professor at Veracruzana University, Mexico, and Member of the Mexican National System of Researchers.

Citizenship and Sustainability in Organizations
Series Editors: David F Murphy and Alison Marshall

Exploring how organizations and citizens respond to and influence current and future global transformations, this book series publishes excellent, innovative and critical scholarship in the fields of citizenship, social responsibility, sustainability, innovation, and place leadership in diverse organizational contexts. These contexts include commercial businesses, social enterprises, public service organizations, international organizations, faith-based organizations (FBOs), non-governmental organizations (NGOs), community groups, hybrids and cross-sector partnerships. The role of the individual as citizen may also be explored in relation to one or more of these contexts, as could formal or informal networks, clusters and organizational ecosystems.

Business Schools, Leadership and Sustainable Development Goals
The Future of Responsible Management Education
Edited by Lars Moratis and Frans Melissen

Smart Organizations in the Public Sector
Sustainable Local Development in the European Union
Hanna Godlewska-Majkowska, Tomasz Pilewicz and Patrycjusz Zarębski

Fair Trade and Sustainable Development
Dispersed Hybrid Markets
Magdalena Śliwińska

Social Sustainability and Good Work in Organizatiosns
Edited by Klarissa Lueg and Simon Jebsen

Ecocentrism for Knowledge Management and Sustainability
Theoretical and Practical Studies in the Post-industrial Era
Edited by David Israel Contreras-Medina, Elia Socorro Díaz Nieto, Sergio Ernesto Medina-Cuéllar and Noé Aguilar-Rivera

For more information about this series, please visit: www.routledge.com

Ecocentrism for Knowledge Management and Sustainability

Theoretical and Practical Studies in the Post-industrial Era

Edited by David Israel Contreras-Medina, Elia Socorro Díaz Nieto, Sergio Ernesto Medina-Cuéllar and Noé Aguilar-Rivera

Routledge
Taylor & Francis Group
NEW YORK AND LONDON

First published 2025
by Routledge
605 Third Avenue, New York, NY 10158

and by Routledge
4 Park Square, Milton Park, Abingdon, Oxon, OX14 4RN

Routledge is an imprint of the Taylor & Francis Group, an informa business

Library of Congress Cataloging-in-Publication Data
Names: Contreras-Medina, David Israel, 1979– editor.
Title: Ecocentrism for knowledge management and sustainability : theoretical and practical studies in the post-industrial era / edited by David Israel Contreras-Medina, Elia Socorro Díaz Nieto, Sergio Ernesto Medina-Cuéllar and Noé Aguilar-Rivera.
Description: New York, NY : Routledge, 2025. | Series: Citizenship and sustainability in organizations | Includes bibliographical references and index.
Identifiers: LCCN 2024012785 | ISBN 9781032731704 (hardback) | ISBN 9781032736037 (paperback) | ISBN 9781003465058 (ebook)
Subjects: LCSH: Knowledge management—Environmental aspects. | Management—Environmental aspects. | Sustainable development. | Environmentalism.
Classification: LCC HD30.2 .E24 2025 | DDC 658.4/083—dc23/eng/20240404
LC record available at https://lccn.loc.gov/2024012785

ISBN: 978-1-032-73170-4 (hbk)
ISBN: 978-1-032-73603-7 (pbk)
ISBN: 978-1-003-46505-8 (ebk)

DOI: 10.4324/9781003465058

Typeset in Galliard
by Apex CoVantage, LLC

Contents

Figures

Tables

Contributors

List of contributors by order of appearance:

David Israel Contreras-Medina, Universidad de Guanajuato, División de Ingenierías Campus Irapuato-Salamanca (DICIS), Departamento Arte y Empresa. Study Areas: Knowledge Management, Innovation, Sustainability.

Elia Socorro Díaz Nieto, Affiliated with ANFECA (Association of Universities and Schools of Accounting and Administration), Member AMET (Mexican Association of Labor Studies), Member of SNI 1 (National System of Researchers). Visiting Professor, Liverpool John Moores University, UK. Research lines: Knowledge Management, Competitiveness and Social Responsibility. Study Areas: Human Resources, Senior Management, Wine sector, Coffee Sector.

Sergio Ernesto Medina-Cuéllar, Universidad de Guanajuato, División de Ingenierías Campus Irapuato-Salamanca (DICIS), Departamento Arte y Empresa. Study areas: Agricultural Economics, Political Economics, Applied Economics.

Noé Aguilar-Rivera, Facultad de Ciencias Biologicas y Agropecuarias. Universidad Veracruzana. Study Areas: Environmental Management, Sustainable Development, Circular Economy in Agro-industries.

Verónica Cerroblanco-Vázquez, Facultad de Contaduría y Administración, Universidad Autónoma de Querétaro. Study Areas: Technology Management, Innovation.

Jessica A. Araujo Rodríguez, Division of Postgraduate Studies and Research, Tecnológico Nacional de México en Celaya, Celaya, Mexico. Study Areas: Image Analysis and Processing, Prediction Systems Development, Database Development, Implementation.

Coral Martínez Nolasco, Department of Mechatronics Engineering, Tecnológico Nacional de México en Celaya, Celaya, Mexico. Study Areas: Aeroponic Systems, Mechatronic Systems, Multispectral Image.

José A. Padilla Medina, Department of Electronics Engineering, Tecnológico Nacional de México en Celaya, Celaya, Mexico. Study Areas: Aeroponic Systems, Image Processing, Thermal Analysis.

Alejandro I. Barranco Gutiérrez, Department of Electronics Engineering, Tecnológico Nacional de México en Celaya, Celaya, Mexico. Study Areas: Greenhouses, Image Processing, Electric Vehicles.

Juan Prado Olivarez, Department of Electronics Engineering, Tecnológico Nacional de México en Celaya, Celaya, Mexico. Study Areas: Bioengineering, Electrical Impedance.

Juan J. Martínez Nolasco, Department of Mechatronics Engineering, Tecnológico Nacional de México en Celaya, Celaya, Mexico. Department of Electronics Engineering, Tecnológico Nacional de México en Celaya, Celaya, Mexico. Study Areas: Aeroponic Systems, Mechatronic Systems, Multispectral Image.

Alejandro Espinosa-Calderón, Tecnológico Nacional de México, Regional Center for Optimization and Development of Equipment (CRODE), Celaya, Guanajuato, Mexico. Study Areas: Digital Signal Processing, Electronic Instrumentation, Electronic Automation.

Héctor Juan Carlos López-Tapia, Tecnológico Nacional de México, Department of Electrical and Electronic Engineering, Celaya, Guanajuato, Mexico. Study Areas: Power Energy Converters, Renewable Energies, Microgrids.

Miguel Ángel Velázquez-Alejos, Center for Applied Innovation in Competitive Technologies (CIATEC), Leon, Guanajuato, Mexico. Study Areas: Technology, Innovation Management.

Esteban Aguirre-Reynoso, Tecnológico Nacional de México, Regional Center for Optimization and Development of Equipment (CRODE), Celaya, Guanajuato, Mexico. Study Area: Electronic Instrumentation.

Georgina Rico-Ojeda, Tecnológico Nacional de México, Regional Center for Optimization and Development of Equipment (CRODE), Celaya, Guanajuato, Mexico. Study Area: Project Management.

Saúl Fuentes-Reyes, Tecnológico Nacional de México, Department of Electrical and Electronic Engineering, Celaya, Guanajuato, Mexico. Study Areas: Battery Chargers, Storage Power Systems, CD-CD Power Converters Control.

María Catalina Rangel-León, Department of Arts and Enterprise, Universidad de Guanajuato, Salamanca, Guanajuato, Mexico. Study Areas: Technology-Based Companies, Entrepreneurship Ecosystems, Sustainable Businesses.

Abraham Olivares-Arriaga, i-Energy Natural Technology Inc., Salamanca, Guanajuato, México. Study Areas: Thermodynamics, Root Cause Analysis, Energy Diagnosis.

Sergio Cano-Andrade, Department of Mechanical Engineering, Universidad de Guanajuato, Salamanca, Guanajuato, Mexico. Study Areas: Thermodynamics, Sustainability and Energy Reliability, Heat Transfer, Fluid Mechanics.

Maria Emilia Camargo, Postgraduate Program in Postgraduate Program in Professional and Technological Education—Federal University of Santa Maria, RS—Brazil and Postgraduate Program in Intellectual Property Science—Federal University of Sergipe—SE, Brazil. Study Areas: Innovation, Knowledge Management, Sustainability, Structural Equation Modeling, Production Chains, Intellectual Property Science.

Aprígio Teles Mascarenhas Neto, Postgraduate Program in Intellectual Property Science—Federal University of Sergipe—SE, Brazil. Study Areas: Innovation, Structural Equation Modeling, Intellectual Property Science.

Walter Priesnitz Filho, Postgraduate Program in Professional and Technological Education—Federal University of Santa Maria—RS, Brazil. Study Areas: Technological Innovation, Stochastic Modeling.

Angela Isabel dos Santos Dullius, Postgraduate Studies in Professional and Technological Education—Federal University of Santa Maria, RS, Brazil. Study Areas: Stochastic Modeling, Intellectual Property Science.

Beatriz Lúcia Salvador Bizotto, Unifacvest University Center—Santa Catarina, Brazil. Study Areas: Innovation, Sustainability, Production Chains.

Angela Pellegrin Ansuj, Department of Statistics—Federal University of Santa Maria, RS, Brazil. Study Areas: Stochastic Modeling.

Leonardo Andrés Carvajal Alvarez, Doctorate in Technology Management and Innovation—PhD (c), Master of Administration (MBA), Electronic Engineering, Professional Studies and Advanced Training in Telecommunications; and Diploma in Blended and Non-personal Education. Affiliations: Partner-Director-Consultant at Global Synergy Ltda. Professor at Universidad Libre (Cali), Pontificia Universidad Javeriana (Cali), Universidad de Caldas (Manizales), among others. Member Colombian Association of Engineers (ACIEM), Valle Chapter (Vice President of the Board of Directors). Study Areas: Strategic Management, Technological Management, Projects, Technology Integration, Telecommunications, ICT.

María del Consuelo Gallardo Aguilar, Tecnológico Nacional de México en Celaya. Study Areas: Environment of Organizations, Organizational Management.

María Teresa de la Garza Carranza, Tecnológico Nacional de México en Celaya. Study Area: Organizational Behavior.

Salustia Teresa Cano Ibarra, Tecnológico Nacional de México en Celaya. Study Area: Prospective Studies of Organizational Performance.

Mónica Servín Cervantes, Tecnológico Nacional de México en Celaya. Study Area: Environmental Engineering.

Luis Miguel Contreras-Medina, Universidad Autonoma de Queretaro, CA bioingeniería básica y aplicada, división de investigación y posgrado, facultad de ingenieríaQuerétaro, Mexico. Study Areas: Electronic, Instrumentation.

Diana Victoria Melo-Sabogal, Universidad Autonoma de Queretaro, CA bioingeniería básica y aplicada, división de investigación y posgrado, facultad de ingenieríaQuerétaro Mexico. Study Area: Biotechnology.

Daphne Ojeda-Rodríguez, Universidad Autonoma de Queretaro, CA bioingeniería básica y aplicada, división de investigación y posgrado, facultad de ingenieríaQuerétaro, Mexico. Study Area: Biotechnology.

Guadalupe Esmeralda Contreras-Morales, Universidad Autonoma de Queretaro, CA bioingeniería básica y aplicada, división de investigación y posgrado, facultad de ingeniería, Querétaro, Mexico. Study Area: Biotechnology.

Margarete Luisa Arbugeri, Professor of the Master's Degree in Design for the Circular Economy at Instituto Superior Manuel Teixeira Gomes—ISMAT—Portugal and member of the Tourism Research Center at the University of Algarve—Portugal. Study Areas: Sustainable Finance, Financial and Non-financial Indicators, Social Innovation, Corporate Governance.

Margarita Schmitt Revilla, Independent Researcher. Study Area: Social Sciences.

Julia Pérez Bravo, Full-Time Professor-Researcher at the Autonomous University of Querétaro. Doctor in Government and Public Administration; Belongs to the National System of Researchers (SNI) Candidate Level, PRODEP Profile, Certified by the National Association of Faculties and Schools of Accounting and Administration (ANFECA) and by the National Certification Council (CONOCER), (ECO 217 Certificate); Belongs to the Mexican Association of Labor Studies (AMET), to the Editorial and Arbitration Committee of the Publishing House of the Single Union of Academic Personnel of the Autonomous University of Querétaro (SUPAUAQ), to the Academic Body Knowledge Management and Social Responsibility of the University Autonomous of Querétaro. Research Lines: Social Responsibility, Knowledge Management. Study Areas: Strategy Administration—Tourism Sector.

Martha Salvador Ledesma, Professor at the Autonomous University of Queretaro, Master in Administration with a Terminal Line in Senior Management; Degree in Business Administration; Higher University Technician in Marketing; Doctoral Student in Administration at the Autonomous University of Queretaro; Active Member of the International Network of Researchers INNOVARED, Innovation & Entrepreneurship. Study Areas: Sustainability, Circular Economy, Tourism.

1 Foundational concepts

An introduction to ecocentrism, knowledge management and sustainability

David Israel Contreras-Medina, Elia Socorro Díaz Nieto, Sergio Ernesto Medina-Cuéllar and Noé Aguilar-Rivera

Introduction

Since the beginning of times, numerous events have manifested in the universe that have created, modified, or eliminated various forms of life on the planet's environment over time, among which is the *Homo sapiens.*

Naturally, human beings have evolved together with other species of plants and animals in the environment, although with an emphasis on the development of the human being. The first interaction (and dependence) between humans and the environment dates back to the appearance of our first bipedal ancestor called "Lucy." This fact gave way to the appearance and application of knowledge under the need to adapt to the environment 4 Ma ago (Polanyi, 2012). This historical episode in which the universe, human life, knowledge and the environment came together could have been the precursor of the concepts currently known as ecocentrism, knowledge management and sustainability as they were represented empirically within an earthly universe.

Over time, the development of human beings became more evident. Possibly the most important milestone that was recorded was their conversion from nomadic to sedentary, lacking a stable place to live to settle in a place based on agricultural activity, giving way to the first civilizations, commerce and technology, favoring private property and the arrival of the industrial revolution (Sagasti, 2011; Servicio de Información Agroalimentaria y Pesquera, [SIAP], n.d.).

With the emergence of the first industrial revolution, productive activities reached another level, favoring the development of capitalism, modifying the production system and developing mechanized production (Universidad Nacional Autónoma de México [UNAM], 2017). This tendency began to be introduced into the organizations of that time; it established itself as a unidirectional and anti-systemic form of thinking where the priority was the economic development of the organizations.

DOI: 10.4324/9781003465058-1

The use of coal and fossil fuels on a large scale, the control of people's time, the release of waste into the land and water and even the perceived risk of greater contamination due to the management of technologies are some of the particular characteristics of this era and that until today there is concern about it (Ghosh et al., 2023; Calderón Ortiz et al., 2010; Shrivastava, 1995).

Given the risk of economic development being influenced, concern about a deteriorating environment was expressed during the Stockholm in 1972. This situation gave rise to the construction of the Brundtland Commission based on the definition of the term sustainability "as the satisfaction of the needs of the present without compromising the ability of the future generations to satisfy their own needs" interrelating the concepts of environment and society (Brundtland, 1987; Alfaro et al., 2014).

This book handles the concepts of ecocentrism that etymologically derives from the Greek oikos (house) and kentron (center), represented by the idea that everything in the natural world has intrinsic value and deserves moral consideration, based on the planet Earth as the house in which all creatures live (ten Have & Patrão Neves, 2021; Darnthamrongkul & Mozingo, 2020). Knowledge management theory, which locates public and private organizations of the 21st century with a vital role in articulating and amplifying knowledge (Nonaka, 1994), creating it, sharing it and managing green practices to achieve goals, describes studies linked with Sustainable Development Goals (SDGs; United Nations, 2015).

Therefore, achieving the goals and objectives of a common sustainable future, SDGs provide a methodological, conceptual, holistic and transversal framework that can guide decision makers in the formulation of strategies, public policies and actions for this future based on (1) addressing essential human needs and well-being, (2) managing climate change and economic stability and (3) sustaining biodiversity and ecosystem services (Leal Filho et al., 2020)

Nonetheless, Saxena et al. (2021) have discussed that there are numerous factors after the COVID-19 pandemic that represent challenges to achieving sustainability such as conceptualization, leadership, implementation and evaluation.

Regarding the book, the first part deals with a theoretical approach regarding:

- Ecocentrism paradigms, taking into account environmental aspects in decision-making, circular economy and investing in sustainable innovations, especially focusing on the green economy or bioeconomy, to recognize ecocentrism paradigms as ways of knowledge management for sustainability in the post-industrial organization in the 21st century, entitled: "Ecocentrism Paradigms as a Way of Knowledge Management for Sustainability in Post-industrial Organizations in the 21st Century."

- The advantages and disadvantages, as quality increases, ecocentric mindset and certifications, but also the problems for the update and applications of regulations based on the economic and infrastructure situation, to identify the advantages and disadvantages of knowledge management for sustainability from an ecocentrism perspective in post-industrial organizations in the 21st century, titled "Knowledge Management for a Posture of Ecocentrism and Organizational Sustainability."
- Theoretical concepts and tools to integrate sustainability via knowledge management, describing the primary, secondary and tertiary sectors in these terms, for exploring theoretical concepts and tools to incorporate sustainability via knowledge management in post-industrial organizations in the 21st century, titled "Theoretical Concepts and Generic Tools to Incorporate Sustainability via Knowledge Management Into Post-industrial Organizations in the 21st century."

The second part studies the SDGs:

- Zero hunger and clean water and sanitation, from the aeroponics' technique focusing on agricultural productivity and the minimum use of and recirculating of (water), to expose an empirical study for quantifying water consumption in aeroponic crops, proposing a prototype for allowing management to sell indoor greenhouses in post-industrial organizations in the 21st, entitled "The Importance of the Aeroponic Cultivation Technique in Sustainable Agriculture: A Study Carried Out With the Cultivation of *Phaseolus vulgaris L.* Var Opus."
- Affordable and clean energy, displaying a historical journey related to sustainable energy as photovoltaic, wind, hydroelectric and geothermal technologies, explaining its benefits but also the complications they have raised, to reveal a study of different technologies related to sustainable energy and how these tools have improved the knowledge acquisition process and the challenges presented in post-industrial organizations in the 21st century, titled "Historical Development of Sustainable Energy Technologies."
- Decent work and economic growth, exposing through research done in a technology-based company, exposing practices for the contribution of (decent work), knowledge management and sustainability, for presenting an empirical analysis of decent work, knowledge management and sustainability in post-industrial organizations in the 21st century, titled "Decent Work, Knowledge Management and Sustainability in a Technology-Based Company: A Case of Study."

- Industry, innovation and infrastructure green management practices exploring the strategies, challenges and options for transitioning from conventional coffee production to green and low-carbon systems to display management strategies for transitioning from traditional to green post-industrial organizations in the 21st century, titled "Management Strategies for Transitioning From Conventional Industries to Green and Low-Carbon Production Systems."
- Sustainable cities and communities present the population of small- and medium-sized apple producers located in the southern states of Brazil and their relationship between sustainable processes, product innovation, absorptive capacity and adaptive capacity to show an empirical study about sustainable organizations and communities in the post-industrial era in the 21st century, entitled "Relationship of Innovative Sustainable Business Strategies With Dynamic Capabilities in the Apple Production Chain in Southern Brazil."

Following the same line:

- Responsible production and consumption, encouraging telecommunications companies to adopt sustainable and ecocentric practices to manage knowledge post the COVID-19 pandemic, to highlight the importance of ecocentrism and sustainability for knowledge management in post-industrial organizations in the 21st century, titled "Sustainable and Ecocentric Change for Knowledge Management in the Telecommunications Subsector."
- Climate action, exposing the activities implemented to promote social responsibility and sustainability in educational institutions, to present an empirical study of climate action green practices with implications for knowledge management in training spaces in post-industrial organizations in the 21st century, titled "University Social Responsibility, Evaluation and Impact on Student Satisfaction as an Opportunity for Knowledge Management and Sustainability."
- Submarine life, showing the importance of microalgae for the CO_2 capture and in the generation of biofuel, food and metabolic compounds exploring the sensors for monitoring its growth process, for describing a study of submarine life involving sensors and signal processing methodologies to generate knowledge in post-industrial organizations in the 21st century, entitled "Sensors and Signal Processing Used to Increase Knowledge Management of Algae Production."
- Life and terrestrial ecosystem conjoined the economic and social development, environmental conservation and sustainable practices in companies and local people of the wine tourism sector to report an empirical study of wine tourism as a driver of knowledge management practices in

post-industrial organizations in the 21st century, titled "Wine Tourism as a Driver of Knowledge Management Practices and the Sustainability of the New Rurality."

- Peace, justice and strong institutions, studying the strength of Mexican companies in the trading sector located in the State of Guanajuato around the ecocentric awareness, attitudes in the line of knowledge sharing dimensions, to assess the environmental awareness in Mexican companies' knowledge management and knowledge governance systems in Guanajuato, titled "Assessing Environmental Awareness in the Organizational Culture and Its Mediating Role in Integrating an Ecocentric Paradigm Into Mexican Companies' Knowledge Management and Governance Systems in Guanajuato."
- Alliances to achieve objectives, exploring partnerships between public and private spheres, particularly the restaurant industry, within the sustainable regulatory framework in Queretaro, Mexico, to examine green practices of the hospitality industry from Queretaro, Mexico, titled "Environmental Responsibility and Knowledge Management in Post-industrial Organizations of the 21st century."

Furthermore, a first chapter is presented, in which the terms "ecocentrism," "knowledge management" and "sustainability" in post-industrial organizations of the 21st century are defined, titled "Foundational concepts: An introduction to ecocentrism, knowledge management and sustainability," besides one last presenting a conclusion about the challenges and options, titled "Challenges and alternatives of ecocentrism, knowledge management and sustainability in post-industrial organizations in the 21st century."

Roots of ecocentrism

Conte and D'Elia's (2018) concept of green economy must be conceptualized; in this sense, it requires first defining economics as the science that studies the way in which societies manage scarce resources to produce goods and services that are distributed to society. Second, define the term "economic growth," which means increasing the gross domestic product of a country and third, economic development, as a more general process that has reference to processes that lead to an increase in the quality of life of a country. So if we reflect on these terms, we can decide that there can be an economy without growth and without development, even though there can be an economy with growth and without development, so that there is green economy does not mean that there is green growth, but there is green growth, that is it does not ensure that there is sustainable development, since if the green economy continues to grow, it does not guarantee fairness in distribution.

Conte and D'Elia's (2018) sustainable development appears as a broader concept, especially when analyzing the preface of the president in charge of the commission that writes Burtland's report, in which it is stated: "What is needed now is a new era of economic growth, growth that is powerful, but also socially and environmentally sustainable." It is important to understand that in the concept of traditional sustainability, the ideas, which in terms of economic growth and environmental sustainability are fine in themselves, but that we must achieve maximum social well-being, defining this based on the values of society. In this context, the objectives of economic and social development must be sustained through adequate management. Furthermore, the environment is the set of resources that can be exploited with economic-social and environmental rationality, to achieve long-term development objectives.

Vargas et al.'s (2017) green economy concept arose from the need to change the brown economy model, from which wealth was achieved, without facing problems such as social inequality or the exhaustion of resources. It is worth mentioning that the green economy does not replace sustainable development, but sustainability continues to be a vital objective in the long term. The green economy concept is not a new concept; it was introduced in 1984 by Pearce, Markandya and Barbier in their book *Blueprint for a Green Economy*, where it is defined as "a system of economic activities related to the production, distribution and consumption of goods and services that result in long-term human well-being, without sacrificing future generations with environmental risks and significant ecological scarcity."

Vargas et al. (2017) thank the current interaction in the economy and the environment. Society has a greater degree of consciousness, while being aware of the damage that productive activities cause to the natural environment, such as the processes of contamination of air, water, soil and diversity. This level of awareness in society has allowed the search for alternatives that are more sustainable and responsible for the environment, in order to achieve a series of actions and regulations on the part of the state and social initiatives to control, minimize, correct and prevent them. The harmful effects of economic activities on the natural system give way to a process of activities that is known in the media as a green economy.

Luque (2015) states that culture since 2006 has become one of the elements of sustainable development, in resolving economic, social and environmental problems that affect all societies. UNESCO has been an institution that has sought the possibility of promoting cultural policies with economic development strategies, based on the concept of cultural diversity. The UNESCO Universal Declaration of Cultural Diversity (2001) indicates how culture expands the possibilities of election, allowing each individual to have greater individual freedom to be able to direct the way of life that they choose, which is their own human development.

Luque (2015) within the III World Congress of United Cities and Local Governments (CGLU), held in Mexico, whose members approved a document called "Culture is the fourth pillar of sustainable development," where it was stated that culture in all its diversity was necessary to face the current challenges of humanity at a time when there was a call to national governments to integrate the cultural perspective to national development plans, establish objectives and actions in concrete areas through culture such as education, economy, science, communication, environment, and cooperation (p. 55).

References

Alfaro, J.M., Limón, B., Martínez, G.Á., & Tijerina, G. (2014). *Ambiente y sustentabilidad: por una educación ambiental.* Grupo Editorial Patria.

Brundtland, G.H. (1987). Report of the World Commission on Environment and Development: Our common future. *United Nations.* https://sustainabledevelopment.un.org/content/documents/5987our-common-future.pdf

Calderón Ortiz, G., Magallón Diez, M.T., & Núñez Estrada, H.R. (2010). A cien años de la administración científica. Análisis de las aportaciones de Taylor. *Gestión y estrategia*, *38*, 31–48. https://doi.org/10.24275/uam/azc/dcsh/gye/2010n38/Calderon

Conte, M., & D'Elia, V. (2018). Desarrollo sostenible y conceptos "verdes". *Problemas del desarrollo*, *49*(192), 61–84. www.scielo.org.mx/scielo.php?script=sci_arttext&pid=S0301-70362018000100061&lng=es&nrm=iso

Darnthamrongkul, W., & Mozingo, L.A. (2020). Challenging anthropocentric stormwater management: Advancing legislation for environmental sustainability in the United States. *Water Security*, *10*, 100064.

Ghosh, J., Chakraborty, S., & Das, D. (2023). El imperialismo climático en el siglo XXI. *El trimestre económico*, *90*(357), 267–291.

Leal Filho, W., Wolf, F., Lange Salvia, A., Beynaghi, A., Shulla, K., Kovaleva, M., & Vasconcelos, C.R. (2020). Heading towards an unsustainable world: Some of the implications of not achieving the SDGs. *Discover Sustainability*, *1*, 1–11. https://doi.org/10.1007/s43621-020-00002-x

Luque, V. (2015). Cultura y desarrollo sostenible. *Periférica*, 51–61. http://dx.doi.org/10.25267/Periferica.2015.i16.05

Nonaka, I. (1994). A dynamic theory of organizational knowledge creation. *Organization Science*, *5*(1), 14–37.

Polanyi, M. (2012). *Personal knowledge.* Routledge.

Sagasti, F. (2011). *Ciencia, tecnología, innovación. Políticas para América Latina.* Fondo de Cultura economica.

Saxena, A., Ramaswamy, M., Beale, J., Marciniuk, D., & Smith, P. (2021). Striving for the United Nations (UN) sustainable development goals (SDGs): What will it take? *Discover Sustainability*, *2*, 1–14. https://doi.org/10.1007/s43621-021-00029-8

Servicio de Información Agroalimentaria y Pesquera [SIAP]. (n.d.). *La agricultura.* http://siaprendes.siap.gob.mx/contenidos/2/01-agricultura/index.html

Shrivastava, P. (1995). Ecocentric management for a risk society. *Academy of Management Review*, *20*(1), 118–137.

ten Have, H., & Patrão Neves, M. (2021). Ecocentrism (See anthropocentrism; biocentrism; environmental ethics; zoocentrism). In *Dictionary of global bioethics.* Springer. https://doi.org/10.1007/978-3-030-54161-3_220

United Nations. (2015). Transforming our world: The 2030 agenda for sustainable development. *Department of Economic and Social Affairs.* https://sdgs.un.org/2030agenda

Universidad Nacional Autónoma de México [UNAM]. (2017). *Historia Universal 1.* https://e1.portalacademico.cch.unam.mx/alumno/historiauniversal1/unidad3/revolucionindustrial/introduccion

Vargas, O.I., Trujillo, J.M., & Torres, M.A. (2017). La economía verde: un cambio ambiental y social necesario en el mundo actual. *Revista de Investigación Agraria y Ambiental, 8*(2). https://hemeroteca.unad.edu.co/index.php/riaa/article/view/2044

2 Ecocentrism paradigms as a way of knowledge management for sustainability in post-industrial organizations in the 21st century

Sergio Ernesto Medina Cuéllar

Introduction

Ecocentrism is an ethical and philosophical perspective that places nature at the center of our concerns and decisions. In the context of 21st-century post-industrial organizations, ecocentrism paradigms can play an essential role in knowledge management to promote bioeconomic sustainability.

Ecocentrism is based on the idea that nature has intrinsic value and should be respected and protected. According to Naess (1989), ecocentrism recognizes the interdependence between humans and the natural environment and seeks to promote a sustainable balance. In 21st-century post-industrial organizations, ecocentrism paradigms can be crucial to promoting bioeconomic sustainability in knowledge management. This perspective contrasts with anthropocentrism, which places humans at the center and considers that nature only has value based on its usefulness to humans, justifying its use and depletion. In social terms, the natural ecosystem must be overexploited until poor people have the same level of wealth as the rich. By achieving this point, the entire world population will be able to work on the ecological aspects of sustainability (Klostermann & Cramer, 2006).

In the context of 21st-century post-industrial organizations, ecocentrism paradigms can be applied as forms of knowledge management to promote sustainability. According to Senge et al. (2008), knowledge management refers to creating, acquiring, storing and applying knowledge within an organization. Ecocentrism can influence how knowledge is managed by promoting incorporating environmental and ethical perspectives into decision-making processes.

One of the ways ecocentrism paradigms can influence knowledge management is by promoting environmental education in organizations. According to Sterling (2001), environmental education can help develop ecological awareness in employees, which can influence how knowledge is shared and used within the organization. This can lead to adopting more sustainable practices and integrating environmental considerations into decision-making.

DOI: 10.4324/9781003465058-2

Furthermore, ecocentrism paradigms can foster collaboration and knowledge sharing among organizations. According to Gray (2002), collaboration between organizations can be crucial to address environmental challenges and promote sustainability. Ecocentrism can provide a common ethical framework that facilitates collaboration and knowledge sharing in search of sustainable solutions.

Ecocentrism paradigms can be essential in managing knowledge for sustainability in 21st-century post-industrial organizations. By promoting environmental education, collaboration and knowledge sharing, ecocentrism can help organizations adopt bioeconomic and more sustainable practices and integrate environmental considerations into decision-making. Organizations must recognize the importance of these perspectives and incorporate them into their knowledge management to contribute to a more sustainable future.

The ecological economy (bioeconomy)

Contemporary marketing practices have wreaked havoc on people's way of life, who are increasingly forced into irrational consumerism, which corresponds to behaviour of which the vast majority of the population is unaware. It is interesting to note, for example, that objects such as clothing, footwear, accessories and miscellaneous items purchased frequently are only used rarely in periods that do not exceed a couple of years, thanks to the planned obsolescence of factories and manufacturing need for a constant flow of production to sustain a society based on a conception of unlimited and impossible economic growth in energy and ecological terms.

Faced with a scenario in which the growing climate deterioration, the energy crisis based on fossil natural resources, and the energy dissipation manifested in various types of waste calls for reflection on the change that humanity is experiencing, which, far from being encouraging, shows a self-destructive tendency that makes the human race reconsider the question of whether the human being is genuinely seeking his own life and that of other species. Hundreds of thousands know what is happening on the planet and what is being done daily. The arrival of the growth limits admitted by planet Earth has become increasingly apparent.

Such is the case of the approach presented by economists like Kenneth Boulding in "The Economics of the Coming Spaceship Earth." He represents the planet Earth as a "spaceship" that goes on a long journey and will have only one external energy source based on solar energy and the more food is exhausted (which is limited), the hope of surviving also decreases unless they find some way to recycle water and materials to generate food sources; Boulding invites us to see the Earth as a closed system in which the economy and the environment have a circular relationship in which the cycle does not close, humans could find themselves on the brink of starvation in the hypothetical spacecraft because of global environmental problems.

The ecological economy tries to value the resources and the environmental effects of the economic process; this doctrine arises from the evolution of the theories raised by the classical economy in which everything that occurred was believed to have a predetermined cost and for the neoclassical economy that, unlike its predecessor, observed that for the implementation of a selling price, it is necessary to take into account other variables such as the availability to pay. On this path of discovery was born the concept of ecology, which began to be conceived in ancient Greece by Hippocrates, Aristotle and Theophrastus. However, it was not until 1866 that Ernst Heinrich Haeckel created the term "ecology" to define the body of knowledge concerning the economy of nature, that is, the study of the relations of animals with the organic and inorganic elements of the environment with which they are in contact.

Economics as a branch of biology

At the beginning of the 20th century, the period of the Great Depression in the United States, during which the failures of the capitalist production system were so evident that the search for answers to its causes called the attention of academics and scientists, Alfred Marshall came to an important conclusion that remains valid:

> Specialists who never look beyond their domains are exposed to see things out of every real proportion . . . does not reach them that light that the progress of all science casts by comparison and analogy on those that surround it . . . . The economy is a branch of the Biology widely interpreted.
>
> Alfred Marshall (1957)

This reconceptualization of the nature of economics as science laid the foundation for the second half of the twentieth century to be the scene where various processes of the search for the naturalization of the social sciences began, which began to adopt within the different thought streams of the human sciences, physical ideas and terms such as ecosystem, energy flows and entropy. Since then and to this day, it is increasingly evident that physical and natural limitations exist in a model of industrial economic growth based on intensive energy consumption without considering the biological conditions of the different ecosystems that provide raw materials to the global market system.

The alert that began to arouse interest in the future that a population that consumes its natural resources without measure can aspire to was the sensitivity of the economic system to fossil fuels with the consequent degradation of the environment, showing the lack of equity in the distribution of control and exploitation of natural resources by the prevailing economic and social system, such as the need for questioning whether different conventional scientific positions can lead to a better understanding of the political and ecological issues.

Economists are at the center of contemporary academic debate on ecological and energy theories within the social sciences, who expressed themselves in advance sensitive to the ecological and political problems mentioned; in this sense, the contribution of Kenneth Boulding stands out with his metaphorical conception of "the Earth spacecraft" with which he emphasizes the natural limitations of the planet for the extraction of resources, as well as for the assimilation of debris (Boulding, 1966).

In the same vein, Nicholas Georgescu-Roegen, in the desire to rethink important aspects of the economy as social science, in his work "The law of entropy and the economic process" carried out an analysis of the economic process from an energetic approach, which stands out for its relevance in pointing out how a mechanical consideration of the economic process that conceives it isolated from the world in a material sense diminishes the validity of accepted economic theory (Georgescu-Roegen, 1971).

Georgescu-Roegen (1971) affirmed that the physical laws of entropy govern the economy as a process that converts elements defined as matter and energy into waste irreversibly and inevitably, stressing that the root of scarcity is entropic ownership of economic processes. Under this concept, economic development occurs at the expense of the disappearance of non-renewable natural resources that cannot be replaced. As demonstrated, the study and analysis of economic development must be approached from the point of view of its impact on nature and the degradation of its resources. This leads us to the forced reflection that unlimited growth is impossible on a planet with finite resources, so integrating sciences such as ecology and economics can be a viable alternative to managing scarce natural resources.

The study of energy use

Assuming the essential aspects of the integrative discourse of the economy and ecology in which Georgescu-Roegen stands out, Martínez-Alier (1984), from a prospective position, argues on such a scientific environment outlining his vision: a liberating environmental program from a transcendent perspective, which states that human ecology differs significantly from the ecology of other species because it involves the use of energy and materials in a way that allows a large number of variations between individuals of the same species.

This fact causes human ecology, identified as the green economy, to consider how individual decisions are determined for cultural and social reasons or concerning human beings' use of energy and raw materials. Therefore, an authentic economic science designed to study the allocation of scarce resources between alternative human purposes is an extended human ecology that considers the analysis of political conflicts, ethical qualities and the price system because various decisions of people are under the influence of specific historical times prices (Martínez-Alier, 1984).

In this position, one can observe the presence of an internal critique about the assumptions established in economic theory and, on the other hand, of an external character concerning the sphere of economic sciences. This approach is remote but not separated from the caution implied by the neo-positivist need to test the scientific concepts that such a position addresses.

In the development of conventional economics theory, economic individualism prevails, whose assumptions about utilitarian calculus and individual rationality cannot address the problems involved in efficient allocation between generations of non-renewable natural resources. This fact makes it clear that in order to study the allocation of scarce natural resources, it must necessarily be linked to the historical knowledge of technological development and natural sciences in order to initiate a consistent act of reflection on the fact that human consumption habits and preferences have a cultural and historical character, the reason why relying on market mechanisms is not enough to achieve a reasonable allocation of resources to generations to come.

The administration of finite resources between generations implies moral and ethical pronouncements and judgments since society's adoption of these values changes historically; in the face of this situation, when the economist values these issues, it must also encompass a historical and social vision of ethics. The green economy covers the field of economic sciences in several aspects, such as the conception of economic goods from a physical and natural approach and how man uses natural resources, taking into account the source of origin of human needs. In this sense, the need arises to transcend the frontiers of the economy in order to make clear that it is necessary to have the capacity to understand and expose the class struggle, the migratory phenomena, property rights and the way moral values are distributed in society to explain how scarce (natural) resources are allocated for alternative human purposes (Martínez-Alier, 1984).

The need for a comprehensive approach has been at the center of the debate on the scope and methods of the green economy because in determining that a social science such as economics can be defined as human ecology, a research scheme of present and past forms of natural resource management is being proposed from a holistic perspective (Martínez-Alier, 1983).

Social sciences and energy theories

The research of theories on the different forms and sources of energy in numerous fields of science has thrown new light on the evolution of the social sciences from the progress and evolution of ideas around the study of the environment. However, the need for systematic studies on various contact points between social reflection with technology and science is evident. The search for the scope that energy and ideas about thermodynamics can have for the social sciences is the common point that shares precursors of the ecological economy with scientists of different natures, among whom are Josef Popper, Frederick Soddy, Patrick Geddes and Lancelot Hogben.

The concept of energy did not exist until the early 19th century; its formulation as a force with the ability to become mechanical work and the theory of its conservation originates between the years 1830 and 1850 with the contributions of Mayer, Faraday and Joule, among others (Kuhn, 1982). In that period, Rudolf Clausius proposed the principle of energy conservation, and later, based on the analysis of the efficiency of the work carried out by the machines, the development of the second law of thermodynamics took place, known as entropy or second law of Clausius, which speaks of the degree of disorder, decay or exhaustion of a closed system depending on the tendency of the energy to diminish as long as it does not receive some external energy input.

From the discovery of the second law of Clausius, it became evident the scope that the thermodynamic principles can have, showing energy as a quantifiable element and linked to a wide range of physical and chemical phenomena in nature in such a way that relevant conclusions can be drawn not only of an ecological character but also of a social and historical nature, in this sense the merit of intellectuals such as Georgescu Roegen and Martínez-Alier, is found in his exhaustive and rigorous analysis of how concepts such as entropy and energy were transferred from the field of natural sciences, to enrich and formalize the field of social sciences.

Under this perspective, under a generalizing approach to the social sciences, the German chemist Friedrich Wilhelm Ostwald proposed an energetic scheme of interpretation of natural phenomena to replace the mechanistic analysis prevalent at the dawn of the 20th century. This approach established that cultural development—how human beings consciously modify nature through instruments, technical resources and procedures—depends on the amount of energy available and the efficiency of its transformation in thermodynamic terms. Referring to this, Max Weber, who is considered one of the forerunners of the modern study of social sciences and public administration, commented that Ostwald's proposal should also consider the fading of matter, which is subordinated to processes of an entropic nature and also the fact that cultural advancement necessarily implies less use of energy to carry out production when there is evidence that the levels of industrial production that characterize contemporary cultural progress consume large amounts of energy.

It is interesting to note that Ostwald's approach proposed a vision that combines the study of energy with the postulates of economic theory; although criticized by Weber, he proposed a fertile path for a physical and natural conception of economic factors, not only monetary ones. This shows its relevance when it becomes evident that the periodicity of different historical stages arises based on the different uses of energy, making it clear that, as the historian Henry Adams claimed, it is feasible to correlate the historical evolution of humanity and the energy expenditure necessary to satisfy the needs of human populations in different times and scenarios (Martínez-Alier, 1983).

Food production is the economic activity that, being determinant for human subsistence, naturally occupies first place as a priority to invest energy, so the analysis of agrarian productivity emerged from the perspective of energy accounting that began at the end of the 19th century by the hand of Sergei Podolinsky who in accordance with the ideas of Marx stated:

> Humanity is thermodynamically perfect through agriculture because, with the energy obtained through labor (food), the boiler itself is supplied.
>
> Sergei Podolinsky

This intellectual with similar ideas to Marx and Engels gave transcendent importance to natural resources in a historical period in which industrial production began to wreak havoc because of its high consumption of fossil natural resources such as coal and oil, which, due to their non-renewability, are of high value. Podolinsky was among the first to assess the significance of the second law of thermodynamics to analyze how economic systems work from the entropy approach.

Podolinsky's reasoning coincides with Georgescu-Roegen's later contributions in the sense that the planet Earth has the characteristic of being a thermodynamic system that, when opened, incoming solar energy balances the entropic processes in which plants fix such energy so that agricultural work increases the amount of energy that can be used to feed humans, so energy units should be the unit of measurement of the effectiveness of work because the flow of solar energy is determinant of human life (Martínez-Alier, 1987).

In the effort to redesign the theory of value-work in terms of energy balances, alongside Podolinsky, Eduard Sacher reflected that historical progress may be influenced by available energy. The thesis generated by both on the efficiency of energy use in agricultural production gives rise to a condensed vision of agriculture and its energy balance so that, when accounting for the inputs required by industrialized agriculture, it can be concluded that the increases in agricultural production volumes are due to a constant increase in external energy inputs (Smil, 1991).

The analysis of human evolution from an ecological point of view proposed by Podolinsky and Sacher generated specific hypotheses about ecological energy ideas and their historical significance, which laid the foundations for concrete criticism of the theory of economic growth based on the recognition of essential correlations between energy consumption and the economy, This allowed the emergence of critical points to the modern industrial system based on energy dissipation as a predominant attribute, entrenched in the increasing use of non-renewable natural resources.

Communion between bioeconomy and ecocentrism

Bioeconomy and ecocentrism are fundamental concepts in the search for sustainable development in the 21st century. So, it is essential to understand the origins of bioeconomy and ecocentrism, identify their common points and analyze their evolution throughout history to reach the complex reality of the 21st century.

The bioeconomy is rooted in economic theories that consider biological resources essential for production and human well-being. From the ideas of Nicholas Georgescu-Roegen on the economy as an economy based on material and energy flows of biological origin (Georgescu-Roegen, 1971) until the contemporary proposals that promote the sustainable use of biological resources for the production of goods and services (McCormick et al., 2013), the economy has undergone a significant evolution.

Ecocentrism, on the other hand, originates in ethical and philosophical concerns about the relationship between humans and nature. Aldo Leopold's work, *A Sand County Almanac* (Leopold, 1949), is a fundamental milestone that proposes an ethics based on the interdependence between humanity and the natural environment. In addition, the contributions of Arne Naess (1989) have driven the development of deep ecology, a current that advocates a deeper and more respectful connection with the biosphere.

Despite their distinct origins, bioeconomy and ecocentrism share common ground. Both approaches recognize the importance of sustainability and the need to consider ecosystem health when making economic decisions. The bioeconomy seeks to optimize the production of biological resources sustainably, while ecocentrism advocates a fundamental change in human perception, promoting the ethical consideration of nature as an end in itself.

In the 21st century, bioeconomy and ecocentrism have intertwined in the search for solutions to contemporary environmental and economic challenges. Growing awareness of resource finiteness and the need to address climate change has led to integrating ecocentric principles into bioeconomic frameworks (Miller et al., 2018). The use of sustainable technologies, the promotion of the circular economy and the valorization of ecosystem services are examples of how these approaches converge to address current problems.

The relationship between bioeconomy and ecocentrism demonstrates the need for an integrated perspective to address the economic and environmental challenges of the 21st century. The evolution of these concepts throughout history reflects a constant search for solutions that balance human needs with ecological integrity. The synthesis of bioeconomy and ecocentrism can offer a path to a sustainable future where human prosperity is understood as intrinsically linked to the health and balance of the natural ecosystem.

Energy management with a bioeconomic approach

In order to optimize the analysis, it was necessary to formalize the set of economic and social elements that aim to carry out effective bioeconomic management of resources to satisfy the needs of human populations; it is necessary to distinguish the energy load that is attributed to the organic matter of vegetable or animal origin; including the biomass constituted by the wastes and organic wastes susceptible of being exploited, for the management of sustainable development (García, 2012). In this regard, they highlight the various efforts made to achieve energy efficiency in the different productive sectors through various modifications to generate energy based on renewable sources with the capacity to generate the same working capacity that has fossil fuels that are considered harmful by their high energy dissipation through the creation of a large amount of waste. When an ideology of sustainable living is tied with a paradigm shift on the forms of generation and transformation of energy, takes place the development and implementation of renewable energies accompanied by multidisciplinary strategies to take advantage of even the entropic processes of the matter as new sources of resources (Kaltschmitt et al., 2007).

Various renewable energy sources can be essential participants in an energy efficiency approach, even if they are not entirely bio-based, which seeks to reduce dependence on oil and harness the benefits of other alternative sources of available energy. Geothermal energy, which exists in most countries and is used mainly for electricity generation, is in the face of high hydrocarbon prices and declining oil reserves, so the agreement to accept the Kyoto Protocol in several countries is favoring the installation of geothermal plants globally (Mercado, 2007).

Another notable energy source is hydroelectric, which is produced by harnessing the force of gravity on the water collected in reservoirs or swamps. It is clean, waste-free and easy to store. In addition, the water stored in reservoirs located in high places allows for the regulation of the flow of the river. Although the dispersion of energy by waste generation is minimal, it has an entropic effect on the environment since the construction of hydroelectric plants is expensive and large power lines are needed; in addition, the reservoirs cause losses of fauna and productive agricultural soil due to the flooding of the land destined for them, in addition to causing the decrease in the flow of rivers and streams under the dams, altering the quality of the water. It is a renewable energy with high energy efficiency and due to the water cycle, its availability is almost inexhaustible without producing toxic emissions during its production. However, in global terms, much remains to be done to lessen its entropic effect on the environment (Gagnon, 1993).

Despite the apparent safety of the energy above sources, the solar source forms the primary energy input to the system constituted by the entire planet due to its quality of transmuting into other forms of energy; since the creation of biomass, even wind energy in determining most biological processes in the environment, but it can also be transformed sustainably into other forms of energy such as heat and electricity thanks to the human technological exploitation of its advantages, among which its inexhaustible, renewable nature stands out (Rodríguez, 2009).

Under this argument, it is precisely the desire for the efficient use of solar energy that gave rise to the term bioindustry, which is associated with that intermediary of intelligent transformation of nature to create products that meet human needs, transcending the need to use fossil fuels and using solar energy first stored in plants to produce biofuels and chemicals. Such bio-processing could enable conventional industries such as petrochemicals and sugar industries to access new markets and meet more needs sustainably (Isserman, 2009).

The trend is toward a better course toward sustainability through bioenergy and biofuels for transport and the industry. The exploitation of natural resources for the production of satisfiers and the issue of the need to identify options for sustainable economic growth are positions that must be reconciled with the essential activities carried out by living beings by their instinct to satisfy their needs for survival in this sense food is the primary requirement and the search for food security is the natural response; focused on examining economic conditions for both the causes that generate failures in the supply of the agricultural sector and the restriction of accessibility to essential consumer products, as for the search for options that improve access to these products (Torres et al., 2003), through the use of inputs in an environmentally friendly manner and the sustainable technical management of land, considering agriculture and the consequent production of food as the primary origin of all the other productive chains that make up a country's economy.

Bioeconomic strategies address food security in various ways. In most cases, biotechnology is a possible solution for increasing yields and improving food safety and nutritional quality (Cimoli, 2015). In the face of the imminent effect of climate change and the constant danger, it poses to food security, with apparent examples ranging from the decline in the world's population of pollinators such as bees to a gradual melting of the poles, why each country must apply the relevant public policies to achieve bioeconomic development, to seek the use of resources, the care of the environment and the sustainable development of production processes.

There is still widespread concern about the sustainability of food production systems because, despite technological advances to meet demand, environmental deterioration persists, bringing a series of economic and ecological problems (Altieri, 2009). The primary purpose of resource development is to sustain the current quality of life and to enable it for future generations through strategies to attract and promote a bioeconomy for social development through approaches such as payment for environmental services, a scheme that seeks to recognize the importance of biodiversity, the scenic beauty and social resources to evaluate the conditions of urban environmental sustainability (Soto, 2002).

Ecocentrism in the bioeconomic use of energy in post-industrial organizations

The term "post-industrial organization" refers to an economic and social entity undergoing significant transformation after the industrial era. This transformation implies a change in the economic base and the nature of the prevailing economic activities. The conceptualization of post-industrial organization is linked to historical development and the economic and social transformations that occurred after the industrial era.

The concept of post-industrialism became popular in the 1960s and 1970s, primarily through the work of sociologist and economist Daniel Bell. In his work "The Sources of the New Society" (Bell, 1973), Bell argued that industrial societies were evolving into post-industrial societies. According to Bell, critical features of a post-industrial society include:

a) Services sector domain: In post-industrial organizations, the production of manufactured goods tends to decrease compared to the importance of the services sector. Economic activities have become more oriented toward information, technology, education, health and other services.
b) Importance of information and knowledge: The post-industrial economy is characterized by a significant dependence on the production, distribution and manipulation of information and knowledge. Post-industrial organizations often focus on industries related to information technology, telecommunications, research and development.

c) Change like work: Work in post-industrial organizations tends to be more intellectual, knowledge-based and focused on creativity than the more physical and routine industrial workforce.
d) Greater flexibility and decentralization: Organizational structures in the post-industrial era tend to be more flexible and decentralized than the hierarchical and centralized structures of industrial organizations.

It is essential to remember that the concept of post-industrial organization does not imply that the manufacturing industry will disappear altogether but that its relative importance diminishes compared with other economic and social activities. The evolution toward a post-industrial society and organizations reflects profound changes in the economy and how institutions are organized.

In the post-industrial era of the 21st century, energy management has become a crucial issue. Bioeconomic approaches to natural resource use are essential to ensure long-term sustainability. In this sense, it highlights the relevance of ecocentrism as the correct paradigm for the bioeconomic use of the energy of the natural ecosystem, emphasizing the limitations of anthropocentrism in contemporary organizations.

Ecocentrism, in its essence, places nature at the center of ethical concerns and holds that all life forms and ecosystem elements have intrinsic value. The ecocentric perspective advocates biological systems the interconnectedness and interdependence of encompasses the idea that the planet's health is crucial for long-term human well-being (Leopold, 1949).

In the context of the bioeconomy, ecocentrism provides an ethical framework that promotes the responsible use of natural resources, avoiding excessive exploitation that could result in negative consequences for biodiversity and ecosystems (Martínez-Alier, 2002). Implementing bioeconomic policies based on ecocentrism seeks to balance human needs with preserving ecological integrity.

In contrast, anthropocentrism has been the basis of many economic and organizational practices in industrial and post-industrial history. This perspective considers the human being as the center of all ethical concerns and values natural resources according to their usefulness for immediate human benefit (Naess, 1989). However, this vision has proven unsustainable as we face increasingly pressing environmental challenges.

Anthropocentrism has led to over-exploitation of resources, environmental degradation, and biodiversity loss (Taylor, 1986). In a post-industrial world, where environmental awareness is essential, persisting in this approach can have devastating consequences for future generations.

Adopting ecocentrism in post-industrial organizations is crucial for moving toward a sustainable economy. Companies must integrate ecocentric principles into their strategies, considering short-term economic benefits and long-term environmental responsibility. Business practices must be aligned with the health and vitality of the natural ecosystem on which they depend.

A notable example is the transition to renewable energy sources. Organizations embracing ecocentrism are leading the energy revolution, investing in clean technologies, and promoting energy efficiency (Sachs, 2015). These initiatives benefit the planet and contribute to sustainable development and the creation of a resilient bioeconomy.

Ecocentrism emerges as the correct paradigm for the bioeconomic use of natural ecosystem energy in post-industrial organizations of the 21st century. The transition to this approach is essential to ensure long-term sustainability, overcoming the limitations of anthropocentrism that have characterized past practices. By embracing ecocentrism, organizations can pioneer a new era of development that values the planet's health as much as human progress.

In contemporary post-industrial organizations, energy management has become a critical element in pursuing sustainable development, so it is crucial to adopt an ecocentric approach to energy management, combined with bioeconomic principles, as an essential response to current environmental challenges.

Ecocentrism, as an ethical perspective, places nature at the center of considerations, recognizing its intrinsic value and the interdependence of biological systems (Leopold, 1949; Naess, 1989). This ethical approach finds a natural convergence with the bioeconomy, which seeks sustainable management of biological resources to balance human needs with the preservation of the environment (McCormick et al., 2013).

Adopting bioeconomic principles in energy management implies a transition to renewable sources and practices that respect the limits of the ecosystem. Sachs (2015) highlights the importance of integrating clean technologies and energy efficiency into organizations' operations to minimize the environmental footprint. This is essential from an ethical perspective and aligned with long-term economic viability.

Anthropocentrism, focused on immediate human benefit, has been an obstacle to sustainable energy management. The overexploitation of non-renewable resources and the excessive emission of greenhouse gases manifest this limited approach (Taylor, 1986). Contemporary post-industrial organizations must overcome these challenges by adopting an ecocentric approach, recognizing that ecosystem health is crucial to long-term human well-being.

Leading companies have shown that it is possible to implement ecocentric energy management with a bioeconomic approach. The transition to renewable sources, optimization of energy processes and incorporation of the circular economy in the supply chain are examples of successful practices (UNEP, 2019). These organizations reduce their environmental impact and create sustainable and resilient business models.

Ecocentric energy management with a bioeconomic approach is the route to a sustainable future in contemporary post-industrial organizations. The convergence of ecocentric and bioeconomic principles not only responds to the ethical demands of our time but also offers practical solutions to environmental and economic challenges. Organizations that adopt this approach contribute to ecosystem preservation and ensure their own resilience and long-term success.

The paradigms of ecocentrism in knowledge management for sustainability: a novel approach in the framework of the ecological economy (bioeconomy)

In the search for sustainable development, knowledge management emerges as an essential component, highlighting the potential of ecocentrism paradigms as an innovative approach to knowledge management within the framework of the green economy, also known as a bioeconomy.

Ecocentrism, as an ethical perspective, recognizes the interdependence of the elements of the ecosystem, advocating the consideration of nature as an end in itself (Leopold, 1949; Naess, 1989). The ecological economy, or bioeconomy, integrates ecological aspects into economic decision-making, promoting sustainability and responsible management of biological resources (Martínez-Alier, 2002; McCormick et al., 2013).

Knowledge management in the context of sustainability involves acquiring, creating, distributing and applying knowledge that promotes sustainable practices (Nonaka & Takeuchi, 1995). Integrating ecocentrism into this process implies recognizing the intrinsic importance of nature and the need for considering its limits in generating and applying knowledge.

Ecocentrism offers an ethical perspective that can transform knowledge management. From problem identification to solution implementation, this approach encourages integrating environmental values at every stage of the knowledge life cycle. Ecocentric ethics guide decision-making toward practices that respect ecological integrity.

Within this framework, the bioeconomy is a valuable analytical tool for assessing the sustainability of knowledge management practices. The proper valuation of ecosystem services, the internalization of environmental externalities and the integration of bioeconomic principles in decision-making ensure that knowledge management is aligned with nature's limits.

Organizations committed to sustainability are already integrating ecocentric paradigms into their knowledge management. Considering environmental aspects in decision-making, promoting the circular economy and investing in sustainable innovations are examples of how ecocentrism can be integrated into knowledge management practices (Rockström et al., 2009).

Integrating ecocentrism paradigms into knowledge management, specifically focusing on the green economy or bioeconomy, represents a novel and promising approach to addressing sustainability challenges. By adopting this ethical approach, organizations can ensure that the knowledge generated and applied contributes to ecosystem health and resilience, ensuring a sustainable future.

References

Altieri, M. (2009). *La agricultura Moderna: Impactos Ecológicos y la Posibilidad de una Verdadera Agricultura sustentable*. Department of Environmental Science, Policy and Management, University of California.

Bell, D. (1973). *The coming of postindustrial society: A venture in social forecasting*. Basic Books.

Boulding, K.E. (1966). The economics of the coming spaceship Earth. In H. Jarrett (Ed.), *Environmental quality in a growing economy. Resources for the Future* (pp. 3–14). Johns Hopkins University Press.

Cimoli, M. (2015). What kind of microfundations? Notes on the evolutionary approach. *CEPAL* (pp. 240–320). https://repositorio.cepal.org/items/73bb21d9-7a7c-4504-ad9c-9a161fc91687

Gagnon, L. (1993). Emissions from hydroelectric reservoirs and comparison of hydroelectricity, natural gas and oil. *INIS*, *25*(11), 568–569.

García, S. (2012). *Centrales termoeléctricas de biomasa*. Renovetec editorial.

Georgescu-Roegen, N. (1971). *The entropy law and the economic process*. Harvard University Press.

Gray, B. (2002). *Collaborating: Finding common ground for multiparty problems*. Jossey-Bass.

Isserman, A. (2009). Ethanol and the local economy industry trends, location factors, economic impacts, and risks. *Economic Development Quarterly*, *23*(1), 71–88. https://doi.org/10.1177/0891242408329485

Kaltschmitt, M., Streicher, W., & Wiese, A. (2007). *Renewable energy: Technology, economics and environment*. Springer Science & Business Media.

Klostermann, J.E.M., & Cramer, J. (2006). The contextual meaning of sustainable development: The case of the Dutch drinking water sector. *Sustainable Development*, *14*(4), 268–276. https://doi.org/10.1002/sd.287

Kuhn, T.S. (1982). *La tensión esencial, México*. Fondo de Cultura Económica.

Leopold, A. (1949). *A sand county Almanac*. Oxford University Press.

Marshall, A. (1957). *Principios de Economía: un tratado de introducción* (Traducción directa de la 8va edición inglesa, 1931). Aguilar.

Martínez-Alier, J. (1983). La ciencia económica y el análisis energético. Discusiones antiguas y recientes. *Papers. Revista de Sociologia*, *19*, 121–143.

Martínez-Alier, J. (1984). *L'ecologisme i l'economia. Història d'unes relacions amagades*. Edicions 62.

Martínez-Alier, J. (1987). *Ecological economics*. Basil Blackwell.

Martínez-Alier, J. (2002). *The environmentalism of the poor: A study of ecological conflicts and valuation*. Edward Elgar Publishing.

McCormick, K., Kautto, N., & Wehrmeyer, W. (2013). The bioeconomy in Europe: An overview. *Sustainability*, *5*(6), 2589–2608. https://doi.org/10.3390/su5062589

Mercado, S. (2007). Medio Ambiente, Geotermia y Toma de conciencia. *Geotermia*, *20*(2), 1–95.

Miller, T.R., Wiek, A., Sarewitz, D., Robinson, J., Olsson, L., Kriebel, D., & Loorbach, D. (2018). The future of sustainability science: A solutions-oriented research agenda. *Sustainability Science*, *9*, 239–246. https://doi.org/10.1007/s11625-013-0224-6

Naess, A. (1989). *Ecology, community and lifestyle*. Cambridge University Press.

Nonaka, I., & Takeuchi, H. (1995). *The knowledge-creating company: How Japanese companies create the dynamics of innovation*. Oxford University Press.

Rockström, J., Steffen, W., Noone, K., Persson, Å., Chapin, III, F.S., Lambin, E.F., & Foley, J.A. (2009). A safe operating space for humanity. *Nature*, *461*(7263), 472–475.
Rodríguez, H. (2009). *Desarrollo de la energía solar en Colombia y sus perspectivas* (pp. 1–7). Universidad de los Andes en Bogotá.
Sachs, J.D. (2015). *The age of sustainable development.* Columbia University Press.
Senge, P.M., Smith, B., Kruschwitz, N., Laur, J., & Schley, S. (2008). *The necessary revolution: How individuals and organizations are working together to create a sustainable world.* Broadway Business.
Smil, V. (1991). *General Energetics: Energy in the biosphere and in civilization* (Sacher, pp. 5, 348). Wiley.
Soto, M. (2002). *Gestión local y participación en torno al pago por servicios ambientales.* Centro Internacional de la Política Económica.
Sterling, S. (2001). *Sustainable education: Re-visioning learning and change.* Green Books.
Taylor, P.W. (1986). *Respect for nature: A theory of environmental ethics.* Princeton University Press.
Torres-Torres, F., Trápaga-Delfín, Y., Delgadillo-Macías, J., Gasca-Zamora, J., Oceguera-Parra, D., Arroyo-Morales, N., Aguilar-Ortega, T., & Cortés, H. (2003). *Seguridad alimentaria: seguridad nacional.* Plaza y Valdés.
UNEP. (2019). *Global resources outlook 2019: Natural resources for the future we want.* United Nations Environment Programme.

3 Knowledge management for a posture of ecocentrism and organizational sustainability

Elia Socorro Díaz Nieto

Introduction

Knowledge management is a concept that is required more every day within organizations that, according to Fierro Moreno and Mercado Salgado (2012), implies the creation of value through the collection and materialization of ideas that the organization can codify and transfer both intra- and inter-organizationally. In this sense, the objective of knowledge management is to provide methodologies and action guides in the practice of effective knowledge administration. This research encompassed three variables, the independent one being knowledge management and the dependent one being ecocentrism and organizational sustainability.

Within this context, Montiel (2008) cited in Morales G. (2016) stated that sustainability is based on an ecocentric philosophical paradigm, based on the intrinsic value of nature, while CSR responds to an anthropocentric paradigm, highlighting the utilitarian value of environmental preservation. Amato et al. (2016) pointed out that CSR was born as a new business dimension concerned with the concept of sustainability, marking a paradigm shift in relation to the economic theory of the company, which maintained that the only responsibility of itself was to make profits (p. 86). The objective of the study was to describe the advantages and disadvantages of knowledge management for sustainability from the perspective of ecocentrism in wine companies that are located on the ecotourism route of Querétaro.

The research problem refers to the need for protecting nature in its different life cycles and nonhuman living beings with which the world is shared. Herrera et al. (2022) defined ecocentrism as a perspective with the nature of an autonomous organism that is composed of life cycles, from this point of view, nature stops being seen as an object at the service of humanity and begins to be considered a subject that must be protected and respected. It should be noted that within ecocentrism itself, there are moderate and radical positions, in response to living beings that are recognized as beings deserving of protection due to their intrinsic value. On the one hand, we find animal ethics that

DOI: 10.4324/9781003465058-3

consider sentient animals, also considered biocentric ethics that include every living, individual organism, and on the other hand, ethics that consider species as a whole and ecosystems, with a holistic approach.

There are countless consequences of human activities in the environment, and the main one is the increase in population and the need for food; in this sense, human life could not survive without nature. In a more specific sense, we can mention (a) the exponential demographic growth of the human population, (b) capacity of the earth's load to produce food, for the entire human population. Food production has increased in all third world countries, due to the increase in population growth, (c) Food needs: Investigation needs to focus on healthy diet and poor nutrition. The research question posed for the study was: What are the advantages and disadvantages of knowledge management for sustainability, from the perspective of ecocentrism in post-industrial organizations of the 21st century?

Biblioteca Jurídica Virtual del Instituto de Investigaciones Jurídicas de la UNAM (2011). Knowledge management has increased in the context of post-industrial organizations which are derived from what has been called the post-industrial society or the knowledge society, which is also what Alvin Toffler described as the third wave of accelerated advancement of humanity. Currently the most important wealth is no longer generated by agriculture, nor by industry but by the knowledge factor reflected in scientific advances and developed cutting-edge technologies which has become the determining element of sustained progress and economic profitability in human communities.

Theoretical framework

Ecocentrism

Ecocentrism seeks the protection of nature with its different life cycles and nonhuman living beings, with which this planet is shared. Morales G. (2016) defined ecocentrism as a perspective with the nature of an autonomous organism that is composed of life cycles. Under this approach, nature stops being seen as an object at the service of humanity and becomes considered a subject that must be protected and respected. Montalván (2020) explained ecocentrism as one of the great contemporary challenges of political philosophy and law, which has achieved an understanding of our role on the planet, and questions us about exclusivity as moral agents, the ideal of justice and, with it, our idea of damage.

According to Universidad de Murcia (2023), there are a number of consequences of human activities in the environment, and the main one is the increase in population and the need for food, in a more specific sense we can mention (a) the exponential demographic growth of the human population is due to the advances in medicine, hygiene and the resources obtained by the agricultural and industrial revolution, the growth of the human population seems to have no limits, advances that provide food and defense against diseases; (b) capacity of the earth's load to produce food for the entire human population: Food production has increased in all third world countries, due to the increase in population growth; however, food production per person has increased very little. It is worth mentioning that these foods have been used to feed the people who can buy them, not the hungry population, and on the other hand, it must be noted that production on land is limited, since it depends on arable land and water. (c) Nutritional needs, healthy diet and poor nutrition: Nutritional needs change from one country to another, for example, many inhabitants of the northern (developed) countries have a diet with an excess of calories, 1.3 billion human beings live in absolute poverty, 850 million have a deficient diet, and 1.4 billion lack drinking water. The supply of food and daily calories is insufficient, through the food consumed, as happens in poor countries. This is what is known as malnutrition, which can occur due to a lack of nutrients or an excess of them. In both cases, there are problems, for example in developed countries, the excess of nutrients causes obesity, since they abuse meat and foods rich in proteins, and in third world countries, they lack proteins such as meat that provides amino acids and other nutrients, since the basis of their diet is vegetables.

According to Universidad de Murcia (2023), the human population currently has an exponential growth, which exceeds 6,000 million and it is estimated that there will be more than 8,000 in 2050. The growth rate today is more than 80 million inhabitants per year of which 80% are born in underdeveloped countries and the greater the number of individuals, the more resources are necessary; the consumption of these resources causes environmental alterations and pollution. In underdeveloped countries, the human population behaves like a superpopulation of individuals who spend resources, while developed countries behave like a consumer superpopulation, since an individual from a developed country consumes about 18 times more resources than an underdeveloped country, but since underdeveloped countries have a larger population, they also produce a countless number of resources.

According to Universidad de Murcia (2023), environmental problems are caused by waste—waste is any material that results from a manufacturing, transformation, use, consumption or cleaning process, when its owner or producer releases it without any care. A residue understood in a simpler way would be any substance or object, from which its owner gets rid of.

The accumulation of waste that a society produces generates environmental and health problems; a large part of these problems derive from the uncontrolled abandonment of this waste. We highlight the following problems:

> Water contamination; contaminated soil; waste with organic matter increases the risk of pests, such as insects, rodents, seagulls and microorganisms, many of them pathogens, which can carry diseases.

Social responsibility

According to Vernier D. (2023), corporate social responsibility (CSR) in Mexico is a central issue for companies that want to positively impact society and the natural environment that surrounds them, being leaders in the Corporate Sustainability Governance issues that concern them, carrying out each of their activities under innovative models proposed within the new ESR distinctive. Not only is it an ethical selection, but it also implies improving the corporate image, which will mean, as a positive effect, the loyalty of the workers, with access to financing with a sustainable focus, since financial institutions are paying attention to sustainability, therefore socially responsible companies can access more efficiently to financing programs and sustainable investment resources by demonstrating solid governance and excellence schemes.

Within the regulations and policies that encourage CSR are: Official Mexican Standard NOM-035-STPS-2018; Psychosocial risk factors at Work-Identification, analysis and prevention; voluntary emissions market in Mexico; General Law for the Prevention and General Management of Waste; and General Law on Climate Change. Compliance with these norms and policies (which fosters Corporate Social Responsibility) avoids legal sanctions, guarantees good functioning and formalizes the company's sustainable commitment. Companies that demonstrate a genuine commitment to society and the environment gain long-term competitive advantages, such as improving the climate work environment, attracting more and better talent, increasing reputation, improving credibility and encouraging financing. CSR in Mexico can be a strategic differentiator in a competitive market.

Social responsibility requires that companies carry out a material analysis, which means knowing which aspects are relevant in their management; this allows them to focus the use of resources well, to generate the maximum positive impact on interest groups, in addition to being a tool that allows companies to make decisions in the easiest way, considering their different stakeholders, all of which creates value independent of the sector to which they belong. Companies obtain significant benefits that can boost both their business performance and their sustainability profile. Let's find out what they are.

Ten most important environmental certificates in Mexico

According to 10 principales certificaciones de sustentabilidad en México Procuraduría Federal de protección al Ambiente (2023).

1. Socially Responsible Company (ESR): The most famous certificate in the country evaluates environmental issues, positive impact on the community and social responsibility. It is annual and has modalities for both large companies and SMEs.
2. Clean industry: Awarded by PROFEPA that recognizes industries that exceed Mexican regulations on emissions, waste and water. The best thing about this recognition is that it is free, so there are no excuses that it costs a lot to obtain an environmental certificate.
3. Family Responsible Company (EFR): Certificate issued by the Secretary of Labor and Social Welfare that recognizes organizations that have a commitment to work-life balance, gender equality and combating workplace violence.
4. Clean transportation: Certificate granted by SEMARNAT and SCIT that seeks to reduce fuel consumption, operating costs and emissions. It is suitable for the transportation of cargo, passengers, tourism and private transportation.
5. LEED: International and most famous certificate on bioconstruction, it recognizes buildings that have elements of sustainability, well-being and energy efficiency.
6. Forest Stewardship Council (FSC): A certificate specialized in wood and forest products, recognizing those resources that come from sustainable and responsible sources; ideal for factories and retailers of wood, cardboard or paper.
7. Tre Distinction: It is an exclusive recognition for companies with a presence in Nuevo León that recognizes outstanding labor practices.
8. 100% Carbon neutral program: Private initiative in Latin America that certifies companies that have plans to be net zero or have already achieved it.
9. Standard NMX-R-025-SCFI-2015 Labor Equality and Non-discrimination: A voluntary Mexican standard that can be certified, the standard deals with norms of gender equality, non-discrimination or labor equality. Suitable for all types of organizations, whether large or small, private or public, regardless of the economic sector.
10. Environmental Quality Distinction: Awarded by PROFEPA to micro-, small- and medium-sized businesses (MSMEs), as well as to rural societies that comply with applicable environmental regulations, efficiently use resources and provide services and products in a sustainable manner. It is free.

In order for MSMEs and rural societies to voluntarily comply with environmental standards and increase the productivity of small and medium-sized businesses and rural societies of each entrepreneur, the Federal Environmental Protection Agency (PROFEPA) promotes environmental self-regulation through the Distinctive Environmental Quality of Mexico, under the following strategies.

- Take advantage of natural resources to produce goods and provide services in a sustainable manner.
- Obtain the Mexico Environmental Quality Distinction (Distintivo), which is a free and direct process between the facility and Profepa, without the intervention of an accredited external auditor.
- Incorporate ejidos, small producers and communities that establish companies to take advantage of their natural resources and provide services.
- Incorporate MSMEs from the commercial, industrial and service sectors.

Sustainability in the Mexican countryside

Carral (2008), the Law of Sustainable Rural Development in the Mexican Countryside (2001), was approved. By the Chamber of Deputies, and since its publication in the Official Gazette of the Federation, on December 7 of this year, in October 2004, it was included in its regulations, which guides and regulates economic activities in rural areas and establishes public policies for the Mexican countryside under a comprehensive approach, the basis of the Sustainable Rural Development Law.

It is worth mentioning that Westra (2003) cited in Carral (2008) addressed integrity from a federalist and democratic planning scheme, and in the legal and administrative framework of constitutional article 27 and the National Development Plan, PND (2001–2006), territorial approach was incorporated (Echeverri et al., 2007 cited in Carral, 2008) (spatial dimension, geographically given resources). However, in a scenario of very strong social pressure, mobilization of multiple peasant groups of coffee growers, ranchers, pineapple growers, corn growers, sugarcane growers, etc., that is, a project of the National Peasant Confederation (CNC), which achieved an imperfect but acceptable to all parties and which was the basis of the Sustainable Rural Development Law (LDRS) (Echeverri et al., 2007, p. 39, cited in Carral, 2008). However, as it will be seen, his neoliberal bias was clear.

Its objectives were to improve the well-being of the rural population; correct disparities in regional development; ensure food sovereignty and security, environmental protection, and recognition of the multifunctional nature of rural society. It is important to note that it was not presented as part of a broader conception of the national economy, mainly in environmental matters.

Wine sector in Mexico

Secretary of Agriculture and Rural Development (2022): Approximately 80 varieties of grapes are grown in Mexico; 50% are for industrial use, mainly for wine. In the last decade, Mexican wine consumption grew 20%. Current production covers only 30% of national demand.

The improvement in grape varieties and technological innovations has increased productivity and performance in the sector. The national wine industry is made up of producers of industrial grapes, fruit and concentrated juice, table wines and liquors (brandy) (Tables 3.1 and 3.2).

Table 3.1 Main entities producing grape varieties for wine, 5,000 tons

States of the Mexican Republic White Inks.	*Inks*	*Inks*
Baja California	**Tempranillo** **Var. Tintas:** Cabernet Sauvignon, Merlot and Tempranillo	**Var. Blancas:** Chenin Blanc, Chardonnay and Sauvignon Blanc
Zacatecas	**Var Inks:** Carignan, Ruby Cabernet Sauvignon and Salvador	**Var Whites:** Saint Emilion, Italia and Muscatel
Coahuila	**Var Inks:** Cabernet-Sauvignon, Merlot and Syrah	**Var Whites:** Chardonnay and Muscatel
Guanajuato	**Var Inks:** Cabernet Sauvignon, Tempranillo, Merlot, Syrah, Petite Sirah	**Var Whites:** Semillón
Querétaro	**Var Inks:** Tempranillo and Cabernet Sauvignon	**Var Whites:** Chenin Blanc, Chardonnay and Sauvignon Blanc

Source: Own elaboration based on Gobierno de México. Secretary of Agriculture and Rural Development. Secretary of Agri-Food and Fisheries Information (SIAP) (2023).

Table 3.2 Production volume by state and type of grape

Grape fruit	*Industrial grapes*	*Raisin*
Sonora	Zacatecas	Sonora
Zacatecas	Baja California	Baja California
Aguascalientes	Aguascalientes	
Baja California	Coahuila	
Jalisco	Guanajuato	
Coahuila	Querétaro	
San Luis Potosí	Sonora	
Puebla	Chihuahua	
Guanajuato	San Luis Potosi	
Baja California Sur	Nuevo León	

Source: Own elaboration based on Secretary of Agriculture and Rural Development. Secretary of Agri-Food and Fisheries Information (SIAP).

Main wine routes in Mexico (2023):

1. Valle de Guadalupe Baja California
2. Zacatecas Wine Route
3. The Guanajuato wine route
4. Art, Cheese and Wine of Querétaro
5. Organic vineyard of Aguascalientes
6. Dinos and Wines Coahuila

Ministry of Agriculture and Rural Development: Secretary of Agri-Food and Fisheries Information (SIAP) (2023) pointed out that the national wine sector generates more than 500,000 jobs only in the primary activity of the vine and 1,200 direct jobs and more than 10,000 indirect jobs, which makes it rank as the second-most important employer in the primary sector.

The Secretariat of Agriculture and Rural Development and the Mexican Wine Council (CMV) held the event Our Wealth: Mexican Wine, where they recognized authors who contribute to the knowledge of the wine sector, considering that Wine Day is celebrated on October 7 with the representation of the Secretary of Agriculture and Rural Development, Víctor Villalobos Arámbula (www.gob.mx/agricultura/prensa/contribuye-sector-vitivinicola-al-crecimiento-productivo-y-economico-en-el-sector-primario-del-pais-agricultura).

On the other hand, the general coordinator of Agriculture, Santiago Arguello Campos, pointed out that improving the level of resilience in the sector is essential for its permanence and growth, with the management of sustainable production systems, under the effects of climate change at a global level. He assured that science and research are the cornerstone to promote innovative processes in the development of technologies, irrigation systems, pest and disease control, as well as integrated agronomic management to increase productivity and yields in primary activity, through support of the public assets of the federal agency (www.gob.mx/agricultura/prensa/contribuye-sector-vitivinicola-al-crecimiento-productivo-y-economico-en-el-sector-primario-del-pais-agricultura).

It was specified that Mexico is considered the oldest wine producer in Latin America and ranks 33rd worldwide. Last year it recorded a planted area of 36 thousand hectares, of which 24,000 were harvested for table grapes, 9,000 for grapes for industrial use (wines and juices) and the rest for raisins. He highlighted the leadership of Baja California, which concentrates 44.4% of the surface area destined for the cultivation of grapes for industrial use, followed by Zacatecas, Aguascalientes, Coahuila, Querétaro, Chihuahua, Guanajuato, Sonora, San Luis Potosí and Nuevo León (www.gob.mx/agricultura/prensa/contribuye-sector-vitivinicola-al-crecimiento-productivo-y-economico-en-el-sector-primario-del-pais-agricultura).

The president of the International Organization of Vine and Wine (OIV), Luigi Maio, welcomed the commemoration of the first year of the

National Mexican Wine Day, which is a great initiative to increase the dissemination and intergenerational transmission of culture of this drink. The author of the book, *Winegrowers of the Hispanic Baja California's, 300 Years of Mexican Traditions*, Rondi Frankel, was recognized for the contribution of her work in which through 25 years of work she exposes the direct historical line between the first winegrowers and the current ones. She highlighted that the roots of the acclaimed California wine are Mexican, not Spanish and come from native and New Spanish hands, responsible for current winemaking.

Methodology

The research was qualitative, exploratory and descriptive, which was carried out in SMEs in the wine sector, located in the Querétaro Cheese and Wine tourist corridor.

Nine scientific articles, one book and 12 websites were reviewed.

Personal visits were carried out to the selected SMEs.

The analysis category was made up of two types of small wine companies.

Two selection criteria for SMEs were used:

First criterion, SMEs dedicated to planting, harvesting, processing, fermenting, bottling, marketing their products and providing services to tourism, of which 12 were identified.

1. Finca Sala Vivé de Freixenet de México
2. La Redonda Vineyards
3. Winery San Juanito Vitivinicola
4. Polo Vineyards
5. Terra Salvador Vinicola
6. Hacienda Atongo
7. Terra Alonso
8. Cote Vineyards
9. Wolf Gate
10. Azteca Vineyards
11. Donato Vineyards
12. El Marquéz Wines

Second criterion, SMEs dedicated to the production and marketing of wine, of which five were selected.

1. Rosales vineyards
2. Rancho San Miguel Agroindustry's
3. Los Tres Sarmientos Vineyards
4. Rancho Santa María
5. Maria and Bernardo

Procedure

Tours were carried out within the vineyards, some as a tourist and others as a researcher, everything depended on the disposition of the SMEs.

An active observation was carried out on them.

Semi-structured interviews were conducted with willing workers.

Research questions

Are you interested in caring for the environment?
What actions were implemented for the care of the environment?
What are the environmental certifications they have been obtained?
How many male and female workers work in the vineyard?
What activities are carried out?
What jobs do they have?

Results

These are the results found:

a) The activities observed in the SMEs studied are focused on ecocentrism and sustainability.
b) Medals awarded by organizations such as the OIV (the international organization of vineyards and wine). It was created in 1924 as the International Wine Office to homogenize the world wine situation. It currently provides grape and wine-producing and wine-consuming countries with information to develop regulations, minimize trade barriers, promote sustainable production and protect consumers (www.oiv.int/es/quienes-somos/presentacion).
c) Puerta de Lobo Vineyards received two medals, obtained on June 28, 2023, Mexico Medal for obtaining the highest score in its categories, according to the Querétaro cluster, according to the website: https://alternativo.mx/vinos-queretanos- creditors-of-31-medals/. Puerta del Lobo received a gold medal thanks to his Tio Neto red wine, which reflects.
d) The work and talent of the team. UEC (Spanish Union of Tasters) announced the 32 major gold medals in the list of winners of 2021. Bacchus international award is endorsed by more than 80 professionals of various nationalities who have rated the 1,692 wines registered (www.vinetur.com/2021052864793/bacchus-2021-estos-son-los-32-mejores-vinos-del-mundo.html). In the Brussels 2022 world competition, it received a silver medal, which places the winery as a benchmark for Queretaro quality and pride.
e) Sala Vivé de Freixenet in Mexico was awarded the following medals:

   Trophy (1 of 18): Terra Madi Blanc de Noirs—For the best sparkling wine from the New World.

Award Japanese Wine Challenge (1 of 3): Terra Madi Blanc de Noirs—Award for the best Mexican wine.
Gold Terra Madi Blanc de Noirs, Terra Madi Brut Reserve
Bronze Living Room Semi Dry

f) For Freixenet México, the Japanese market continues to be the largest in terms of exports, so it is a pride to be classified by the Japan Wine Challenge as the winery that produces the best Mexican wine, as well as the best sparkling wine of all the new world (https://vagabundeando.mx/blog/78/Freixenet-Mexico-vinicola-de-Queretaro-gana-4-medallas-en-el-Japan-Wine-Challenge).
g) 25th edition Japan Wine Challenge 2022, held every year, is the oldest and most prestigious competition in all Asia. A total of more than 1,200 wines from the main producing countries participated and a very experienced jury, made up of eight of the main wine experts, were in charge of choosing the best, after a blind tasting, thus guaranteeing their neutrality.
h) Winery San Juanito Vitivinicola obtained Neutral Carbon recognition from the MéxiCO2 organization, Mexican Carbon Platform, and has managed to neutralize its carbon emissions.
i) It is worth mentioning that Winery San Juanito Vitivinicola won 92 medals for its Exquisite Wines, and each bottle tells a story of passion and effort, from deep reds to fresh whites.
j) Los Rosales Vineyards, from its website: https://vinedoslosrosales.com/ is a wine-producing house located in Tequisquiapan, heart of the Querétaro wine region. After a few decades of producing grapes for other wine producers, the firm decided to re-engage and start producing its own label wines. They are located at kilometer 27 of the Tequisquiapan–Ezequiel Montes Highway.
k) Los 3 Sarmientos Vineyards have a comprehensive project, in which they plant and harvest the fruit of the vine, to make red wine with their own brand that they produce artisanally on the organic farm, where they prepare their own insecticides and fertilizers for pest control. The family vineyard is located in Santa Matilde (El Sol de San Juan del Rio, www.elsoldesanjuandelrio.com.mx/circulos/vinedos-tres-sarmientos-proyecto-sensorial-1945758.html
l) La Redonda Vineyards. He won Mexico Medal on June 28, 2023, for obtaining the highest score in its categories, according to the Querétaro cluster, obtained from the website: https://alternativo.mx/vinos-queretanos-acreedores-de- 31-medals/.
m) Agroindustry's Rancho San Miguel. They are dedicated to growing grapes for the wine industry, conventional and organic blueberries for export, as well as alfalfa and forage for the country's dairy industry, http://rancho-sanmiguel.com/

n) Donato Vineyards (https://donato.com.mx/nosotros.php) is located in Bernal. It has obtained six medals, the last one on June 28, 2023. Mexico Medal by obtaining the highest score in its categories, according to the Queretano cluster.
o) https://alternativo.mx/vinos-queretanos-acreedores-de-31-medallas/
p) Ibarra Lozano expressed his pride and highlighted that 31 medals were obtained in the Mexico International Wine Competition 2023 and are recognition of the quality and excellence of Queretaro wines. Liliana Cedillo, director of the Querétaro Wine Cluster, highlighted that 29 Querétaro wines received a gold medal, following the standards of the OIV, and two labels were honored with the Mexico Medal for obtaining the highest score in their categories. In total, Bodegas de Cote received 10 gold medals, the Cluster obtained two medals (including the Mexico medal), Donato received six medals, Freixenet from Mexico obtained three medals, Puerta del Lobo and San Juanito received two medals each, and Bodegas Valdozor, Azteca, Viñedos del Polo and La Redonda each took a medal. https://alternativo.mx/vinos-queretanos-acreedores-de-31-medallas/

Advantages of knowledge management

Take advantage of natural resources to produce goods in a sustainable way.

- Improve quality.
- Improve the image of the company.
- Be aware of social responsibility.
- Obtain recognitions in Mexico and the world, through quality medals in wine, as well as environmental certificates.
- Constant update in employee training.
- Have an ecocentric mindset.

Disadvantages of knowledge management

- Updates on and application of new regulations.
- Updating on controls.
- Increase in costs.
- Loads of work.

Discussion

We are all witnesses that we live in a world of continuous changes, and in this scenario, Nonaka (2007), cited in Garcia (2016), pointed out that "markets change, technologies proliferate, competitors multiply, products become obsolete, so successful companies consistently create new knowledge, they disseminate it widely throughout the organization and quickly incorporate it into new products and technologies" (p. 1).

Nonaka (2007), cited in Garcia (2016), alluded to another way of perceiving knowledge and its role in business organizations, through extremely successful Japanese competitors, such as Honda, Canon, Matsushita, NEC, Sharp and Kao, who had the ability to respond with agility to customers, creating new markets developing products and mastering emerging technologies. Executives everywhere recognize the serendipitous nature of innovation. The Japanese core is recognizing that creating new knowledge is not simply about processing objective information, rather than taking advantage of the tacit and often subjective ideas, institutions and hunches of individual employees, which must be made available to the company, in general. New knowledge always begins with a person, a worker who gathers ideas over years of experience to generate an innovation, converting tacit knowledge into explicit knowledge, which means having a way to express the inexpressible.

Mejía and Colín (2013) show that the wine SMEs on the route of art, cheese and wine have an interest in an ecocentric position of respect for all nonhuman living beings, with whom they share this planet. Mejía and Colín (2013) state, innovative knowledge management has been necessary to know that the organization is being differentiated from its competitors, placing it as a leader at least in its own sector. The Tiwana company described three types of knowledge, considering that innovative knowledge is what achieves favorable differentiation, and in this sense, an ecocentric position can be established within innovation.

In the SMEs studied, we found activities that are carried out in order to obtain the ten most important Environmental Certificates in Mexico, which is why there are activities related to an ecocentric and sustainable posture for the organization and the environment, but that requires management of the knowledge.

1. Corporate social responsibility: Dignified treatment of workers and clients was observed, which is related to ethics and human rights, cleanliness in all its facilities and of course, a focus on quality.
2. Clean industry: Awarded by PROFEPA that recognizes industries that exceed Mexican regulations on emissions, waste and water. General cleaning was observed in all its facilities, sales areas, restaurants, bathrooms, green areas, gardens and rest spaces for clients.
3. Family Responsible Company (EFR): Certificate issued by the Secretary of Labor and Social Welfare. The SMEs studied have between 60% and 70% male workers in their workforce and the rest women, which would seem to be a lack of gender equality; however, the nature of the work requires more men.
4. (Certificate number 8) 100% Carbon neutral program: Private initiative in Latin America that certifies companies that have plans to be net zero or have already achieved it. Only Winery San Juanito Vitivinicola

obtained the Carbon Neutral recognition by the MéxiCO2 organization, the Mexican Carbon Platform, which managed to neutralize its carbon emissions, through a combination of reducing internal emissions and investing in carbon offset projects, which contributes significantly to the mitigation of climate change. This achievement is a testament to the power of collaboration and shared vision. This company is honored to lead the way toward a more sustainable and environmentally friendly future.

Gutierrez P.J. (2007) defined the position of the ecocentrist, as one that considers that it is up to this modern society to get along with nature, to use production techniques, in accordance with each natural environment and with the minimum of artificial inputs, for which it has devised various forms of production. of food. However, today's society has become rigid by admitting two opposing positions. The first position focuses on the preservation of nature, while the second is hyper-intensively committed to the resources of nature for the personal purposes of the industrial, transformative, consumer and user classes, without much concern for the future of humanity or of nature. In the case of the SMEs studied, an ecocentric position was found, focused on the awareness of preserving nature. These were the statements of workers at all levels, which were expressed clearly and spontaneously during visits to the companies.

Gutierrez P.J. (2007) explained that ecology is not seen as a social problem; it is not a priority in development plans, in any area or at any political level, neither municipal, state nor national, since environmental issues are only touched on three occasions: electoral campaigns, when an environmental impact causes some direct or indirect damage to human health, when poor management of natural resources or toxic or industrial waste has detrimental consequences on the local economy, regional or global. However, the current perception of those who are part of wine SMEs is opposite, since ecology is identified as something in which we are all responsible.

It is worth mentioning that the responsibility for the creation of new knowledge is not the responsibility of a group or a department of experts. Managers, middle management employees and rank-and-file employees all have their share of responsibility. Managers must address this confusion. When rank-and-file employees develop an idea that makes sense, they may find it difficult to gauge the importance of their contributions to others, because the knowledge is not received positively, but rather each person interprets it and adjusts it to their own needs, own situation and perspective. That is, what makes sense in one context may change or not make sense in another, resulting in the new knowledge disseminated in the organization creating confusion (Valhondo, 2010).

It is important to identify appropriate individuals at each level, knowledge integrators: editors, writers, technicians, scientists and so forth who have the ability to structure and make knowledge understandable, that is, knowledge workers, in the case of wine SMEs, whose main activity is the cultivation of the vine, which is followed by other activities such as the production of wine, marketing of grapes, wine and other products that they also commercialize such as cheese and restaurants services. Some of these SMEs are even in the real estate sector. They require enologists, wine tasters, grape growers and marketers as the select group of knowledge workers for these companies.

In this context and according to Valhondo (2010), a knowledge management model is required to structure knowledge management initiatives in organizations. Likewise, establish the practices that place knowledge management as a business activity, with defined roles and responsibilities that must be established and disseminated in organizations. In the SMEs studied, the organizational structures are defined, although most of the positions are overloaded with functions and in many cases, one person executes activities of two or even three positions. It is worth mentioning that key positions such as enologists, wine tasters, marketers, administrators and office workers are occupied by people who have formal studies supported by public and private universities.

In relation to an organizational model of knowledge management in the SMEs studied, it was not observed that the concept as such exists in any of them; however, there are very clear activities related to this concept, that is, new ideas are managed, all staff are motivated to think and improve in the search for quality, especially in wine and customer service. There is a delegation in all people to achieve it

Sustainability is a process that aims to find the balance between the environment and the use of natural resources. Sustainability in these wine SMEs can be observed in the national and international medals obtained for their quality in the production and marketing of wine; the context in which these two activities are carried out attests to their approach to sustainability.

Limitations of the study was time, since, to carry out interviews with managers of all types, it was necessary to depend on the dates and times of these people. The willingness for these interviews was very limited. The nature of the business or activity of these companies in all months of the year is of a lot of work.

Conclusion

The SMEs studied have an ecocentric stance and a focus on organizational sustainability, as they carry out activities in order to obtain the ten most important environmental certifications in Mexico. It is worth mentioning that San Juanito Winery is the only company in this wine sector that obtained Carbon Neutral recognition from the organization MéxiCO2, Mexican Carbon Platform, and has managed to neutralize its carbon emissions.

The activities of SMEs studied, such as zero chemical fertilizers in the planting of vineyards, the use of production techniques in accordance with each natural environment and with the minimum of artificial inputs, the focus on all wine-quality processes, are a proof of its desire to live with nature and respect it, having knowledge management as its main basis and organizational sustainability as its purpose.

References

Alternativo. https://alternativo.mx/vinos-queretanos-acreedores-de-31-medallas/

Amato, C.N., Buraschi, M., & Peretti, M.F. (2016). Orientación de los empresarios de Córdoba-Argentina hacia la sustentabilidad y la responsabilidad social empresarial: identificación de variables asociadas a cada constructo. *Contaduría y administración*, *61*(1), 84–105. https://doi.org/10.1016/j.cya.2015.10.001

Biblioteca Jurídica Virtual del Instituto de Investigaciones Juridicas de la UNAM. (2011). *Nuestra Sociedad Posindustrial y las tendencias a la concentración económica* (pp. 21–41). https://archivos.juridicas.unam.mx/www/bjv/libros/9/4123/5.pdf

Carral, G. (2008). La Ley de Desarrollo Rural Sustentable y el campo mexicano. *Revista de Geografía Agrícola*, (40), 55–72. www.redalyc.org/articulo.oa?id=75711534006

El Sol de San Juan del Rio. www.elsoldesanjuandelrio.com.mx/circulos/vinedos-tres-sarmientos-proyecto-sensorial-1945758.html

Fierro Moreno, E., & Mercado Salgado, P. (2012). La gestión del conocimiento y la cultura centrada en el conocimiento en mandos medios y directivos de hospitales públicos del Estado de México. *Investigación administrativa*, *41*(109), 7–19. www.scielo.org.mx/scielo.php?script=sci_arttext&pid=S2448-76782012000100007&lng=es&tlng=es

Garcia, A. (2016). Creación, conversión, facilitación y espacios del conocimiento: las aportaciones de Ikujiro Nonaka a la teoría organizacional. *Entreciencias: Diálogos en la Sociedad del Conocimiento*, *4*(9), 73–88. www.redalyc.org/journal/4576/457645340006/html/

Gobierno de México. (2023). Contribuye sector vitivinícola al crecimiento productivo y económico en el sector primario de país: Agricultura. *Secretaría de Agricultura y Desarrollo Rural* [SIAP]. www.gob.mx/agricultura/prensa/contribuye-sector-vitivinicola-al-crecimiento-productivo-y-economico-en-el-sector-primario-del-pais-agricultura

Gutierrez, P.J. (2007). Configuración ecológica del medio ambiental como bien jurídico. *Revista Aranzadi de derecho ambiental*, *2*(12), 263–285. https://dialnet.unirioja.es/servlet/articulo?codigo=2723238

Herrera, D., Marmolejo, Pérez, V., & Ávila, P. (2022). Derechos de la naturaleza: Una aproximación desde la práctica jurisprudencial. *Centro de Estudios Constitucionales SCJN*. www.sitios.scjn.gob.mx/cec/blog-cec/derechos-de-la-naturaleza-una-aproximacion-desde-la-practica-jurisprudencial

Las 10 Principales Certificaciones de Sustentabilidad en México. (2023). www.csrconsulting.com.mx/2023/06/30/las-10-principales-certificaciones-de-sustentabilidad-en-mexico/

Mejía, M.I., & Colín, M. (2013). Gestión del conocimiento y su importancia en las organizaciones. *Trilogía Ciencia Tecnología Sociedad*, *5*(9), 25–35. www.redalyc.org/articulo.oa?id=534366871003

Montalván, D. (2020). Justicia ecológica. *Eunomía. Revista en Cultura de la Legalidad*, (18), 179–198. https://doi.org/10.20318/eunomia.2020.5272

Morales, G. (2016). La categoría *ambiente*. Una reflexión epistemológica sobre su uso y su estandarización en las ciencias ambientales. *Revista Electrónica Nova Scientia*, *8*(2), 579–613. www.scielo.org.mx/scielo.php?script=sci_arttext&pid=S2007-07052016000200579

Organización Internacional de la Viña y el Vino. www.oiv.int/es/quienes-somos/presentacion

Procuraduria Federal de Proteccion al Ambiente. (2023). *Convocatoria Distintivo de Calidad Ambiental México.* www.gob.mx/profepa/documentos/convocatoria-distintivo-de-calidad-ambiental-mexico-336256

San Miguel Agroindustria. http://rancho-sanmiguel.com/

Secretary of Agriculture and Rural Development. Secretary of Agri-Food and Fisheries Information (SIAP). (2023). *Contribuye sector vitivinícola al crecimiento productivo y económico en el sector primario de país: Agricultura.* www.gob.mx/agricultura/prensa/contribuye-sector-vitivinicola-al-crecimiento-productivo-y-economico-en-el-sector-primario-del-pais-agricultura

Universidad de Murcia. (2023). *Los principales problemas ambientales.* www.um.es/sabio/docs-cmsweb/materias-pau-bachillerato/tema_9._problemas_ambientales.pdf

Vagabundeando. https://vagabundeando.mx/blog/78/Freixenet-Mexico-vinicola-de-Queretaro-gana-4-medallas-en-el-Japan-Wine-Challenge

Valhondo, D. (2010). Gestión del conocimiento del mito a la realidad. *Diaz de Santos.* https://books.google.co.ve/books?id=MClLAQAACAAJ&printsec=copyright&hl=es#v=onepage&q&f=false

Vernier, D. (2023). Impacto Proyecto. *Responsabilidad Social Empresarial en México.* www.proyectaimpacto.com/2023/10/responsabilidad-social-empresarial-en-mexico/

Vinetur. www.vinetur.com/2021052864793/bacchus-2021-estos-son-los-32-mejores-vinos-del-mundo.html

4 Theoretical concepts and generic tools to incorporate sustainability via knowledge management into post-industrial organizations in the 21st century

David Israel Contreras-Medina and Verónica Cerroblanco-Vázquez

Introduction

From its beginning, the concept of "sustainability" was based on empirical facts that gave rise to theoretical questions about what is known today as sustainable development. The first of these practical events occurred in the 19th century, when the poor relationship between human beings and their environment was detected, becoming evident in the excessive use of natural resources without replacement (Lowenthal, 2015).

This first fact gave way to the second in which, derived from the previous actions, concern was expressed that the poor relationship with the environment would affect economic growth by the representatives of various countries within the Stockholm summit, but it was not until the establishment of the Brundtland Commission in which sustainability was established by defining as "meeting the needs of the present without compromising the ability of future generations to meet their own needs," relating the social and economic aspects to the environment at the end of 20th century (Brundtland, 1987; UN, 2023; Alfaro et al., 2014).

The empirical meaning transferred to the theoretical is not new. Possibly the most representative event was the creation of technology, in which, based on the experience of people dedicated to agriculture, technical solutions were provided to problems, allowing the result of a genetic reservoir, giving way to a theoretical establishment applicable to the context, and setting the precedent of theory over practice (Sagasti, 2011).

In line with the definition of sustainability and now under the theoretical-empirical intersection, at the beginning of the 21st century, various nations and organizations began to manage support and programs as concepts to develop actions to benefit the environment, the economy and society. In the case of countries, for example, in Mexico, the Trust Established in Relation to Agriculture (FIRA acronym in Spanish), in coordination with the European Union and

DOI: 10.4324/9781003465058-4

the French Development Agency, established the support program for sustainable projects, facilitating access to credit and technical support for investment projects in the agricultural, forestry and fishing sectors that generate benefits to the environment (FIRA, 2022). Portugal, from the tourism industry, has managed to balance the social, economic and environmental aspects, considering variables such as seasonality, value generation and employment, which has earned it the ITB Earth Award for the success of its strategy and its example of global leadership against climate change (Turismo de Portugal, 2019). Ethiopia's forestry sector focuses on plating plants to create jobs, stimulate post-COVID-19 recovery and improve health (ONU, 2020).

For organizations, the transfer of theoretical (concepts) to empirical (practices) has evolved through the creation of various paradigms and technological tools. An important era for this was marked by the arrival of the First Industrial Revolution, in which the appearance of the steam engine, the origin of energy, shifted from human beings to the use of different tools and technologies, registering a first model shift by replacing manual work with mechanical work, giving way to industrialization concept in the 18th century (González-Hernández et al., 2021; Peñaloza, 2007).

Industrialization, defined as the process of industries in a country or an area (Oxford, n.d.), focused on mass production, was gradually introduced to organizations. This concept was strengthened after the Second Industrial Revolution, mainly with the conceptualization of Taylorism, which established the division of labor and time study as part of its meaning at the beginning of the 19th century (Valencia Castrejón, 2020).

With the arrival of the Third Industrial Revolution, the transition toward renewable energies was introduced, introducing the concept of information and communication technologies and the use of computers in the 1980s. This same term is transferred to the Fourth Industrial Revolution, introducing the so-called Industry 4.0 with more sophisticated technological tools in the second decade of the 21st century (Rodríguez, 2017; Martínez Valdez et al., 2018).

During the period of the Industrial Revolution in its different stages, there was a transition from the industrial era to the post-industrial, characterized by the new presence of knowledge, which preceded the arrival of the so-called knowledge society (Cairós Barreto, 2001).

With the beginning of the era of the knowledge society, in 1969, a higher growth rate began to be marked and organizations began to prioritize knowledge as an important part of their development (Steinmueller, 2017; Aróstica Fernández, 2014), giving way to knowledge management concept.

The knowledge management concept is openly defined as a multidisciplinary approach process that creates, stores, shares, uses and manages knowledge to achieve the objectives of an organization through technological tools (CEPAL, 2020).

One of its most important representatives, Ikujiro Nonaka, has stated that knowledge is created by combining tacit and explicit knowledge, generating new concepts and ideas (Nonaka, 1994). This mixture represents an organization's epistemological and ontological philosophies, starting from the socialization of people's tacit knowledge and ending in internalization through the SECI model.

Over time, the concept of knowledge management has been harshly criticized for emphasizing technological tools for use; however, although the ghost of industrialization could be present, post-industrialization creates a more balanced context, focusing knowledge and its management on human beings before technology.

At the beginning of the 21st century, particularly speaking of the second decade, the sense of emphasizing the importance of the human being is promoted by the European Commission through programs such as Science With and For Society (Comisión Europea, 2020); by the Organization for Economic Co-operation and Development (OECD), with the employment program focused on people (OECD, 2021); or by the incoming Industry 5.0 that takes people as a pivot for the implementation of technologies for achieving sustainability (Nahavandi, 2019). This concurrence of knowledge management, concepts, tools/technologies and sustainability is installed in the direction of countries and organizations, even with their respective worldwide social, economic, technological and environmental vicissitudes. Therefore, this study explores the theoretical concepts and tools/technologies used to integrate sustainability under the common thread of knowledge management in post-industrial organizations of the 21st century.

Methodology

Based on the approach of systematic review, the information was obtained from the SCOPUS database in September 2023 using the Boolean operator as a validated methodology for developing studies following Tamburino et al. (2020); Scells et al. (2019) and Contreras-Medina et al. (2022). From this, titles, abstracts and keywords of scientific articles from 2000 to 2023 in English and Spanish were extracted, exploring keywords, concepts, tools, technology, sustainability, knowledge and management. Additionally, an exploration has been carried out since 1960 in the so-called post-industrial era under the same terms.

The sequence of the words is recorded as follows:

Concepts AND tools OR technology AND sustainability AND knowledge AND management AND PUBYEAR > 1960 AND PUBYEAR < 2025 AND (LIMIT-TO (DOCTYPE, "ar")) AND (LIMIT-TO (LANGUAGE "English") OR LIMIT-TO (LANGUAGE, "Spanish")).

The operators' operability was based on their definition within the context of the various studies. In concept, the idea with the greatest emphasis used in the study (Oxford, n.d.a); for tools/technology, the instruments/technologies (Oxford, n.d.b); in sustainability, the sustainable economic, social, or environmental aspects considered (Brundtland, 1987); while for knowledge management, the common thread that articulates and amplifies knowledge (Nonaka, 1994).

The information preparation began by classifying the various Excel files issued by the SCOPUS database and extracting the empirical articles based on the study's objective.

Analysis, order and organization for displaying information

The articles were analyzed and organized based on knowledge management as the guiding thread of the work, including: 1) the concept, extracting the term or idea with greater emphasis; 2) tools or technologies, such as technological elements referred into the study; 3) sustainability, dimension or record that is given in the document. All classified by industry according to economic sector, productive activity and place of the research.

Results

A total of 151 documents were displayed and 51 documents with the keywords concepts, tools, technology, sustainability and knowledge management as the guideline of the review. Within the primary sector, six papers were found in the line of agriculture, food production and silk. The secondary 14 texts were in manufacturing, textile, technology and aluminum. Regarding tertiary, 31 studies were discovered as a part of education, public sector, research and development and biotechnology, information technologies and telecommunications, deposit-taking savings and credit cooperative societies, tourism and hospitality, healthcare and commercialization, with the following details:

Primary

- Agriculture:
  - Mexico encloses the SECI model as a knowledge management process combined tacit/explicit, using SECI and roadmapping as concepts, including emerging technologies as fiber optic refractometer, metal rooftop, horizontal distiller-fractionator, metal containers and glass bottles as a proposal to implement; pursuing the sustainability of the process (Contreras-Medina et al., 2021).

- Mexico considers tacit and explicit knowledge management conversion, using road mapping as the main concept, detecting emerging technologies (digital quality management, advanced and statistical process control) and searching for sustainable practices (Contreras-Medina et al., 2020).
- Brazil includes knowledge exchange; the concept considers actions and resources, tools, knowledge and tangible products, searching for economic, social and environmental impact (Silva et al., 2019).
- Italy considers knowledge management as a tool, incorporating the sustainability of knowledge management as a concept and searching for sustainable management (Zecca & Rastorgueva, 2017).

- Food production:
  - Pakistan uses knowledge management adoption and implementation, employing managerial barriers as the concept, exemplifying the innovation and technological barrier, with the goal of a sustainable supply food chain (Nazam et al., 2020).
- Silk:
  - Thailand includes knowledge integration capability; the concept is also knowledge integration capability to obtain, apply, transform and aggregate internal and external sources; the tools are the information technology to manage production knowledge, considering competitive positioning (Wichitsathian & Nakruang, 2019) (Figure 4.1).

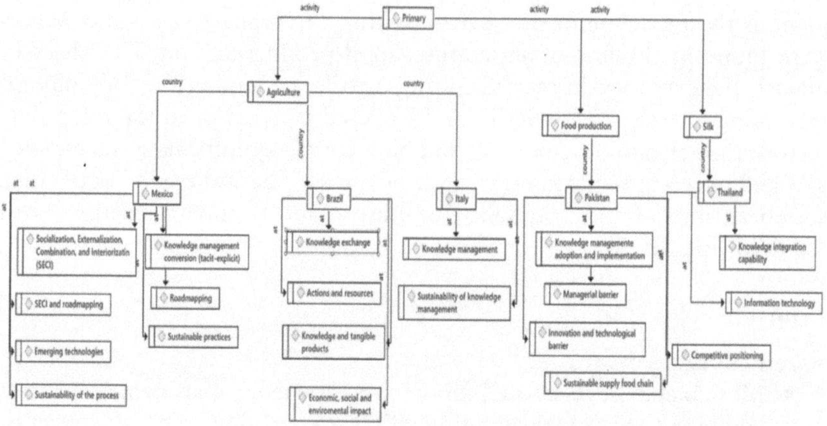

Figure 4.1 Concepts, tools, technology, sustainability and knowledge management in the primary sector.

Source: Contreras-Medina et al. (2021); Contreras-Medina et al. (2020); Silva et al. (2019); Zecca and Rastorgueva (2017); Nazam et al. (2020) and Wichitsathian and Nakruang (2019).

Secondary

- Manufacturing:
    - China includes the knowledge management dimensions through knowledge acquisition and application, handling the knowledge-based view concept, incorporating blockchain as a tool and relating sustainable organizational performance as a goal (Sun et al., 2022).
    - Ethiopia contains the knowledge management dimensions as knowledge sharing, conversion and storage, taking this term as a concept driving knowledge provider and receiver, involving platform as a tool, indicating innovative advantage as a goal (Erena et al., 2023).
    - Pakistan comprises knowledge management as acquisition, dissemination and application; annexing corporate green innovation as a concept; mentioning the important aspects for technological adoption; and connecting organizational sustainability through sustainable development practices (Shahzad et al., 2021).
    - South Korea involves knowledge transfer, registering the sustainable technological human resource concept by combining technologies and know-how, comprising technological innovation as a tool and having sustainable technological human resources as a goal (Lee & Ma, 2021).
    - Malaysia contains knowledge management under the concept of organizational performance, comprising information, innovation and technology capability as the tools for searching business sustainability (Muthuveloo et al., 2021).
    - Sweden encloses a knowledge management platform considering skill development, training and change, encompassing sustainable product development as the concept and guideline, besides digitalization as the tool (Hallstedt et al., 2020).
    - India uses project knowledge management under the project performance concept, big data analytics as a tool and the line of sustainability (Mangla et al., 2021).
    - China contains knowledge acquisition, integration and application; uses lean concept; technology is handled concurrent engineering focusing on lean sustainability (Zhang et al., 2020).
    - Pakistan encompasses knowledge management capabilities such as knowledge distribution, new knowledge and knowledge use; it includes looking at sustainable competitive advantage as a tool, considering technology infrastructure as hardware, software, networks and data storage (Akram et al., 2018).
    - The United States includes a knowledge management strategy, which uses the concept of interaction of people, technology and techniques; the tool is a technology management strategy for achieving sustainable manufacturing (Mandal & Bagchi, 2016).

- Textile:
  - Thailand considers knowledge management as performing the work, efficiency, developing production processes, and acquiring new knowledge and the necessary knowledge to work; the concept is about knowledge management regarding training and education before working; contemplating technology management parameters as the tools; pursuing sustainability in the industry (Lueadthahan et al., 2021).
  - Vietnam uses knowledge creation, sharing and storage; it incorporates and searches for social sustainability as social responsibility, work conditions, communications, collaboration and transparency; and it uses information technology as a tool (Lim et al., 2017).
- Technology:
  - Thailand employs logistics knowledge management, combining these terms as the concept (Management and logistics knowledge) in tools incorporating contemporary technologies for sustainable logistic innovation (Leepaitoon et al., 2020).
- Aluminum:
  - The United States and Iceland (multinational) focus on knowledge sharing; the concept is centered on knowledge/environmental sustainability; the tools are business intelligence, mobile devices, data visualization and social networking for achieving sustainable management (Spangler et al., 2014) (see Table 4.1).

Tertiary

- Education services:
  - Lithuania includes the acquisition of knowledge, storage, sharing, application and creation were registered; incorporating knowledge management as the concept; using Information and Communication Technologies ICT, internet and intranet (in knowledge storage); linking the sustainable development (Raudeliūnienė et al., 2020).
  - Malaysia includes technical knowledge management, cultural, human and structural approaches, emphasizing the concept of human knowledge; robot technology is included as a tool for career sustainability (AlQershi et al., 2023).
  - Saudi Arabia includes knowledge sharing, application and access which are managed using the concept of knowledge sharing as the emphasis of the study, including the tools of Massive Open Line Courses MOOCs, incorporating sustainable development (Alyoussef, 2023).

Table 4.1 Concepts, tools, technology, sustainability and knowledge management in the secondary sector

Secondary					
Activity	*Place*	*Knowledge management*	*Concept*	*Tools technology*	*Sustainability*
Manufacturing	China	Knowledge acquisition and application	Knowledge based view	Blockchain	Sustainable organizational performance
	Ethiopia	Knowledge sharing, conversion and storage	Knowledge provider and receiver	Platform	Innovative advantage
	Pakistan	Knowledge acquisition, dissemination and application	Corporate green innovation	Technological adoption	Sustainable development practices
	South Korea	Knowledge transfer	Sustainable technological human resource	Technological innovation	Sustainable technological human resource
	Malaysia	Knowledge management	Organizational performance	Information, innovation and technology capability	Business sustainability
	Sweden	Knowledge management platform	Sustainable product development	Digitalization	Sustainable product development
	India	Project knowledge management	Project performance	Big data analytics	Sustainability
	China	Knowledge acquisition, integration and application	Lean	Concurrent engineering	Lean sustainability
	Pakistan	Knowledge distribution, new knowledge and using knowledge	Sustainable competitive advantage	Hardware, software, networks and data storage	Sustainable competitive advantage
	United States of America	Knowledge management strategy	Interaction of people, technology and techniques	Technology management strategy	Sustainable manufacturing
Textile	Thailand	Perform the work, efficiency, develop production processes, new knowledge for use, and necessary knowledge to work	Training and educate them before working	Technology management parameters	Sustainability
	Vietnam	Knowledge creation, sharing and storage	Social sustainability	Information technology	Social sustainability
Technology	Thailand	Logistics knowledge management	Management & logistics knowledge	Contemporary technologies	Sustainable logistic innovation
Aluminum	United States of America & Iceland	knowledge sharing	Knowledge/environmental sustainability	Business intelligence, mobile devices, data visualization, and social networking	Sustainable management

Source: Author's elaboration based on Sun et al. (2022); Erena et al. (2023); Shahzad et al. (2021); Lee and Ma (2021); Muthuveloo et al. (2021); Hallstedt et al. (2020); Mangla et al. (2021); Zhang et al. (2020); Akram et al. (2018); Mandal and Bagchi (2016); Lueadthahan et al. (2021); Lim et al. (2017); Leepaitoon et al. (2020) and Spangler et al. (2014).

    - China includes knowledge exploitation and exploration; these are used as concepts relating to the performance for exploitation and experimentation in exploration; the tools are R&D projects with the aim of University performance (Centobelli et al., 2019).
    - Poland contains knowledge management, defined as having the right information at the right time as a concept, exposing the lack of technology in tools and having sustainable development as a goal (Ulewicz & Blaskova, 2018).
    - Spain employs knowledge transfer (sharing and application), uses epistemological and ontological concepts and includes the conceptual model as an innovative tool for sustainable and transferable education (Fidalgo-Blanco et al., 2015).
    - Italy uses knowledge management, includes metacognitive knowledge as the concept, incorporates social online environments as a tool and has sustainability related to the cognitive process as a goal (Cinque & Martini, 2012).
    - Multinational involves personal knowledge management using the concept of massive open online courses (MOOC), with open and distance learning in the sense of sustainability plans (Fini, 2009).

- Public sector:

    - In Malaysia, knowledge creation, acquisition, sharing and applications were considered strategies, driving green innovation combined with management as concepts and using innovation practices as tools to achieve green innovation practices (Rahim et al., 2023).
    - Brazil uses the knowledge management process, which incorporates the concept of sustainable public procurement, including costs and environment, as a tool for the appropriate technologies for environmental, economic and social sustainability (Cader Da Silva et al., 2018).
    - South Africa includes the knowledge transfer, which uses the knowledge management concept. Information and communication technologies are the tools and sustainable management is a goal (Conger, 2015).

- Research and development and biotechnology:

    - In Iran, the creation of knowledge, transfer and application is managed through a conceptual model mediated by social media to achieve business sustainability (Tajpour et al., 2022).
    - China uses knowledge and performance management; the concept is open innovation from an enterprise perspective; it uses this same term as a tool, sustainably proposing network convergence (Ma et al., 2018).

- Spain includes knowledge management focused on exogenous and endogenous aspects. It uses the concepts of complexity exogenous and endogenous, including technological innovation, to get sustainable technological innovations as a goal (García-Muina et al., 2010).

- Information Technologies and Telecommunications (TICs):
    - In India, knowledge management is considered the common thread, recording its practice as a concept and moderator, including information technology and managing sustained competitive advantage (Shea et al., 2023).
    - Malaysia includes knowledge management in codification and personalization, managing the concept of strategic fit as a tool for innovation and focusing on sustainable competitive advantage (Khan et al., 2021).
    - Vietnam incorporates knowledge creation, sharing and integration; it comprises an open innovation concept with innovation capability as a tool for sustainable creation (Lam et al., 2021).
    - Brazil uses knowledge sharing and ingenuity as a form of knowledge management; the tools are also ingenuity to incorporate innovation and integrate sustainability in the supply chain project (Siqueira & Honig, 2019).
    - Malaysia integrates knowledge improved through management techniques and tools, technology (knowledge and implementation) and business, as the concept incorporates corporate sustainability, while the tools technology transfer (Fazal et al., 2017).
    - Russia includes knowledge management for exploration and exploitation, uses strategic entrepreneurship as a concept, involves technologies, patents, licenses, professional managers, qualified employees and searches for sustainable competitive advantage (Shirokova et al., 2013).

- Deposit-taking savings and credit cooperative societies:
    - In Kenya, knowledge sharing is managed using this same concept of registering online internal communication as tools, searching for sustainable competitive advantage (Waititu & Barker, 2023).

- Tourism and hospitality:
    - Taiwan uses knowledge management as mediation and moderation, includes the concept of consumer interest, contains blockchain technology as a tool and manages sustainable marketing (Liu & Dong, 2021).

    - Algeria considers knowledge management in four dimensions: conversion, mapping, storage and sharing, including customer relationship management, as the concept of CRM technology as a tool looking for sustainable competitive advantage (Brahami et al., 2020).

- Healthcare:

    - Thailand incorporates knowledge management in an exploration and exploitation sense, integrates the systematic management architecture as the concept, includes technological capabilities and combines the social, economic and environmental dimensions under the meaning of green human resources practices, quality management and chain collaborators, healthcare inventory control system and green innovation (Tseng et al., 2020).
    - Greece includes critical elements of knowledge management relating to perception, synthesis, dissemination, collaboration, means and leadership; the concept focuses on knowledge management enablers such as organizational structure, IT, strategy and culture; the tool is the information and communication systems; to have a sustainable care system (Karamitri et al., 2020).
    - England contains knowledge mobilization; the concept is about knowledge management focusing on how the knowledge and evidence could be used; the tool is decision-making for sustaining change (Day & Goswami, 2020).
    - Iran includes knowledge management, particularly in knowledge sharing, storage, acquisition and creation; it uses the concept of ambidexterity and open innovation as the tools and social, economic and environmental goals for sustainable, balanced performance (Sofiyabadi et al., 2020).
    - Colombia (hospital and academic institutions) uses knowledge sharing, involves knowledge management as the concept, details the implications of technological resources and focuses on continuity and sustainability strategies (Torres Narváez et al., 2014).

- Commercialization:

    - Asia, Europe, North America and Africa include the knowledge management activities; considering this same as a concept in the sense of exploration and knowledge sharing; incorporating the technology commercialization as a tool; and searching the sustainable management activities in an economic sense (Kim et al., 2020).
    - Thailand uses the knowledge creation, incorporates the concept of Pracharat and includes the trademark as a tool while looking for sustainability (Phimolsathien, 2020).

- Construction:
  - Hong Kong, the UK, Singapore and Sri Lanka include knowledge sharing; it contains the relationally integrated value networks as the concept; it has information and communication technology as the tools; and it comprises the sustainably built infrastructure (KW Wong et al., 2014) (Table 4.2).

The intersection between concepts, tools, technology, sustainability and knowledge management, as the guide, shows significant differences in these aspects. The tertiary sector shows a greater number of studies focusing on educational services. The concept is about knowledge management; while tools are related to innovation combined (open innovation), the purpose is to be sustainable, emphasizing knowledge sharing as the guide to knowledge management in post-industrial organizations in this sector. The results align with Sriratanaviriyakul and El-Den (2019) when referring to the significance of the knowledge sharing of internal and external elements in students.

Regarding the secondary, the surveys focus on manufacturing firms, with the concept of knowledge/management; the intention is also to be sustainable, whereas the tool is technology, centering mostly on the acquisition as the line of knowledge management in post-industrial organizations. In the use of technology, this study is in line with Ericsson and Avdic (2002) when considering the impact of internal elements in this industry and the importance of acquiring knowledge.

Concerning the primary post-industrial organizations, the investigations concentrate on agriculture, using the concept of barriers, the term of sustainability and the tools are technologies, focusing on tacit and explicit knowledge as the channel of knowledge management in post-industrial organizations. The focus of the results on tacit and explicit knowledge is in line with what was expressed in the United Nations Permanent Forum by recognizing and respecting the traditional knowledge (tacit-explicit) immersed in peasants and indigenous people around the world (UN, 2019).

Conclusion

Establish that knowledge management theory is located within organizations and is vital in articulating and amplifying knowledge (Nonaka, 1994). The basis for post-industrial organizations of the 21st century, in the primary, secondary and tertiary sectors, is recognized from different perspectives.

For the primary, the emphasis is on converting of tacit to explicit knowledge, transferring people's experiences into tangible elements; for the secondary, it is based on the acquisition of new or improved knowledge obtained from stakeholders; while for the tertiary, it is about knowledge

Table 4.2 Concepts, tools, technology, sustainability and knowledge management in the tertiary sector

Tertiary					
Activity	*Place*	*Knowledge management*	*Concept*	*Tools technology*	*Sustainability*
Education services	Lithuania	Acquisition of knowledge, storage, sharing, application and creation	Knowledge management	Information and communication technologies	Sustainable development
	Malaysia	Technical knowledge management, cultural, human and structural	Human knowledge	Robot technology	Career sustainability
	Saudi Arabia	Knowledge sharing, application, and access	Knowledge sharing	Massive open line courses	Sustainable development
	China	Knowledge exploitation and exploration	Performance for exploitation/ Experimentation in exploration	R&D projects	University performance
	Poland	Knowledge management	Knowledge management	Lack of technology	Sustainable development
	Spain	Knowledge transfer	Epistemological and ontological	Conceptual model	Sustainable and transferable education
	Italy	Knowledge management	Metacognitive knowledge	Social online environments	Cognitive process
	Multinational	Personal knowledge management	Massive open online course	Open and distance learning	Sustainability plans
Public sector	Malaysia	Knowledge creation, acquisition, sharing and applications	Green innovation and management	Innovation practices	Green innovation practices
	Brazil	Knowledge management process	Sustainable public procurement	Appropriate technologies	Environmental, economic and social sustainability
	South Africa	Knowledge transfer	Knowledge management	Information and communication technologies	Sustainable management
R & D/Biotech	Iran	Knowledge creation, transfer and application	Conceptual model	Social media	Business sustainability
	China	Knowledge and performance management	Open innovation	Open innovation	Network convergence
	Spain	Knowledge management/ exogenous and endogenous	Complexity exogenous/ endogenous	Technological innovation	Sustainable technological innovations
TICs	India	Knowledge management	Knowledge practice	Information technology	Sustained competitive advantage
	Malaysia	Knowledge management/ codification-personalization	Strategic fit	Innovation	Sustainable competitive advantage
	Vietnam	Knowledge creation, sharing and integration	Open innovation	Innovation capability	Sustainable creation

	Brazil	Knowledge sharing	Ingenuity	Ingenuity	Sustainability in the supply chain project
	Malaysia	Management techniques and tools, technology (knowledge and implementing), and business	Corporate sustainability	Technology transfer	Corporate sustainability
	Russia	Knowledge management exploration/exploitation	Strategic entrepreneurship	Technologies, patents, licenses, professional managers, and qualified employees	Sustainable competitive advantage
Deposit-taking savings/credit societies	Kenya	Knowledge sharing	Knowledge sharing	Online internal communication	Sustainable competitive advantage
Tourism and hospitality	Taiwan	Knowledge management as mediation and moderation	Consumer interest	Block chain	Sustainable marketing
	Algeria	Knowledge management (conversion, mapping, storage, and sharing)	Customer relationship management	CRM	Sustainable competitive advantage
Healthcare	Thailand	Knowledge management in exploration and exploitation	Systematic management architecture	Technological capabilities	Social, economic and environmental
	Greece	Knowledge management relating to perception, synthesis, dissemination, collaboration, means and leadership	Knowledge management enablers as organizational structure IT, strategy and culture	Information and communication systems	Sustainable care system
	England	Knowledge mobilization	Knowledge and evidence	Decision-making	Sustain change
	Iran	Knowledge sharing, storage, acquisition and creation	Ambidexterity	Open innovation	Sustainable balanced performance
	Colombia	Knowledge sharing	Knowledge management	Technological resources	Sustainability strategies
Commercialization	Asia, Europe, North America, and Africa	Knowledge management activities	Exploration and knowledge sharing	Technology commercialization	Sustainable management activities in economic sense
	Thailand	Knowledge creation	Pracharat	Trademark	Sustainability
Construction	Hong Kong, United Kingdom, Singapore, and Sri Lanka	Knowledge sharing	Value networks	Information and communication technology	Sustainable built infrastructure

Source: Author's elaboration based on Raudeliūnienė et al. (2020); AlQershi et al. (2023); Alyoussef (2023); Centobelli et al. (2019); Ulewicz and Blaskova (2018); Fidalgo-Blanco et al. (2015); Cinque and Martini (2012); Fini (2009); Rahim et al. (2023); Cader Da Silva et al. (2018); Conger (2015); Tajpour et al. (2022); Ma et al. (2018); García-Muina et al. (2010); Shea et al. (2023); Khan et al. (2021); Lam et al. (2021); Siqueira and Honig (2019); Fazal et al. (2017); Shirokova et al. (2013); Waititu and Barker (2023); Liu and Dong (2021); Brahami et al. (2020); Tseng et al. (2020); Karamitri et al. (2020); Day and Goswami (2020); Sofiyabadi et al. (2020); Torres Narváez et al. (2014); Kim et al. (2020); Phimolsathien (2020) and KW Wong et al. (2014)

sharing among individuals and organizations. All studies use a wide range of concepts and tools/technology to be sustainable or obtain sustainability.

In light of the previous results and under the argument of being the sector that supplies raw materials directly or indirectly, it is important to propose and develop studies within the primary sector, as it is a fundamental part of the growth of industries and, above all of the sustainability of human beings and the world.

Acknowledgments

To the Universidad de Guanajuato for its support for developing research and extension as part of its substantive activities.

To the Consejo Nacional de Humanidades, Ciencias y Tecnologias, for the support of research through the scholarship.

References

Akram, M.S., Goraya, M.A.S., Malik, A., & Aljarallah, A.M. (2018). Organizational performance and sustainability: Exploring the roles of IT capabilities and knowledge management capabilities. *Sustainability*, *10*(10), 1–20. https://doi.org/10.3390/su10103816

Alfaro, J.M., Limón, B., Martínez, G.Á., & Tijerina, G. (2014). *Ambiente y sustentabilidad: por una educación ambiental.* Grupo Editorial Patria.

AlQershi, N., Saufi, R.B.A., Yaziz, M.F.B.A., Permarupan, P.Y., Muhammad, N.M.N., Yusoff, M.N.H.B., & Ramayah, T. (2023). The threat of robots to career sustainability, and the pivotal role of knowledge management and human capital. *Journal of Innovation & Knowledge*, *8*(3), 1–10. https://doi.org/10.1016/j.jik.2023.100386

Alyoussef, I.Y. (2023). The impact of Massive Open Online Courses (MOOCs) on knowledge management using integrated innovation diffusion theory and the technology acceptance model. *Education Sciences*, *13*(6), 1–18. https://doi.org/10.3390/educsci13060531

Aróstica Fernández, P. (2014). *China en transición a la sociedad del conocimiento: implicaciones para América Latina* (pp. 1–31). Naciones Unidas & CEPAL colección documentos de proyectos.

Brahami, M., Adjaine, M., Semaoune, K., & Matta, N. (2020). The influences of knowledge management and customer relationship management to improve hotels performance: A case study in hotel sector. *Information Resources Management Journal (IRMJ)*, *33*(4), 74–93. https://doi.org/10.4018/IRMJ.2020100105

Brundtland, G.H. (1987). Report of the world commission on environment and development: Our common future. *United Nations.* https://repositorio.cepal.org/server/api/core/bitstreams/a880c14d-f051-403b-afb7-747784c6356f/content

Cader Da Silva, R., Betiol, L., Villac, T., & Nonato, R. (2018). Sustainable public procurement: The Federal Public Institution's shared system. *Revista de Gestão*, *25*(1), 9–24. https://doi.org/10.1108/REGE-11-2017-001

Cairós Barreto, D.M. (2001). La sociedad post-industrial y sus consecuencias en las relaciones laborales. *Anales de la facultad de derecho*, *18*, 123–139.

Centobelli, P., Cerchione, R., & Esposito, E. (2019). The mediating role of knowledge exploration and exploitation for the development of an entrepreneurial university. *Management Decision*, *57*(12), 3301–3320. https://doi.org/10.1108/MD-11-2018-1240

CEPAL. (2020). Gestión del Conocimiento (GDC). *Biblioteca de la CEPAL*. https://biblioguias.cepal.org/GestionDelConocimiento

Cinque, M., & Martini, A. (2012). Metacognition, motivation and self-efficacy in a socio-cognitive online environment: First results of a survey at the University of Pisa. *Journal of e-Learning and Knowledge Society*, *8*(1), 53–69.

Comisión Europea. (2020). Mission-oriented SwafS to advance innovation through co-creation. *Comisión Europea*. https://doi.org/10.3030/101006382

Conger, S. (2015). Knowledge management for information and communications technologies for development programs in South Africa. *Information Technology for Development*, *21*(1), 113–134. https://doi.org/10.1080/02681102.2014.899960

Contreras-Medina, D.I., Camargo, M.E., & Díaz-Nieto, E.S. (2022). Scientific and technological knowledge: A review of sustainable benefits on the coffee sector. *Coffee Science*, 15–23.

Contreras-Medina, D.I., Contreras-Medina, L.M., Pardo-Nuñez, J., Olvera-Vargas, L.A., & Rodriguez-Peralta, C.M. (2020). Roadmapping as a driver for knowledge creation: A proposal for improving sustainable practices in the coffee supply chain from Chiapas, Mexico, using emerging technologies. *Sustainability*, *12*(14), 1–26. https://doi.org/10.3390/su12145817

Contreras-Medina, D.I., Medina-Cuéllar, S.E., Sánchez-Gómez, J., & Rodríguez-Peralta, C.M. (2021). Innovation of women farmers: A technological proposal for mezcalilleras' sustainability in Mexico, based on knowledge management. *Sustainability*, *13*(21), 1–24. https://doi.org/10.3390/su132111706

Day, A., & Goswami, L. (2020). Driving change with evidence and knowledge: Transforming knowledge services for the NHS across England. *Business Information Review*, *37*(1), 10–18.

Erena, O.T., Kalko, M.M., & Debele, S.A. (2023). Organizational factors, knowledge management and innovation: Empirical evidence from medium-and large-scale manufacturing firms in Ethiopia. *Journal of Knowledge Management*, *27*(4), 1165–1207. https://doi.org/10.1108/JKM-11-2021-0861

Ericsson, F., & Avdic, A. (2002). Information technology and knowledge acquisition in manufacturing companies: A Scandinavian perspective. In E. Coakes, D. Willis, & S. Clarke (Eds.), *Knowledge management in the sociotechnical world: Computer supported cooperative work* (pp. 121–135). Springer. https://doi.org/10.1007/978-1-4471-0187-1_11

Fazal, S.A., Al Mamun, A., Wahab, S.A., & Mohiuddin, M. (2017). Host-country characteristics, corporate sustainability, and the mediating effect of improved knowledge: A study among foreign MNCs in Malaysia. *Multinational Business Review*, *25*(4), 328–349. https://doi.org/10.1108/MBR-07-2017-0042

Fidalgo-Blanco, Á., Sein-Echaluce, M.L., & García-Peñalvo, F. (2015). Epistemological and ontological spirals: From individual experience in educational innovation to the organisational knowledge in the university sector. *Program*, *49*(3), 266–288. https://doi.org/10.1108/PROG-06-2014-0033

Fini, A. (2009). The technological dimension of a massive open online course: The case of the CCK08 course tools. *The International Review of Research in Open and Distributed Learning*, *10*(5), 1–26. https://doi.org/10.19173/irrodl.v10i5.643

FIRA. (2022). Programa de apoyo a proyectos sostenibles. *FIRA*. www.fira.gob.mx/Nd/prosostenible.jsp

García-Muina, F.E., Pelechano-Barahona, E., & Navas-López, J.E. (2010). The development of sustainable technological innovations: The mediating effect of complexity in the biotechnology sector. *Innovar*, *20*(38), 95–110.

González-Hernández, I.J., Armas-Alvarez, B., Coronel-Lazcano, M., Maldonado-López, N., Vergara-Martínez, O., & Granillo-Macías, R. (2021). El desarrollo tecnológico en las revoluciones industriales. *Ingenio Y Conciencia Boletín Científico De La Escuela Superior Ciudad Sahagún*, *8*(16), 41–52. https://doi.org/10.29057/escs.v8i16.7118

Hallstedt, S.I., Isaksson, O., & Öhrwall Rönnbäck, A. (2020). The need for new product development capabilities from digitalization, sustainability, and servitization trends. *Sustainability*, *12*(23), 1–26. https://doi.org/10.3390/su122310222

Karamitri, I., Kitsios, F., & Talias, M. A. (2020). Development and validation of a knowledge management questionnaire for hospitals and other healthcare organizations. *Sustainability*, *12*(7), 2730.

Khan, M.S., Saengon, P., Cheungsirakulvit, T., & Kanchanathaveekul, K. (2021). The moderating effect of strategic fit enhances business performance: Empirical evidence from the telecommunication industry. *Business Strategy & Development*, *4*(3), 229–236. https://doi.org/10.1002/bsd2.146

Kim, J.H., Seok, B.I., Choi, H.J., Jung, S.H., & Yu, J.O. (2020). Sustainable management activities: A study on the relations between technology commercialization capabilities, sustainable competitive advantage, and business performance. *Sustainability, 12*(9), 7913.

Lam, L., Nguyen, P., Le, N., & Tran, K. (2021). The relation among organizational culture, knowledge management, and innovation capability: Its implication for open innovation. *Journal of Open Innovation: Technology, Market, and Complexity*, *7*(1), 1–16. https://doi.org/10.3390/joitmc7010066

Lee, J.Y., & Ma, Y. (2021). The impact of the exchange of sustainable technological HR innovation knowledge within Chaebols on the performance of global subsidiaries. *Journal of Korea Trade*, *25*(4), 108–127. https://doi.org/10.35611/jkt.2021.25.4.108

Leepaitoon, S., Lata, P., & Worawattanaparinya, S. (2020). Guidelines for innovation development for increasing logistics efficiency of manufacturing industrial in Thailand. *Academy of Strategic Management Journal*, *19*(6), 1–12.

Lim, M.K., Tseng, M.L., Tan, K.H., & Bui, T.D. (2017). Knowledge management in sustainable supply chain management: Improving performance through an interpretive structural modelling approach. *Journal of Cleaner Production*, *162*, 806–816. https://doi.org/10.1016/j.jclepro.2017.06.056

Liu, C.H.S., & Dong, T.P. (2021). Discovering the relationship among knowledge management, sustainability marketing and service improvement: The moderating role of consumer interest. *International Journal of Contemporary Hospitality Management*, *33*(8), 2799–2816. https://doi.org/10.1108/IJCHM-12-2020-1468

Lowenthal, D. (2015). Marsh's man and nature at 150. *George Wright Forum*, *32*(3), 227–237. www.jstor.org/stable/44131219

Lueadthahan, Y., Sawangrat, N., & Roopsing, T. (2021). Guidelines for Thailand's textile industrial development for sustainability. *Academy of Strategic Management Journal*, *20*(5), 1–10.

Ma, L., Qian, C., Liu, Z., & Zhu, Y. (2018). Exploring the innovation system of the animation industry: Case study of a Chinese company. *Sustainability*, *10*(9), 1–15. https://doi.org/10.3390/su10093213

Mandal, P., & Bagchi, K. (2016). Strategic role of information, knowledge and technology in manufacturing industry performance. *Industrial Management & Data Systems*, *116*(6), 1259–1278. https://doi.org/10.1108/IMDS-07-2015-0297

Mangla, S.K., Raut, R., Narwane, V.S., Zhang, Z., & Priyadarshinee, P. (2021). Mediating effect of big data analytics on project performance of small and medium enterprises. *Journal of Enterprise Information Management*, *34*(1), 168–198. https://doi.org/10.1108/JEIM-12-2019-0394

Martínez Valdez, R.I., Catache Mendoza, M.D.C., & Huerta Cerda, Z.M. (2018). *La Cuarta Revolución Industrial (4RI) y la Educación de Negocios: Un estudio comparativo de programas de posgrado en México y Estados Unidos de América* (pp. 1–6). Universidad Autónoma de Nuevo León UANL, Facultad de Contaduría Pública y Administración FACPYA & Vincula Tégica EFAN.

Muthuveloo, R., Fang, K.W., Ping, T.A., & Kiumarsi, S. (2021). The influence of organisational capabilities on organisational performance in the manufacturing sector. *International Journal of Management and Enterprise Development*, *20*(3), 273–294. https://doi.org/10.1504/IJMED.2021.118418

Nahavandi, S. (2019). Industry 5.0—A human-centric solution. *Sustainability*, *11*(16), 1–13. https://doi.org/10.3390/su11164371

Nazam, M., Hashim, M., Baig, S.A., Abrar, M., & Shabbir, R. (2020). Modeling the key barriers of knowledge management adoption in sustainable supply chain. *Journal of Enterprise Information Management*, *33*(5), 1077–1109. https://doi.org/10.1108/JEIM-09-2019-0271

Nonaka, I. (1994). A dynamic theory of organizational knowledge creation. *Organization science*, *5*(1), 14–37. https://doi.org/10.1287/orsc.5.1.14

OECD. (2021). Active labour market policies: Connecting people with good jobs. *OECD*. www.oecd.org/els/emp/activation.htm

ONU. (2020). Estos 10 países restaurarán la naturaleza para impulsar sus economías tras la COVID-19. *ONU*. www.unep.org/es/noticias-y-reportajes/reportajes/estos-10-paises-restauraran-la-naturaleza-para-impulsar-sus

Oxford. (n.d.). Industrialization. *Oxford.com Dictionary*. Retrieved September 20, 2023, from www.oxfordlearnersdictionaries.com/us/definition/english/industrialization#:~:text=%2F%C9%AAn%CB%8Cd%CA%8Cstri%C9%99l%C9%99%CB%88ze%C9%AA%CA%83n%2F,a%20country%20or%20an%20area

Oxford. (n.d.a). Concept. *Oxford.com Dictionary*. Retrieved September 28, 2023, from www.oxfordlearnersdictionaries.com/definition/american_english/concept#:~:text=concept-,noun,the%20basic%20concepts%20of%20mathematics

Oxford. (n.d.b). Tools. *Oxford.com Dictionary*. Retrieved September 28, 2023, from www.oxfordlearnersdictionaries.com/definition/english/tool_1#:~:text=an%20instrument%20such%20as%20a,a%20cutting%20tool

Peñaloza, M. (2007). Los paradigmas de la producción y su impacto en el mercado laboral. *Fermentum. Revista Venezolana de Sociología y Antropología*, *17*(49), 455–477.

Phimolsathien, T. (2020). Milestones in intellectual property rights promotion (Trademark) and OTOP business in Thailand under the public concept of "Pracharat". *International Journal of Innovation, Creativity and Change*, *13*(6), 442–457.

Portugal. (2019). Portugal melhor da Europa no ITB Earth Award 2019. *Unión Europea*. www.turismodeportugal.pt/pt/Noticias/Paginas/portugal-vence-itb-earth-award.aspx

Rahim, R.A., Ong, M.H.A., Wahab, L.N.A., & Anwar, N. (2023). Knowledge management strategies and green innovation practices: Empirical evidence from the Malaysian public sector. *International Journal of Industrial Engineering*, *34*(2), 1–11. http://dx.doi.org/10.22068/ijiepr.34.2.2

Raudeliūnienė, J., Tvaronavičienė, M., & Blažytė, M. (2020). Knowledge management practice in general education schools as a tool for sustainable development. *Sustainability*, *12*(10), 1–11. https://doi.org/10.3390/su12104034

Rodríguez, J.M. (2017). Transformaciones tecnológicas, su impacto en el mercado de trabajo y retos para las políticas del mercado de trabajo. In G. Bensusán, W. Eichhorst, & J.M. Rodríguez (Eds.), *Las transformaciones tecnológicas y sus desafíos para el empleo, las relaciones laborales y la identificación de la demanda de cualificaciones* (pp. 33–80). CEPAL.

Sagasti, F. (2011). *Ciencia, tecnología, innovación. Políticas para América Latina.* Fondo de Cultura económica.

Scells, H., Zuccon, G., & Koopman, B. (2019). A comparison of automatic Boolean query formulation for systematic reviews. *Information Retrieval Journal, 24*, 3–28. https://doi.org/10.1007/s10791-020-09381-1

Shahzad, M., Qu, Y., Zafar, A.U., & Appolloni, A. (2021). Does the interaction between the knowledge management process and sustainable development practices boost corporate green innovation? *Business Strategy and the Environment, 30*(8), 4206–4222. https://doi.org/10.1002/bse.2865

Shea, T., Usman, S.A., Arivalagan, S., & Parayitam, S. (2023). "Knowledge management practices" as moderator in the relationship between organizational culture and performance in information technology companies in India. *VINE Journal of Information and Knowledge Management Systems, 53*(4), 719–747. https://doi.org/10.1108/VJIKMS-12-2020-0232

Shirokova, G., Vega, G., & Sokolova, L. (2013). Performance of Russian SMEs: Exploration, exploitation and strategic entrepreneurship. *Critical Perspectives on International Business, 9*(1/2), 173–203. https://doi.org/10.1108/17422041311299941

Silva, S.S.D., Feldmann, P.R., Spers, R.G., & Bambini, M.D. (2019). Analysis of the process of technology transfer in public research institutions: The Embrapa agrobiology case. *Innovation & Management Review, 16*(4), 375–390. https://doi.org/10.1108/INMR-05-2018-0024

Siqueira, A.C.O., & Honig, B. (2019). Entrepreneurs' ingenuity and self-imposed ethical constraints: Creating sustainability-oriented new ventures and knowledge. *Journal of Knowledge Management, 23*(10), 1965–1983. https://doi.org/10.1108/JKM-11-2018-0707

Sofiyabadi, J., Feiz, D., & Kolahi, B. (2020). Ambidexterity and sustainable balanced performance in knowledge-based organisations: Investigating the role of open innovation. *International Journal of Business and Systems Research, 14*(4), 489–509. https://doi.org/10.1504/IJBSR.2020.110769

Spangler, W., Sroufe, R., Madia, M., & Singadivakkam, J. (2014). Sustainability-focused knowledge management in a global enterprise. *Journal of Computer Information Systems, 55*(1), 70–82. https://doi.org/10.1080/08874417.2014.11645742

Sriratanaviriyakul, N., & El-Den, J. (2019). Pedagogical discussion cases in higher education: The role of knowledge sharing in students' learning. *Procedia Computer Science, 161*, 215–225. https://doi.org/10.1016/j.procs.2019.11.117

Steinmueller, W.E. (2017). *Las economías basadas en el conocimiento y las tecnologías de la información y comunicación* (pp. 1–17). UDGVirtual & DSPACE.

Sun, Y., Shahzad, M., & Razzaq, A. (2022). Sustainable organizational performance through blockchain technology adoption and knowledge management in China. *Journal of Innovation & Knowledge, 7*(4), 1–11. https://doi.org/10.1016/j.jik.2022.100247

Tajpour, M., Hosseini, E., Mohammadi, M., & Bahman-Zangi, B. (2022). The effect of knowledge management on the sustainability of technology-driven businesses in emerging markets: The mediating role of social media. *Sustainability, 14*(14), 1–15. https://doi.org/10.3390/su14148602

Tamburino, L., Bravo, G., Clough, Y., & Nicholas, K.A. (2020). From population to production: 50 years of scientific literature on how to feed the world. *Global Food Security*, *24*, 1–8. https://doi.org/10.1016/j.gfs.2019.100346

Torres Narváez, M., Cruz Velandia, I., & Hernández Jaramillo, J. (2014). Knowledge management: Experiences in academic and clinic environments. *Revista Ciencias de la Salud*, *12*(2), 169–181. https://doi.org/10.12804/revsalud12.2.2014.03

Tseng, M.L., Tan, P.A., Wu, K.J., Lin, R.C.W., Todumrongkul, N., Juladacha, P., & Christianti, G. (2020). Sustainable total resource management in Thailand healthcare Industry under uncertain situations. *Sustainability*, *12*(22), 1–23. https://doi.org/10.3390/su12229611

Ulewicz, R., & Blaskova, M. (2018). Sustainable development and knowledge management stakeholders' point of view. *Polish Journal of Management Studies*, *18*(2), 363–374. https://doi.org/10.17512/pjms.2018.18.2.29

UN. (2019). The United Nations permanent forum on indigenous issues. *UN*. www.un.org/development/desa/indigenouspeoples/wp-content/uploads/sites/19/2019/04/Spanish-Traditional-Knowledge-backgrounder-FINAL_ES.pdf

UN. (2023). Sustainability. *UN*. www.un.org/en/academic-impact/sustainability

Valencia Castrejón, S. (2020). Imperialismo capitalista. *Portal académico*. https://portalacademico.cch.unam.mx/historiauniversal2/imperialismo-capitalista

Waititu, P., & Barker, R. (2023). Employees' perceptions on the use of online internal communication for knowledge sharing. *Electronic Journal of Knowledge Management*, *21*(2), 103–113. https://doi.org/10.34190/ejkm.21.2.2947

Wichitsathian, S., & Nakruang, D. (2019). Knowledge integration capability and entrepreneurial orientation: Case of Pakthongchai Silk Groups residing. *Entrepreneurship and Sustainability Issues*, *7*(2), 977–989. http://doi.org/10.9770/jesi.2019.7.2(13)

Wong, K.W., Kumaraswamy, M., Mahesh, G., & Ling, F.Y.Y. (2014). Building integrated project and asset management teams for sustainable built infrastructure development. *Journal of Facilities Management*, *12*(3), 187–210. https://doi.org/10.1108/JFM-05-2013-0025

Zecca, F., & Rastorgueva, N. (2017). Knowledge management and sustainable agriculture: The Italian case. *Calitatea*, *18*(159), 97–104.

Zhang, B., Niu, Z., & Liu, C. (2020). Lean tools, knowledge management, and lean sustainability: The moderating effects of study conventions. *Sustainability*, *12*(3), 1–20. https://doi.org/10.3390/su12030956

5 The importance of the aeroponic cultivation technique in sustainable agriculture

A study carried out with the cultivation of *Phaseolus vulgaris L.* Var Opus

Jessica A. Araujo Rodríguez, Coral Martínez Nolasco, José A. Padilla Medina, Alejandro I. Barranco Gutiérrez, Juan Prado Olivarez and Juan J. Martínez Nolasco

Introduction

Good use of water and mitigating or reducing hunger are priority problems worldwide. Water is considered the main element of life and one of the resources most exploited in industrial and agricultural activities, thus giving rise to awareness of its use individually and collectively. Agriculture alone consumes around 70% of the world's water (Qin et al., 2018). Agricultural activities currently focus mostly on the use of soil to grow various foods such as legumes, vegetables and fruits inside or outside greenhouses.

In this way, throughout the crop's life, water use is necessary for development and effective production, considering a brief decrease in drinking water consumption when the phenological stage of the crop occurs in the rainy season. However, the same does not happen in arid or semi-arid regions, where water stress constantly occurs in agriculture (Kader et al., 2019), therefore soilless cultivation techniques have been considered in recent years for the production of food, mainly encouraging the efficient use of water under greenhouse conditions on large, medium and minor scales, thus giving way to techniques such as aeroponics and hydroponics that by using recirculating systems allow the consumption of this resource to be minimal. This is because the water supply is focused directly on the root area of the plants, providing the necessary nutrients for their growth, development and production, avoiding filtration outside the crop furrows and reducing evaporation when hot climates occur.

It is expected that by 2050, the urbanization of cities will increase by nine billion and ten billion people worldwide, generating greater concern in countries such as Mexico, India and China, among others (Khan et al., 2021; Gao, 2021). This will generate a decrease in rural areas, decreasing

DOI: 10.4324/9781003465058-5

agricultural production and generating food shortages. In addition to this, soil erosion is considered one more reason for this decrease in agricultural production. It is expected that in the coming years, the demand for food and production will increase, generating concern for the quality and nutritional value of food (Khan et al., 2021), given that this demand will not be able to be satisfied using the same agricultural practices and crop varieties (Voss-Fels et al., 2019) being used at present. In Mexico and other countries, various strategies have been carried out to recover agriculture, considering the recovery of nutrients in the soil and generating resistance in crops against multiple types of infestation, calling this strategy conservation agriculture, focused on farmers and producers, emphasizing intercropping, crop replacement and the use of biomass. The biomass is used by creating a type of leaf mulch that conserves moisture in the soil by reducing water evaporation, generating a reduction in temperature in the area and reducing soil erosion (Kader et al., 2019). The principle of intercropping is to plant two crops of different species in the same planting area at the same time and the relay aims to maintain a single crop of the same species in a planting area and at the end of its harvest, replace it with a crop of a different species, thus generating the recovery of nutrients that the soil has lost. However, considering the decrease in the area of arable land, the initiative to implement greenhouses in homes is considered, thus taking advantage of small spaces such as patios and rooftops, in this way each greenhouse can grow various species of food without the need for land use or substrate. In recent years, various soilless techniques have been used, mainly hydroponics and aeroponics, which allow the crop to be maintained in controlled conditions for its survival by providing water with nutrients in the root area of the plants (Lakhiar et al., 2018).

Hydroponics is a soilless cultivation technique that keeps the seedling in a basket to make way for the root area that is in water with a nutrient solution, which is recirculated, thus improving water use. In the first instance, for both techniques, there is a saving of 98% of consumption (Lakhiar et al., 2018), since the root area only uses the water that the seedling requires. Regarding the aeroponics technique, it is similar to the previous technique, with the difference that the supply of water to the root area is not constant. It is carried out by direct spraying to the root or misting to the walls of the root structure containing the seedlings. These sprays are carried out intermittently, where the activation occurs for a few seconds and the waiting time for a few minutes, in the same way recirculating the excess water that the root does not retain. Thus, the minimum water use is considered since it is provided only when required. The above allows the design of an agricultural system without the need for the use of land and under greenhouse conditions to encourage farmers to continue with sustainable agricultural practices, also mitigating excessive water consumption.

In this way, it is considered to contribute to the various applications proposed by the United Nations (UN) in the Sustainable Development Agenda for 2030, which includes 17 global objectives supported by 169 initiatives, contributing mainly to two of the 17 objectives called "zero hunger" and "clean water and sanitation."

According to data recorded by FAO et al. (2023), there is mention that in 2020 approximately 720 million to 811 million people in the world starved due to the increase in the cost of food and lack of accessibility to it. Faced with this problem, an option was presented that proposed the construction of small- and medium-sized greenhouses that efficiently consume water for the cultivation of economical, fresh and organic foods, getting involved in their production and promoting the exchange of these foods between different communities, thus encouraging the consumption of local foods, doubling production at any time of the year, with minimal transportation costs and generating the circulation of the economy of the communities involved.

Contributions to agriculture

It has been shown that production in greenhouses is high due to pest control and the climatic variables that occur inside of these. In addition, hydroponics and aeroponics enable efficient use of the nutrients used for plant development. In both cases, nutrients based on nitrogen (N), phosphorus (P) and potassium (K) are mixed in the water, in addition to considering other micronutrients in smaller quantities such as zinc (Zn), iron (Fe), manganese (Mn), nickel (Ni), boron (B), molybdenum (Mo), chlorine (Cl) and copper (Cu), which are essential elements to achieve the highest crop yield (Dhaliwal et al., 2022). The need for diluting these compounds in water is due to the lack of soil or substrate that allows these nutrients to be obtained directly from the soil. A recirculating hydroponic crop allows you to control the plant's nutrition through the continuous movement of water and nutrients.

The root part of the plant is constantly submerged in water using this technique. Regarding aeroponic cultivation, the root part of the plant is suspended in the air, protected from UV rays by the wall of the aeroponic structure. The root is kept moist by the spraying carried out by valves, which are activated for a few seconds, giving the root time to obtain the nutrients it requires. Upon completion of the activation seconds, the system remains off waiting for the next activation, generating various nebulization intervals (Lakhiar et al., 2018). This system creates a micro-environment with a high percentage of relative humidity that allows root growth (Mateus-Rodriguez et al., 2014). Furthermore, when spraying directly on the root area, the leaves of the plant do not have contact with the water, preventing the appearance of fungi. Consequently, this technique allows the plant's root area to take only the required amount of nutrients for its hydration and nutrition, avoiding waste by being recirculated and reused in future sprays. This allows significant savings in nutrients since only five millilitres are used.

Materials and methods

An aeroponic growth chamber was designed, installed and tested in Celaya, Guanajuato, Mexico, 20¢ 31^{2} North Latitude, 100¢48^{2} East Latitude, 1,762 meters above sea level. The chamber measures 2.55 meters long, 1 meter wide and 1.27 meters high on one side and 1.29 meters high on the other in order to generate a slope that facilitates water recycling. It was installed in a glass greenhouse, without artificial lighting and with conventional extractors using a culture of *Phaseolus Vulgaris L.* Var Opus. The structure made of corrosion-resistant material was placed inside the chamber to promote water recirculation. Initially, a 600-caliber virgin polyethylene cover was placed on the sides for ultraviolet radiation resistance (UV). In the upper part, it has an expanded polystyrene cover to hold the baskets of the seedlings of the tested crop. In the lower part of the aeroponic system, there are bases of polyethylene sheets joined by plastic cells that will retain the water to avoid filtration and waste.

Use of water and nutrients in the aeroponic growth chamber

The aeroponic growth structure consists of polyvinyl chloride (PVC) tubes resistant to salts contained in water and nutrients. The tubes are interconnected for recirculating of water (not used by the root for hydration), which is carried out as soon as the sprinklers are activated. Spraying in the aeroponic structure is carried out using water pumps submerged in containers of water with diluted nutrients, the ignition of the pumps is controlled by asymmetric timers. The horsepower of the water pump should be set depending on the height and length of the system to be used; however, for a small greenhouse of approximately 40 to 50 plants, 1 HP is enough.

The aeroponic structure used reduces water consumption, the pipe system that composes it allows recirculation to the main container and the lower area where the base of the growth chamber is located prevents water filtration, generating its accumulation in a secondary container which is then recirculated to the main container. In this way, water consumption is reduced, therefore, the waste of nutrients, using only those required by the crop in each of its phenological stages, considering the increase of these by 25% (1.25 ml per liter) in the germination stage at 100% (5 ml per liter) when the reproduction stage begins in the case of vegetable crops.

Average crops per year in a growth chamber

According to Organización de las Naciones Unidas para la Alimentación (2009), food production will have to be improved and increased between 60% and 70% to cover global demand by 2050. However, in recent years there has been a reduction in the cultivated area as a result of the growth of urban areas and soil erosion. Therefore, the use of greenhouses is an alternative that allows replacing the use of soil, using substrates in specific areas within them and obtaining better use of the supplied nutrients. In addition, it is possible to reduce plant diseases and pests, allowing various crops to be harvested outside the usual period. Therefore, it is important to evaluate aeroponic and hydroponic techniques for greenhouse crops.

To check the efficiency of an aeroponic system, a culture of *Phaseolus Vulgaris L.* Var Opus was developed considering that it is a fabaceae with a determined growth habit and a life cycle of no more than 95 days. It is shrubby and consists of a vegetative phase and a reproductive phase, each of them with 5 stages. The vegetative phase has the germination (V0), emergence (V1), primary leaves (V2), first trifoliate leaf (V3) and third trifoliate leaf (V4) stages. In the reproductive phase, pre-flowering (R5), flowering (R6), pod formation (R7), pod filling (R8) and maturation (R9) occur. In a growth chamber, it is possible to obtain 3 crops a year. The study was carried out with green beans due to their nutritional importance, according to Férnandez Valenciano and Sánchez Chávez (2017), green beans present a high concentration of fiber, carbohydrates and protein compared to grain beans. At harvest, a proximal chemical analysis was carried out (González Montemayor et al., 2021) to determine nutritional quality.

Monitoring leaf and root areas of plants

Agricultural production is reduced between 10% and 28% due to crop infestations according to data recorded by the FAO; however, it is not the only cause of the decrease in production. The report (FAO, Versión resumida de Repercusiones de las catástrofes en la agricultura y la seguridad alimentaria 2023: Evitar y reducir las pérdidas mediante la inversión en la resiliencia, 2023) mentions that in total there is a 5% total loss of crops worldwide, where 26% is due to extreme temperatures, 26% to floods due to overflows or intense rains, 19% to droughts in the area and 10% to fires, generating a greater incidence of these events as a consequence of climate change. There is a decrease in the impact of environmental factors when using greenhouses, given the control of climatic variables within them. However, plague control is one of the main concerns due to its rapid reproduction and late detection. For this reason, it is important to monitor the leaf and root area to determine the appearance of infestation (biotic factors); however, it turns out to be complex due to the difficulty of locating and identifying the insects involved and may confuse leaf necrosis given to the phenological stage with necrosis caused by plague.

Some of the physiological processes of plants are accelerated when high temperatures occur. However, extreme environmental factors tend to be counterproductive, including the appearance of plague, which generates stress in various parts of the plant. Plants have a thermoregulatory system whose response is slow when biotic or abiotic stress occurs, which produces heating in the leaf and root area of the plant. This process is difficult to observe and is confused with water stress. One of the main advantages that the aeroponic cultivation technique provides is the characterization of the root area of the plant (Chang et al., 2008). This is due to the fact that the root is exposed within the growth chamber, which allows the presence of stress in this area to be identified timely due to the formation of fungus on root or excess water. The proper development of the crop using the aeroponic technique occurs thanks to the fact that the chamber follows the same environmental principles as the traditional technique, that is, the root is kept in complete darkness and with a relative humidity of 80%. In this way, the root area is maintained in optimal conditions for crop development. The continuous monitoring of thermal characterization allows the timely identification of the condition present in the plant, reducing the loss of agricultural production caused by some external factor.

In this study, the root area of the plants was monitored as well as the thermal changes present throughout the phenological life of the plant. In parallel, leaf area and thermal changes of the leaves were monitored. Leaf and root temperatures tend to differ by between one and two degrees Celsius, considering the root to be colder; temperature changes are associated in the first instance with the positive correlation that exists with ambient temperature. However, this tends to change, behaving in a normal way according to the time of day. Though, when the plant presents stress denoted by abiotic or biotic factors, its temperature tends to increase significantly in both parts and this can be seen in thermal images.

The thermal characterization of both areas allows the identification of stress levels in the plant to determine whether they are caused by biotic factors such as phytopathogens or fungi or by abiotic factors such as water stress, lack of nutrients in water or high temperatures.

Aeroponic cultivation allowed us to observe the thermal and visible behaviour of the root area and the root, being able to evaluate stress due to abiotic (see Figure 5.1) or biotic factors (see Figure 5.2); alternatively, it was possible to evaluate the leaf area of the plant. Permanent monitoring of the foliar and root areas allows reducing damage caused to plants by some type of stress. When it comes to water stress, the fertigation time is increased or the waiting time is decreased. This will be observed in the dryness of the

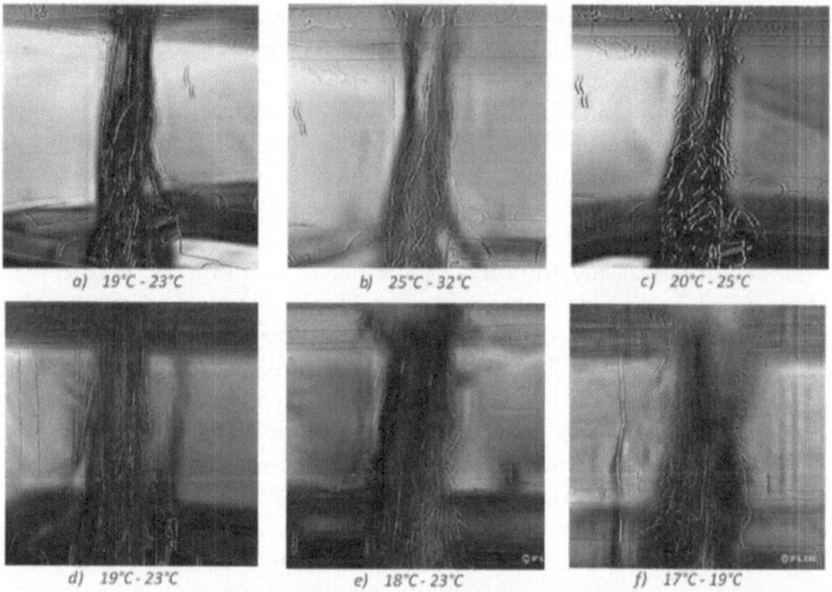

Figure 5.1 (a) Growth stage; (b) presence of water stress; (c) temperature regulation of the root area; (d) and (e) root area growth process; (f) normalization of temperature thermoregulation in the root and beginning of the reproduction stage.

Figure 5.2 (a) Temperature changes in various areas of the plant due to the presence of Thysanoptera; (b) areas infected by Thysanoptera, visible image.

root, that is, if the waiting time between one spray and another is reduced but the root has dry areas, the fertigation time should be increased, this generally occurs when arid climates occur, generally in summer where climates of up to 36°C occur. Otherwise, if the root presents decomposition, the waiting time is between one fertigation and another increases. Since it's a biotic condition, we proceeded with treatments to control the decomposition in the leaf area of the plant, considering natural products.

The cultivation began on August 15, 2023, beginning its reproductive stage on September 15, 2023, the pods appeared 10 days later, starting with the first cut on October 4, 2023, and the tenth and last cut on November 10, 2023, completing a biological cycle of 90 days. Figure 5.3 shows the fruit density obtained. A density of 11.76 plants/m^2 and a yield of 790.56 gr/m^2 and 196.47 green beans/m^2 were obtained, obtaining better results compared to the work presented by Salinas-Ramírez et al. (2013) where a density of 6.25 plants/m^2, a yield of 521 gr/m^2 and 141 green beans/m^2 was obtained in soil cultivation. The duration of the biological cycle of the green bean shows differences across the various environments and depends on the variety, growth habit, sowing date and the environmental conditions present during the development of the crop, this determines a parallel performance of the yield, However, it is important to note that the flowering period occurs earlier when there are no water restrictions.

Likewise, the recording and measurement of the energy and water consumption of the aeroponic system was carried out, obtaining a consumption

Figure 5.3 Density of pods present on the branches of the *Phaseolus Vulgaris L.* Var Opus crop.

of 0.546 kilovolts per hour (kW/h), considering that the sprinklers remain off for 24 minutes and on for 30 seconds, the conversion is carried out, thus a consumption of 0.00015167 kW/30 seconds. Therefore, approximately 60 activations of the submersible water pump are determined, giving a total of 0.0091002 kW/day, considering a total of 0.819018 kW in the total phenological cycle of the plant. Regarding water consumption, each nozzle fertigates 0.1667 liters; however, 0.1613 liters are returned to the main container, which gives an efficient consumption of 0.0053 liters per nozzle. Considering 30 nozzles, there is a consumption of 0.1596 liters/fertigation. In one day, 60 sprays are made with a consumption of 9.54 liters. Therefore, the phenological cycle of the crop uses 858.6 liters of water, which is equivalent to 336.7058 liters per square meter or 0.3367 cubic meters. Comparing with the work presented by Ríos Flores et al. (2017), which presents a water consumption of 14994.6 liters in the complete bean cycle or 14.9946 m^3, using the traditional soil cultivation technique, generating a saving of 97.75% of water using the aeroponic cultivation technique compared to that used in the aforementioned study, which is 2.25% of the total use indicated.

In addition, a proximal chemical analysis was carried out (González Montemayor et al., 2021) to determine the amount of carbohydrates present in the moisture and dry base of the pods obtained in the reported cuts, obtaining similar proportions of fat, protein and fiber to the reported by the Center for Research in Food and Development (CIAD) and different proportions in Potassium (K), Calcium (Ca), Iron (Fe), Zinc (Zn) and Phosphorus (P) (Table 5.1).

Discussion

In this study, a culture of *Phaseolus Vulgaris L.* Var Opus was carried out to evaluate an aeroponic growth chamber in terms of consumption of electrical energy, water and nutrients, in addition to the yield obtained in each cut made during the green bean harvest. This process was carried out in order to take the study toward sustainable agriculture, giving communities an option to include small greenhouses where they can produce various crops

Table 5.1 Comparisons of nutritional quality in traditional cultivation and aeroponic cultivation

	CIAD study	*Study carried out*
Potassium (K)	117 mg	198 mg
Calcium (Ca)	74 mg	36 mg
Iron (Fe)	2 mg	0.9 mg
Zinc (Zn)	0.6 mg	0.19 mg
Phosphorus (P)	37 mg	38 mg

at low cost that help recirculate the economy and improve the acquisition of safe food at any time of the year promoting hunger mitigation.

Positive results were obtained in the yield of green beans compared to the soil cultivation technique. These results suggest the possibility for aeroponics to be an alternative for small-scale food production in Mexico, especially in arid areas and in communities far from urban areas and with difficult access. In the study presented by Wasilewska-Nascimento et al. (2020), it was concluded that the production of an aeroponic crop technique is greater than that of soil cultivation. Their study focuses on the production of minitubers with the aeroponic technique where they obtained 250 to 300 minitubers per potato plant, unlike soil production, which was 50 to 100 minitubers per plant. Likewise, in the study presented, they mention that hydroponic systems are capable of generating a greater number of tubers per plant. However, those tubers obtained by the aeroponic technique have a larger size and weight. Additionally, the authors recommend installing an aeroponic system in locations that consider a fluctuation-free electrical supply.

In hydroponic crops, it is possible to adjust the variables used so that their life cycle is carried out appropriately during their phenological cycle, having a yield and nutritional quality equal to or greater than that obtained with the traditional technique. This can be inferred by the similarity in the behaviour of hydroponic and aeroponic systems, since in both cases, a suitable environment is generated for the development of the plant. In the study by Zha et al. (2023), a comparison was made of three cultivation methods, hydroponics, substrate and in soil of two vegetables, cabbage and lettuce, using green rose lettuce and red rose lettuce, obtaining a better nutritional quality in the cultivation in the substrate; however, it is shown that the best properties for the cultivation of red rose lettuce were obtained under the hydroponic technique, this is due to the presence in a lower amount of nitrate and vitamin C. Likewise, the authors carried out a study of the costs obtained in the total production of the vegetables used in the experiment, giving a higher cost for cultivation in the substrate and a lower cost in cultivation in soil. However, when considering the infrastructure and equipment, the costs in the hydroponics and substrate techniques are much higher than soil cultivation. In addition, the substrate technique entails higher input and labor costs compared to the technique in hydroponics. In conclusion, the authors determined that the systems under the hydroponic technique have a higher yield compared to other cultivation techniques; However, they consider that possible inconsistencies in the planting cycle can affect the result, in the same way the growth rate of the plants is correlated with the efficient nutritional supply, so it is possible that poor crop management density and inadequate environmental management cause non-uniformity in plant growth, given the limitation of root development and poor air circulation in the plant canopy. A study by Gartmann et al. (2023) was carried out with lettuce cultivation in three techniques, hydroponics, bioponics and soil, inside a greenhouse, where the growth behaviour of the crops did not show visual differences, on the other hand, when analyzing chlorophyll, a greater amount was obtained in those grown through bioponics and hydroponics. However, with the hydroponic system, the yield trough was greater compared to bioponics and soil techniques, giving a greater fresh weight and a lower amount of dry matter, in the same way a better texture and resistance was determined in the products obtained by the hydroponic and soil techniques. That is, with hydroponics and biponics techniques, a better nutritional composition (bioponics) and a greater quantity (hydroponics) of the harvest is obtained. Wimmerova et al. (2022) conclude that there is a need for the use of non-conventional techniques (aeroponics and hydroponics) to obtain higher production performance and reduce the pretreatment procedure, to reduce the environmental impact. That is, the consumption of fertilizers, fuel, water and electricity is reduced, expanding the valorization of the waste obtained and water is recovered through the recirculation system, also considering the use on a larger scale of green energy sources, such as photovoltaic and wind for the operation of these systems. Nevertheless, studies are still necessary to adequately control the nutrients and the environment to which the crops are subjected. It is possible to identify that, in a large number of studies, there is optimal production performance, although the implementation costs are high, yields and savings in fertilizer, electricity and water are the main elements that allow for a re-evaluation of these cultivation techniques that allow for a better impact on agricultural production in Mexico.

Conclusion

Aeroponics is a technique that provides nutrients directly to the root of a given crop taking advantage of the water resource by up to 97% compared to the conventional technique and that, compared to the hydroponics technique, the consumption of this resource is up to 90% less (Khan et al., 2020). Consequently, the aeroponics technique is a good alternative because, currently, the agriculture consumes approximately 68% to 70% of available drinking water, which is why the importance of focusing agriculture on more sustainable techniques that allow maximum use of water resources and the improvement of the productivity of various foods under other techniques. Given the above, there is an intention to carry out a study with various grains considering that the four main grains are corn, sorghum, beans and rice. The humidity conditions produced by the growth chamber generate an environment that is optimal for rice production, which is the focus of future studies on the cultivation of this grain. It is expected that by

2050, the need for food consumption will increase and in parallel a decrease of 20% less arable area per person is expected; therefore, the concern about generating food quickly, safely and using only essential resources is necessary to increase productivity and ensure food for each person.

Likewise, the planting, production and management of crops in a sustainable manner are intended to achieve food security, giving importance to Goals 1, 3 and 4 established in UN Objective 2 called zero hunger, focusing the work presented on agricultural productivity and sustainability and ensuring food for people in vulnerable situations.

References

Chang, D.C., Park, C.S., Kim, S.Y., Kim, S.J., & Lee, Y.B. (2008). Physiological growth responses by nutrient interruption in aeroponically grown potatoes. *American Journal of Potato Research*, *85*, 315–323. https://doi.org/10.1007/s12230-008-9024-4

Dhaliwal, S.S., Sharma, V., & Shukla, A.K. (2022). Impact of micronutrients in mitigation of abiotic stresses in soils and plants—A progressive step toward crop security and nutritional quality. *Advances in Agronomy*, *173*, 1–78. https://doi.org/10.1016/bs.agron.2022.02.001

FAO. (2023). *Versión resumida de Repercusiones de las catástrofes en la agricultura y la seguridad alimentaria 2023: Evitar y reducir las pérdidas mediante la inversión en la resiliencia*. www.fao.org/documents/card/fr/c/CC8500ES

FAO, FIDA, OMS, PMA, & UNICEF. (2023). *El estado de la seguridad alimentaria y la nutrición en el mundo 2023. Urbanización, transformación de los sistemas agroalimentarios y dietas saludables a lo largo del continuo rural-urbano*. www.fao.org/3/cc3017es/cc3017es.pdf

Férnandez Valenciano, A.F., & Sánchez Chávez, E. (2017). Estudio de las propiedades fisicoquímicas y calidad nutricional en distintas variedades de frijol consumidas en México. *Nova scientia*, *9*(18), 133–148. https://doi.org/10.21640/ns.v9i18.763

Gao, C. (2021). Genome engineering for crop improvement and future agriculture. *Cell*, *184*(6), 1621–1635. https://doi.org/10.1016/j.cell.2021.01.005

Gartmann, F., Hügly, J., Krähenbühl, N., Brinkmann, N., Schmautz, Z., Smits, T.H., & Junge, R. (2023). Bioponics—An organic closed-loop soilless cultivation system: Yields and characteristics compared to hydroponics and soil cultivation. *Agronomy*, *13*(6), 1–28. https://doi.org/10.3390/agronomy13061436

González Montemayor, A.M., Solanilla Duque, J.F., Flores Gallegos, A.C., López Badillo, C.M., Ascacio Valdés, J.A., & Rodríguez Herrera, R. (2021). Green bean, pea and mesquite whole pod flours nutritional and functional properties and their effect on sourdough bread. *Foods*, *10*(9), 1–15. https://doi.org/10.3390/foods10092227

Kader, M.A., Singha, A., Begum, M.A., Jewel, A., Khan, F.H., & Khan, N.I. (2019). Mulching as water-saving technique in dryland agriculture: Review article. *Bulletin of the National Research Centre*, *43*(147), 1–6. https://doi.org/10.1186/s42269-019-0186-7

Khan, M.M., Akram, M.T., Janke, R., Qadri, R.W., Al-Sadi, A.M., & Farooque, A.A. (2020). Urban horticulture for food secure cities through and beyond COVID-19. *Sustainability*, *12*(22), 1–21. https://doi.org/10.3390/su12229592

Khan, N., Ray, R.L., Raza Sargani, G., Ihtisham, M., Khayyam, M., & Ismail, S. (2021). Current progress and future prospects of agriculture technology:

Gateway to sustainable agriculture. *Sustainability*, *13*(4883), 1–31. https://doi.org/10.3390/su13094883

Lakhiar, I.A., Gao, J., Syed, T.N., Chandio, F.A., & Buttar, N.A. (2018). Modern plant cultivation technologies in agriculture under controlled environment: A review on aeroponics. *Journal of Plant Interactions*, *13*(1), 338–352. https://doi.org/10.1080/17429145.2018.1472308

Mateus-Rodriguez, J.F., De Haan, S., & Rodríguez-Delfín, A. (2014). Genotype by environment effects on potato mini-tuber seed production in an aeroponics system. *Agronomy*, *4*(4), 514–528. https://doi.org/10.3390/agronomy4040514

Organización de las Naciones Unidas para la Alimentación. (2009). *La agricultura mundial en la perspectiva del año 2050*. www.fao.org/fileadmin/templates/wsfs/docs/Issues_papers/Issues_papers_SP/La_agricultura_mundial.pdf

Qin, S., Li, S., Yang, K., & Hu, K. (2018). Can plastic mulch save water at night in irrigated croplands? *Journal of Hydrology*, *564*, 667–681. https://doi.org/10.1016/j.jhydrol.2018.07.050

Ríos Flores, J.L., Torres Moreno, M., Torres Moreno, M.A., & Cantú Brito, J.E. (2017). Eficiencia y productividad del cultivo de frijol en un sistema de riego por bombeo en Zacatecas, México. *Ciencia Ergo Sum*, *24*(2), 152–163. www.redalyc.org/articulo.oa?id=10450491007

Salinas-Ramírez, N., Escalante-Estrada, J.A., Rodríguez-González, M.T., & Sosa-Montes, E. (2013). Rendimiento, calidad nutrimental y rentabilidad del frijol ejotero de temporal en San Pablo Ixayoc, México. *Revista Chapingo Serie Horticultura*, *19*(3), 333–342. https://doi.org/10.5154/r.rchsh.2010.08.031

Voss-Fels, K.P., Stahl, A., & Hickey, L.T. (2019). Q&A: Modern crop breeding for future food security. *BMC Biology*, *17*(1), 1–7. https://doi.org/10.1186/s12915-019-0638-4

Wasilewska-Nascimento, B., Boguszewska-Mańkowska, D., & Zarzyńska, K. (2020). Challenges in the production of high-quality seed potatoes (*Solanum tuberosum* L.) in the tropics and subtropics. *Agronomy*, *10*(2), 1–15. https://doi.org/10.3390/agronomy10020260

Wimmerova, L., Keken, Z., Solcova, O., Bartos, L., & Spacilova, M. (2022). A comparative LCA of aeroponic, hydroponic, and soil cultivations of bioactive substance producing plants. *Sustainability*, *14*(4), 1–14. https://doi.org/10.3390/su14042421

Zha, L., Wang, Z., Huang, C., Duan, Y., Tian, Y., Wang, H., & Zhang, D. (2023). Comparative analysis of leaf vegetable productivity, quality, and profitability among different cultivation modes: A case study. *Agronomy*, *14*(1), 1–16. https://doi.org/10.3390/agronomy14010076

6 Historical development of sustainable energy technologies

Alejandro Espinosa-Calderón, Héctor Juan Carlos López-Tapia, Miguel Ángel Velázquez-Alejos, Esteban Aguirre-Reynoso, Georgina Rico-Ojeda and Saúl Fuentes-Reyes

Introduction

Globally, renewable energy has been recognized as an imperative to meet the growing long-term electricity needs of the developed and developing worlds. There are different technologies related to sustainable energy, such as:

- **Photovoltaic**: The use of energy from solar radiation for the production of electrical energy takes the form of photovoltaics and its potential is directly linked to the geographical latitude of the place (hours of daily light) as well as the cloudiness regime and the clarity index of the area (ISA, 2022). The electrical energy generated by solar energy uses two technologies: photovoltaic energy and concentrated solar thermal energy (concentrated solar power [CSP]). However, according to data from the International Renewable Energy Agency (IRENA), in 2023, solar thermal energy, concerning the installed capacity of renewable energies, only represents 0.2% worldwide; that is, there is only 6,876.44 MW, against 1,412,092.54 MW of photovoltaic energy, that is, it represents 36.5%. Likewise, in 2021, only 13,634.01 GWh of electricity generation was obtained, 0.2% worldwide, against 1,020,376.46 GWh, which represents 13.0% obtained from photovoltaic energy. In such a way that in the section on photovoltaic energy, information regarding solar thermal energy has been added in a summarized manner so that said technology is taken into account.
- **Wind**: The use of wind energy. The energy is obtained through wind turbines that take advantage of the wind's kinetic energy, transforming it into electrical energy. This resource can be classified as perpetual and the amount potentially obtainable in a specific geographical area depends on the wind regime and the orography of the place (Letcher, 2023).

DOI: 10.4324/9781003465058-6

- **Hydroelectric**: Water is used to produce electrical energy in hydroelectric plants. The amount of energy that can be extracted from water in a specific geographical area depends on the available volume and the orographic characteristics of the terrain through which it passes. Hydraulic plants are subdivided into adjustable, flowing and pumping (Daza Vargas, 2023).
- **Geothermal**: This is a renewable energy that is generated from subsoil heat. This technique consists of taking advantage of the heat that resides in the deepest layers of the earth, achieving different services for which ordinary electricity is used (Bruni, 2014; Liming, 2012).

The production of renewable energy worldwide has steadily increased from 1965 to 2022, as seen in the figure. Hydroelectric power energy has experienced relatively constant growth, while wind and solar energy have increased exponentially since 2007 and 2010, respectively. However, they still represent a smaller proportion than hydroelectric power, and together, they only account for a small percentage of humanity's total energy needs. It is important to remark that renewable energy also mitigates the adverse effects of climate change. Social and political perspectives become essential for renewable energy technologies or projects. The impacts of these perspectives may accelerate the adoption cycle or challenge the feasibility of implementing the technology under consideration. Social and political effects are often used interchangeably and are interrelated. Within this journey, we carry out a comparative analysis of the technologies described, explaining how these tools have improved knowledge acquisition processes and the challenges they have posed.

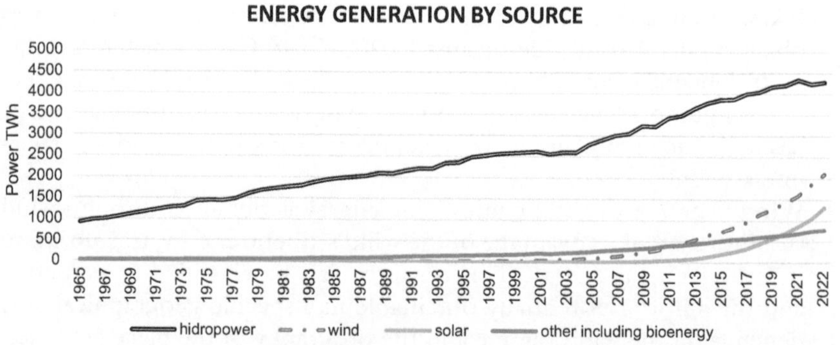

Figure 6.1 Modern renewable energy by source in the world (Our World in Data, 2024)

Photovoltaic solar energy

Photovoltaic solar energy is obtained by taking advantage of solar radiation to get electrical power, thanks to the photovoltaic effect that some materials have that are capable of absorbing light particles (photons), which produces the release of electrons from the structure of said materials. materials which generate the electric current. The devices to carry out this process are called solar cells, made of monocrystalline, polycrystalline or amorphous silicon, a semiconductor material. It should be noted that the solar cells are, in turn, grouped into solar panels.

History of photovoltaic solar energy

After several experiments using metal electrodes, French physicist Alexandre-Edmond Becquerel discovered the photovoltaic effect in 1839 and found that electricity could be generated through solar radiation. In 1883, American inventor Charles Fritts built the first functional solar cell that used gold-coated selenium, which had an efficiency of 1%. However, it was in the 1950s that Bell Laboratory scientists Gerald Pearson, Calvin Fuller and Daryl Chapin developed the first modern solar panel made of silicon, a semiconducting material, reaching an efficiency of 6%. Among its first applications was the supply of electrical energy in the telecommunications sector, specifically in satellites, with the Vanguard 1 and Telstar satellites being the first to use photovoltaic solar energy. It was not until 1973, the first energy crisis, that countries such as Germany, the United States, France and Japan began the first investments in research and development of solar panels. Such research led to developing technologies in the 1990s, such as polycrystalline and monocrystalline silicon cells, which led to significant progress in the marketing of solar panels and improved efficiency. These efforts have led to technological developments that, in turn, allow photovoltaic solar energy to become increasingly affordable and with increasingly greater efficiencies, as well as an increase in its use (Solarama, 2019).

Geographic areas with photovoltaic potential

As mentioned earlier, photovoltaic solar energy involves capturing solar radiation, so it is essential to consider their orientation and inclination to achieve the most significant amount of electric power production to obtain the most excellent efficiency from solar panels. It is important to consider weather conditions, pollution, time of day and time of year. Some photovoltaic system applications are:

- Telecommunications
- Agricultural and livestock applications
- Building electrification

- Domestic and public lighting
- Electric mobility, that is, such as charging stations for electric vehicles
- Irrigation system
- Air conditioning and heating
- Hot water.
- Transportation, although it is still scarce

Photovoltaic systems

As stated, photovoltaic solar energy requires solar panels to capture solar radiation. However, other components are required to carry out the entire process of transforming solar energy into electrical energy. These components are called a photovoltaic system, which can be connected to the conventional electrical supply network or an isolated system.

A photovoltaic system is made up of:

- **Solar panels**: In solar panels, solar cells are grouped into modules that capture solar radiation. Due to the photovoltaic effect, electrons are released that produce an electric, direct current.
- **The inverter**: The inverter converts the electric current to an alternating current, compatible with the electrical grid and appliances.
- **Batteries**: In some systems, the battery can be omitted; it stores unused electrical energy.
- **Regulators**: This device controls the energy flow between the solar panels, the batteries and the consumption, thus avoiding overcharging or deep discharge of the batteries, protecting their helpful life.

It is essential to highlight that a photovoltaic system must be designed before installation. This involves studying its application, whether it will be connected to the electrical grid or isolated. For these reasons, the energy demand must be satisfied, and the geographical area, among other administrative aspects, must be known. The geographical location is vital since solar radiation is not constant throughout the year and during different hours of the day.

Photovoltaic generation capacities

Next is the electricity generation capacity and installed capacity in the world from 2012 and 2022, according to data from the International Renewable Energy Agency (IRENA) on July 28, 2023, concerning photovoltaic solar energy.

Electricity generation capacity:

- Africa in 2012 had 1,101 GWh and in 2021 it reached a level of 19,620 GWh.

- Asia in 2012 had 14,120 GWh and in 2021 it reached a level of 549,776 GWh.
- Central America and the Caribbean in 2012 had 253 GWh, and in 2021, it reached a level of 6,128 GWh.
- Eurasia in 2012 had 18 GWh and in 2021 it reached a level of 15,641 GWh.
- Europe in 2012 had 72,160 GWh and in 2021 it reached a level of 186,558 GWh.
- Middle East in 2012 had 459 GWh and in 2021 it reached a level of 18,284 GWh.
- North America in 2012 had 11,332 GWh and in 2021 it reached a level of 177,622 GWh.
- Oceania in 2012 had 2,359 GWh and in 2021 it reached a level of 28,294 GWh.
- South America in 2012 had 176 GWh and in 2021 it reached a level of 32,002 GWh.

Installed capacity:

- Africa in 2012 had 1,363 MW and in 2022 it reached a level of 12,542 MW.
- Asia in 2012 had 16,258 MW and in 2022 it reached a level of 604,097 MW.
- Central America and the Caribbean in 2012 had 196 MW and in 2022 it reached a level of 3,947 MW.
- Eurasia in 2012 had 13 MW and in 2022 it reached a level of 11,552 MW.
- Europe in 2012 had 73,631 MW and in 2022 it reached a level of 225,278 MW.
- Middle East in 2012 had 317 MW and in 2022 it reached a level of 13,438 MW.
- North America in 2012 had 9,452 MW and in 2022 it reached a level of 127,698 MW.
- Oceania in 2012 had 3,830 MW and in 2022 it reached a level of 30,302 MW.
- South America in 2012 had 168 MW and in 2022 it reached a level of 32,821 MW.

The first ten countries are presented concerning electricity capacity and generation according to the last update from IRENA on July 18, 2023. Electrical capacity is the amount of electricity a power plant can generate and electrical generation is how much energy the power plant produces in a given time.

Ranking of the top ten countries in reference to electricity generation in 2021:

- China with 327,551.1 GWh
- The United States with 148,153.3 GWh
- Japan with 86,094 GWh
- India with 65,581.4 GWh
- Germany with 49,340 GWh
- Australia with 27,712 GWh
- Vietnam with 25,717.5 GWh
- Italy with 25,039 GWh
- Republic of Korea with 23,394 GWh
- Spain with 21,922 GWh

Ranking of the top-ten countries in reference to electrical capacity in 2022:

- China with 392,435.8 MW
- The United States with 111,535 MW
- Japan with 83,055 MW
- Germany with 66,662 MW
- India with 62,850.3 MW
- Australia with 29,676 MW
- Italy with 25,076.6 MW
- Brazil with 24,078.1 MW
- Republic of Korea with 24,078.1 MW
- The Netherlands 18,848.7 MW

Advantages and disadvantages of photovoltaic solar energy (BESUN Energy, 2024)

Advantages

- Fast initial investment recovery (few years).
- Clean and free energy.
- Reduction of the CO_2 footprint by avoiding greenhouse gas emissions.
- Low maintenance cost.
- Renewable and sustainable energy.
- Reduction of the dependence on fossil fuels.
- Reduction of dependence on foreign supply.
- Versatility and adaptability.

Disadvantages

- Dependence of the amount of energy generation concerning solar intensity and orientation.

- Necessity of an ample installation space.
- Low performance of the photovoltaic plans (approximately 20%).
- Mandatory connection to the conventional electrical grid.
- High initial economic investment.

In the Solargis report presented to the World Bank on Global Photovoltaic Energy in June 2020, it is established that 93% of the world's population lives in countries where the average daily photovoltaic potential is in the range of 3.0 and 5.0 kWh/kWp (Global Solar Atlas, 2024). Around 20% of the world's population lives in 70 countries that have excellent conditions for photovoltaic energy, where long-term daily PVOUT averages exceed 4.5 kWh/kWp, among which is Mexico and which is in the mid-range favorable, between 3.5 and 4.5 kWh/kWp represent 71% of the world population, including China and the United States, which are currently the countries with the greatest generation and capacity of photovoltaic energy. Interestingly, they indicate that Japan is located in regions with an average PVOUT of less than 3.5 kWh/kWp. The kWp is the unit of measurement that specifies the ability of a photovoltaic system to generate energy at its peak performance and the kWh is the unit of measurement for the total amount of electricity that a photovoltaic system generates in a year (Merritt & Flowers, 2024).

Wind power

The use of wind as a source of energy for different human activities dates back to ancient times for uses such as transportation on sailing ships in the time of the Egyptian empire or for the grinding of grains of various peoples of ancient Mesopotamia (Letcher, 2023). In the Netherlands, windmills have been used to pump water to generate dry areas for human settlements or farmland. These wind exploitation systems have evolved to improve their efficiency and extract more and more power from this renewable energy source. The main improvements focused on the blades are increasing the contact surface and aerodynamics, as well as reducing weight through lightweight materials. The need to reduce CO_2 emissions and mitigate climate change led to harnessing wind energy to replace the energy produced by burning fossil fuels.

Since the appearance of the first electric turbine in 1887, developed by Charles F. Brush, significant progress has been made to improve its efficiency through the development of better magnetic or ferromagnetic materials and production processes, added to the development of blades with composite materials have reduced the costs of producing electrical energy by wind means (Krouse, 2011).

Every year, electricity generation projects through wind means have increased, thanks to the stimulus of the CO_2 emissions reduction goals. The accumulated installed capacity from 2001 to 2022 has reached 906 GW and is expected to more than double in less than ten years. Globally, 77.6 GW of new installed capacity was interconnected to the electrical grid in 2022, increasing 9% compared to 2021. Of the total installed capacity, approximately 71% of global installations were carried out in China, the United States, Brazil, Germany and Sweden. The United States and China are the countries with the largest wind market in the world (Wu et al., 2023).

Theoretical reserves of wind energy

Global wind energy reserves can be estimated through the design of mathematical models, as presented by Wu et al. (2023). This is immensely helpful in determining the amount of energy that can be extracted in different regions of the world. Measured at 100 meters above the ground, the total theoretical reserves of global wind energy is 4,986 PetaWatts hour (PWh) per year, with 2002 PWh per year from onshore wind energy. The theoretical reserves of wind energy estimated by the model presented in PWh (Wu et al., 2023) are:

- North America: 746 PWh onshore and 482 PWh offshore. Global contribution: 24.6%.
- Asia: 429 PWh onshore and 587 PWh offshore. Global contribution: 20.4%.
- Europe: 733.7 PWh onshore and 257 PWh offshore. Global contribution: 19.9%.
- Oceania: 508.4 PWh onshore and 147 PWh offshore. Global contribution: 13.1%.
- Africa: 283.19 PWh onshore and 360 PWh offshore. Global contribution: 12.9%.
- Central and South America: 283.7 PWh onshore and 169 PWh offshore. Global contribution: 9.1%.

From the distribution of the theoretical reserves across six continents, it is notable that North America, Asia and Europe lead the global rankings. Considering geographical conditions, the central onshore wind energy reserves are predominantly situated in Asia and North America. In contrast, offshore wind energy is primarily concentrated in Europe and North America, particularly in the North Sea, Iceland, Greenland, Alaska and other aquatic regions.

Every year, the number of electricity generation projects through wind power has increased, driven by the stimulus of CO_2 emission reduction goals. Cumulative installed wind power capacity worldwide, in Gigawatts (GW) (Wu et al., 2023):

- 2001: 24 GW
- 2002: 31GW
- 2003: 39 GW

- 2004: 48 GW
- 2005: 59 GW
- 2006: 74 GW
- 2007: 94 GW
- 2008: 121 GW
- 2009: 159 GW
- 2010: 198 GW
- 2011: 238 GW
- 2012: 283 GW
- 2013: 319 GW
- 2014: 370 GW
- 2015: 433 GW
- 2016: 488 GW
- 2017: 540 GW
- 2018: 591 GW
- 2019: 650 GW
- 2020: 745 GW
- 2021: 830 GW
- 2022: 906 GW

Weighted average cost (US dollars/kW) for installed offshore and onshore wind energy (Wu et al., 2023):

- 2010: $5,217/kW offshore and $2,179/kW onshore
- 2011: $5,976/kW offshore and $2,143/kW onshore
- 2012: $5,288/kW offshore and $2,039/kW onshore
- 2013: $5,589/kW offshore and $2,099/kW onshore
- 2014: $5,884/kW offshore and $2,030/kW onshore
- 2015: $5,902/kW offshore and $1,843/kW onshore
- 2016: $4,647/kW offshore and $1,848/kW onshore
- 2017: $5,249/kW offshore and $1,849/kW onshore
- 2018: $5,134/kW offshore and $1,755/kW onshore
- 2019: $4,114/kW offshore and $1,662 /kW onshore
- 2020: $3,483/kW offshore and $1,496 /kW onshore
- 2021: $3,052/kW offshore and $1,418/kW onshore
- 2022: $3,461/kW offshore and $1,274/kW onshore

The cost of installing a wind power system has changed from 2010 to 2022, with a difference of $1,756 per kilowatt (kW) for offshore and $905/kW for onshore (Statista, 2023). This market price is possible, thanks to improvements in the production processes of wind generator components (Office of Energy Efficiency & Renewable Energy, 2023) and the fiscal incentives provided to promote the installation of these systems

(WINDExchange, 2024). From 2017 to 2021, the installation cost consistently decreased for both offshore and onshore, with a difference of \$2,197 and \$431 per kW, respectively.

Hydroelectric power

The first hydroelectric power plants were implemented in 1882. These were small plants located in England, the United States and France. They emerged due to the invention of the turbine, which is the device that allows harnessing hydraulic energy. Pioneers in its development were Eourneyuron, Jonval, Girad, Thomson, James Francis and Lester Pelton (Moreno Jiménez, 2022).

Hydropower is a renewable energy source that harnesses the movement of water. It enables electricity generation by leveraging the kinetic and potential energy of streams, rivers, waterfalls and tides through mills or dams. Hydropower accounts for 17% of global energy generation and 45% of the renewable energy generation capacity worldwide. Furthermore, this energy source has an untapped global economic potential of at least 47% (Daza Vargas, 2023). The installed capacity worldwide has grown from 573 GW in 1990 to 1168 GW in 2020, which is expected to reach 1397 GW by 2030. World historical capacity of hydropower in GW:

- 1990: 573.9 GW
- 1995: 629.4 GW
- 2000: 680.9 GW
- 2005: 758.7 GW
- 2010: 895.9 GW
- 2015: 1,066.3 GW
- 2020: 1,168 GW
- 2030: 1,397 GW

Global historical generation of hydropower in TeraWatt hour (TWh) (IEA, 2021):

- 1990: 2,140 TWh
- 1995: 2,474.5 TWh
- 2000: 2,612.8 TWh
- 2005: 2,934.5 TWh
- 2010: 3,448.6 TWh
- 2015: 3,893.9 TWh
- 2020: 4,332.9 TWh
- 2025: 4,795.3 TWh
- 2030: 5,114.4 TWh

While global historical generation has doubled from 1990 to 2020, it is anticipated that by 2030, global generation will reach 5,114.4 TWh. It is essential to differentiate between installed capacity, which represents a power plant's ability to generate electricity based on its facilities and electrical generation, which quantifies the energy produced by a power plant during a specific period.

Currently, the average cost for the installation of hydroelectric projects stands at $2,881 per kW, with an average cost of electricity generation of $0.061 per kilowatt-hour (kWh). Average electricity cost of hydropower in $/Kw (IRENA, 2023):

- 2010: $0.042/kW
- 2011: $0.039/kW
- 2012: $0.041/kW
- 2013: $0.045/kW
- 2014: $0.045/kW
- 2015: $0.039/kW
- 2016: $0.052/kW
- 2017: $0.054/kW
- 2018: $0.043/kW
- 2019: $0.044/kW
- 2020: $0.049/kW
- 2021: $0.052/kW
- 2022: $0.061/kW

Asia is the region that generates the most hydroelectric power and has seen significant development. This fact is primarily due to China, which has several hydroelectric power stations installed, including the Three Gorges Dam, the largest in the world. Meanwhile, the region that generates the least and has yet to develop in this aspect is the Middle East and Africa, mainly because they are desert regions.

Hydropower generation by region in TWh:

- Asia-Pacific
  - 1990: 399.2 TWh
  - 1995: 483.4 TWh
  - 2000: 521.6 TWh
  - 2005: 727.9 TWh
  - 2010: 1,097.02 TWh
  - 2015: 1,566.85 TWh
  - 2020: 1,864.64 TWh
  - 2022: 1,911.45 TWh

- South and Central America
    - 1990: 368.8 TWh
    - 1995: 463.74 TWh
    - 2000: 550.31 TWh
    - 2005: 619.23 TWh
    - 2010: 693.99 TWh
    - 2015: 663.19 TWh
    - 2020: 696.86 TWh
    - 2022: 746.24 TWh
- North America
    - 1990: 612.45 TWh
    - 1995: 672.88 TWh
    - 2000: 662.6 TWh
    - 2005: 656.09 TWh
    - 2010: 645.82 TWh
    - 2015: 659.54 TWh
    - 2020: 696.26 TWh
    - 2022: 692.71 TWh
- Europe
    - 1990: 502.57 TWh
    - 1995: 564.9 TWh
    - 2000: 617.76 TWh
    - 2005: 571.77 TWh
    - 2010: 650.79 TWh
    - 2015: 637.36 TWh
    - 2020: 660.96 TWh
    - 2022: 566.89 TWh
- Africa
    - 1990: 211.24 TWh
    - 1995: 220.32 TWh
    - 2000: 208.43 TWh
    - 2005: 223.53 TWh
    - 2010: 216.84 TWh
    - 2015: 215.43 TWh
    - 2020: 263.24 TWh
    - 2022: 247.78 TWh

Different types of hydroelectric power plants

Various types of hydroelectric power plants are classified on the basis of their production capacity or the water source they use to generate electricity.

They are divided into three types based on their power and capacity to store hydroelectric energy (Ricaurte, 2015):

- Micro plants: Have a capacity of up to 1 MW.
- Mini plants: Have a capacity between 1 MW and 10 MW.
- Large power plants: Have capacities greater than 10 MW.

Classification by location or flow (Unidad de Planeación Minero Energética, 2015):

- Reservoir hydroelectric plants.
- Run-of-river hydroelectric plants.
- Reversible or pumped-storage hydroelectric plants.

Social impact of hydropower plants

Hydroelectric projects are beneficial in increasing local wealth through construction and maintenance, providing electricity and preventing river overflow. However, especially in large plants, they also generate negative impacts such as land and property loss, changes in livelihoods, loss of cultural identity and displacement of communities (Osorio Londono, 2017). Implementing policies for benefit redistribution and complementary actions by local authorities is crucial to mitigate these effects. Despite challenges, hydroelectric plants contribute positively by improving environmental health, propelling economic growth and elevating overall quality of life.

Environmental impact of hydropower plants

Hydropower reduces greenhouse gas emissions by replacing fossil fuel energy without consuming or polluting water. Reservoir construction improves river water management, benefits aquatic life and reduces the impacts of droughts and floods (Reed et al., 2010).

Large hydroelectric plants can cause adverse environmental impacts depending on the dam's size, reservoir and other structures. Some of these impacts include local disruption during construction, town flooding, affecting cultural sites and productive lands, displacement of wildlife, obstruction to fish migration, fish injury or death in turbines, alteration of flow regimes and sediment transport, reservoir water pollution and emission of carbon dioxide and methane from decomposing flooded vegetation (Daza Vargas, 2023).

Economic impact of hydropower plants

In hydroelectric plants, the most significant costs occur during the construction phase, as once operational, they do not pose a significant expense.

Additionally, the lifespan of these plants is long and many older plants are refurbished to continue production instead of being dismantled.

The primary economic costs of installing a hydroelectric plant are its construction, operation and maintenance. These costs include land acquisition and plans for reducing social and environmental impacts (Osorio Londono, 2017). On the other hand, both social and economic benefits are obtained. These include regional industrial development, job creation and benefits derived from energy production itself (Daza Vargas, 2023).

Geothermal energy

Geothermal, a word with Greek etymological roots, geo—Earth, thermos—heat, is the study and use of thermal energy, that is, the use of natural heat coming from the core for the generation of energy, which does not depend on climatic conditions compared to other energy generation alternatives, it is renewable and clean. In order to know the amount of heat emitted by the Earth, the surface heat flow is calculated, which is the product of the geothermal gradient and the thermal conductivity, the geothermal gradient being the variation that the Earth has at a certain depth and the thermal conductivity being with how easily a material transmits heat (World Bank, 2016).

History of geothermal energy

The Greek civilization used heat from the earth for medicinal purposes, public baths and heating homes; that is, they made use of "Geothermal," which comes from the Greek etymology geo "Earth," thermos "heat." However, it was not thanks to the discovery of boric acid in the water vapor coming out of the earth in Tuscany, Italy, in 1777, which led to its extraction; however, it was not until 1818 that a large-scale extraction was achieved. The French engineer François Jacques de Larderel who later took advantage of the hot flow that emerged to evaporate the boric water in 1827 gave way to the Prince of Trevignano, Gionori Conti, in the years 1904 and 1905, respectively, to begin the first attempts to the production of electricity with geothermal energy. Achieving that in 1913, the first electric power plant was produced producing 250 kW in the Landerello field, Italy, and in 1950, it reached 300 MW (Spain, 2024; Palacio-Villa et al., 2020).

Geographic areas with geothermal potential

The areas that are considered geothermal deposits are classified according to their temperature as:

- Low enthalpy with temperatures less than 90 °C
- Medium enthalpy with temperatures between 90 °C and 150 °C
- High enthalpy

Geothermal energy applications

The guide of the Energy Foundation of the Community of Madrid (Spain, 2024) establishes the uses of geothermal energy depending on temperature.

- High temperature, more than 150 °C, allows water vapor to be transformed into electrical energy.
- Medium temperature, between 90 °C and 150 °C, allows the production of electrical energy through an exchange fluid.
- Low temperature, between 30 °C and 90 °C, is suitable for heating buildings and some industrial processes.
- Very low temperature less than 30 °C is for heating and air conditioning.

Regarding its use for the production of electricity, it is carried out by transforming the thermodynamic energy of fluids (steam or water) into electrical energy. The deposits must have some requirements such as (Liming, 2012):

1. The seal layer is an impermeable rock that acts as an insulator.
2. Geothermal reservoirs are generally formed by hot and permeable rocks that allow fluids (water) to be stored and circulated. If circulating water is unavailable, it can be supplied from the surface.
3. The heat source is at a technically and economically viable depth, a depth that can compensate for the lack of high temperature.
4. Supply of sufficient geothermal fluid is water in a liquid or vapor state.
5. There must be a reservoir refill mechanism.

Types of geothermal power plants

Most of the power plants in operation are dry steam plants or flash plants with high temperatures. However, low- and medium-temperature reservoirs are currently beginning to be used for electricity generation or for combining heat and electricity through the operation of binary cycle plants (Palacio-Villa et al., 2020).

Direct steam plants (dry steam): They are plants where the fluid in their reservoir is vaporized, so they use steam-condensing turbines to extract it. The thermal energy of the steam is transformed into electrical energy and the condensed fluid is returned to the reservoir, ensuring the system's sustainability. The steam must be at a temperature of 150 °C or higher and the percentage must be 99.95% dry to avoid damage to the pipe. They generate between 8 MW and 140 MW.

Indirect steam plants (flash): The plants are very similar to dry steam plants. In them, the reservoir has the fluid in a liquid state, so to obtain electrical energy, a process called flashing is used to obtain steam, which will enter turbines that will transform the thermal energy into electrical energy. The generated liquid is returned to the system by returning it to the reservoir or the flashing process. Flash plants work at temperatures greater than 180 °C and generate between 0.2 MW and 150 MW.

Binary cycle plants: For plants that are used in low and medium enthalpy geothermal fields and in these plants a heat exchanger is used where, in a closed circuit, the geothermal fluid heats a mixture of ammonia-water or hydrocarbons, causing the evaporation of the mixture and the steam obtained. It is used to transform thermal energy into electrical energy. Binary plants work between 100 °C and 250 °C, generating between 1 MW and 50 MW.

Geothermal energy system capabilities

According to the International Renewable Energy Agency's (IRENA's) publication "Global Perspectives on Energy Transitions 2023," direct geothermal consumption in 2020 was 0.9 EJ. It is expected that in 2030, there will be a consumption of 1.4 EJ and, by 2050, a consumption of 2.2 EJ; however, there is no progress in this type of renewable energy.

The electricity generation trend worldwide, by geothermal techniques, according to IRENA, is:

- In 2011 with 69,796 GWh.
- In 2012 with 70,877 GWh.
- In 2013 with 72,408 GWh.
- In 2014 with 77,344 GWh.
- In 2015 with 81,229 GWh.
- In 2016 with 83,264 GWh.
- In 2017 with 85,989 GWh.
- In 2018 with 89,465 GWh.
- In 2019 with 91,980 GWh.
- In 2020 with 94,645 GWh.
- In 2021 with 95,251 GWh.

The trends in electrical capacity worldwide, by geothermal techniques, according to IRENA, are:

- In 2012 with 10,518 MW.
- In 2013 with 10,786 MW.
- In 2014 with 11,249 MW.
- In 2015 with 11,847 MW.
- In 2016 with 12,173 MW.
- In 2017 with 12,754 MW.
- In 2018 with 13,205 MW.
- In 2019 with 13,798 MW.

- In 2020 with 14,132 MW.
- In 2021 with 14,407 MW.
- In 2022 with 14,621 MW.

According to the last update from IRENA on July 18, 2023, the first ten countries are presented concerning electricity capacity and generation. Electrical capacity is the amount of electricity a power plant can generate and electrical generation is how much energy the power plant produces in a given time. The Ranking of the top ten countries in reference to electricity generation in 2021 is:

1. United States with 19,076.8 GWh.
2. Indonesia with 15,899 GWh.
3. Türkiye with 10,793.2 GWh.
4. Philippines with 10,681.4 GWh.
5. New Zealand with 8,447 GWh.
6. Italy with 5,913.8 GWh.
7. Iceland with 5,801.6 GWh.
8. Kenya with 5,182.7 GWh.
9. Mexico with 4,242. 9 GWh.
10. Japan with 3,008 GWh.

The ranking of the top-ten countries in reference to electrical capacity in 2022 is:

1. The United States with 2,652.6 MW.
2. Indonesia with 2,360.3 MW.
3. Philippines with 1,932 MW.
4. Türkiye with 1,691.3 MW.
5. New Zealand with 1,043 MW.
6. Mexico with 998.5 MW.
7. Kenya with 949.1 MW.
8. Italy with 771.8 MW.
9. Iceland with 756.2 MW.
10. Japan with 437 MW.

Advantages and disadvantages of geothermal energy

Advantages

- It is a renewable source of continuous production.
- Stable energy does not depend on changes in wind or solar radiation.
- There are enough geothermal resources to meet human needs.
- Geothermal plants require little maintenance.
- The plants do not generate outside noise.

- The waste from geothermal plants is minimal because they mainly generate steam and the gas emission is minimal, so it has a low carbon footprint.
- According to IRENA, around 100,000 people around the world are employed in activities related to geothermal energy.
- Temperature changes in groundwater or the rocks forming part of the soil are minimal.

Disadvantages

- The initial investment has a high cost because an exploration study is necessary before the construction of the plant.
- There is a high risk of insufficient geothermal resources in the drilling location.
- Changes are generated in the terrain caused by the exploration and subsequent construction of the geothermal plants.
- Hydrogen sulfide emissions produce foul odors.
- In some cases, soil subsidence occurs due to exploration.

In the IRENA report on the costs of renewable energy for 2022, at the end of that year, geothermal generation plants represented 0.4% of the total renewable energy generation plants installed worldwide, with an installed capacity of around 14.9 GW, 45% more than in 2010 (IRENA, 2023). Geothermal energy is a mature and commercially proven technology in geographies with high-temperature conventional geothermal resources close to the Earth's surface; however, the costs are significantly higher for developing unconventional geothermal resources where more specialized drilling is required. More specialized drilling requires evaluation of subsoil resources.

Compared to hydroelectric power generation, solar photovoltaic energy and onshore wind energy, geothermal energy generation projects have a relatively higher cost as they involve field preparation, production wells, reinjection and the power plant. Drilling costs depend on economic trends in the oil and gas industry, while plant installation costs depend on the site to be exploited, as well as the quality of the reservoir. In addition to the number of wells, the nature and extent of the reservoir, its thermal properties, its fluids and depth, it is worth mentioning that binary plants are more expensive because they maximize sustainability, reinjecting 100% of the geothermal fluid, maintaining thus the pressure of the reservoir. The total installed costs of flash power plants for which IRENA has information are between $2,260/kW and $5,580/kW. At the same time, binary plants are between $2,890/kW and $5,210/kW. The initial cost of exploring and drilling between three and five geothermal wells ranged between 20 million and 30 million dollars in 2016, according to the World Bank's

"Comparative Analysis of Strategies to Mitigate the Risks Associated with Geothermal Resources."

Social and political impact of sustainable energies

Social impact can be defined as the effect on society and the well-being of the community and its members (i.e., families and individuals). Social impact also refers to the consequences for human populations of any public or private action that alters how people live, work, play, relate to each other, organize to meet their needs and generally, face each other as members of society. The term also includes cultural impacts involving changes in the norms, values and beliefs that guide and rationalize their knowledge of themselves and society. Society may be affected by decisions on renewable energy and may also affect plans or decisions regarding renewable energy deployments or developments (Sheikh et al., 2016). That is the reason why, worldwide, this impact has gained significant relevance. For example, Kenya, one of the African countries with the most critical investment to meet the growing energy demand through renewable energies, including geothermal, wind and solar, has defined the significance of society's contribution in the planning for each project, meaning that the community of the place where the renewable energy plant is going to be installed must be involved, in order to avoid subsequent conflicts, and contemplate the social benefits of the region (Omenge et al., 2020). Regarding Colombia, some studies show that in communities with primary socioeconomic conditions, citizen participation in political and regulatory matters is practically nil, so it is necessary to implement strategies to involve them more actively in search of common interests, focusing on the outreach of emotional intelligence development, coexistence and self-care (Garces et al., 2021). Meanwhile, de Sena et al. (2016) conclude that social acceptance regarding solar and wind energy in the state of Río Grande do Norte, Brazil, generally has positive acceptance by society regarding the existence of plants for renewable energy generation. de Sena et al. (2016) also state that there is social acceptance regarding solar and wind energy in the region, which also has a population susceptible to social impact.

The political impact can be defined as enacting government policies and regulations that impact renewable energy's development, deployment, growth, supply and overall effects. Special market interests or lobbies and the predisposition of electricity companies also play an essential role in defining the political impact. Sociopolitical impacts exist in the four main stages of the life cycle of a renewable energy project: planning and policy development, construction and implementation, operations and maintenance and decommissioning or abandonment. Therefore, the criteria should also reflect these temporary impacts.

Social perspective

As with any energy source that has a potentially ubiquitous impact on large communities or nations, renewable energy must be analyzed concerning its relationship with society for long-term acceptance, assimilation and support. The social perspective typically involves the study of social interactions, social organization and behavioral patterns of groups. It also involves understanding the thoughts, feelings and motivations of individuals as members of society. The social perspective involves evaluating the reaction of renewable energy and the benefits and threats to society to enable a sustainable strategy aligned with established social constructs. Sometimes, the impact on people is the most crucial consideration. Therefore, for a study to be meaningful, a social impact assessment must be part of a comprehensive evaluation framework. Four main criteria have been identified from the social perspective:

- Public perception
- Employment
- Health and security
- Local infrastructure development

The criterion or metric most found in the literature is the generation of employment through renewable energies. The metrics for social perception in the implementation of renewable energy are usually the influence of technology on the identity and cultural heritage of the local community and the increased immigration of foreign workers and students. The education metric shows the resident population's education level or the acceptance of new renewable technologies. Otherwise, the educational metric is one of the determinants of human development, increasing the human capital of residents and making it positive when related to renewable energy. Therefore, from a social point of view, the appropriate application of social measurements can facilitate the choice of the location of the energy plants to be installed. It is also essential to consider the risks due to the implementation of different renewable energies. For example, some risks of wind power are disturbances derived from noise caused by wind farm turbines, which generate anxiety and stress due to the decrease in lack of sleep, among other repercussions, so it will be essential to consider them to counteract the risks, and thus ensure, to a greater extent, the assimilation of the technologies by people. Other recommendations in this regard are:

- Analyze metrics throughout the entire renewable energy implementation process.
- Estimate and calculate the social and environmental impacts of said metrics.
- Define the advantages and disadvantages.

Public perception of renewable energies

Public perception is a social phenomenon based on popular opinion, media coverage, cultural foundations and existing opinions. It is a virtual truth that may or may not be based on facts. Individuals or companies can try to do the right thing, but if the public perception of the entire industry or technology is harmful, moving in the desired direction becomes challenging. Public perception may consist of several sub-criteria. Some have been identified in this document and summarized in Table 6.1.

Table 6.1 Sub-criteria related to sustainable energy

Sub-criteria of public perception regarding sustainable energies		
Subcriterion	*References*	*Comments*
Esthetic	(Ioannidis & Koutsoyiannis, 2020; Torres Sibille, 2011)	Aesthetics is concerned with the appreciation of beauty, especially in the sense of artistic appeal.
Visual impact	(Sánchez-Pantoja et al., 2018)	For example, solar photovoltaics (PV) impact the landscape through glare due to the reflection of direct sunlight.
heterogeneous interests, Values and worldviews	(Chuang et al., 2020)	Public perception is also determined by varying (and potentially conflicting) interests, values and perspectives or frames of reference (worldviews).
Public engagement policy	(Chuang et al., 2020; Bryant et al., 2020)	Public perception is becoming an important consideration in renewable energy policy and in public reviews of energy planning.
Conflict with what was planned landscape	(Sánchez-Pantoja et al., 2018; Ioannidis & Koutsoyiannis, 2020)	Globally, renewable energy deployments must fit into existing landscape planning, especially in urban environments. Conflicts can significantly delay or even lead to the cancellation of projects.
Synergistic with quality of life improvement Policies	(Chuang et al., 2020; Bryant et al., 2020)	Public perception is affected by the synergy that exists with policies to improve quality and living standards.
Impact on lifestyle	(Soeiro & Dias, 2020)	The trend is toward promoting a higher quality or standard of living and any sub-criteria that align with this trend is received favorably.
Easy/convenient to use	(Lubowiecki-Vikuk et al., 2021)	This implies that consumers and households should not face any difficulty or hesitation in accessing or adopting the new form of energy source.
Social benefits	(Lubowiecki-Vikuk et al., 2021)	In studies and research, the identification of social benefits is key to obtaining approval of renewable energy projects.
Social acceptance	(Cuesta et al., 2020; Lubowiecki-Vikuk et al., 2021)	Studies on renewable and sustainable energy have been conducted to determine social acceptance indicators for renewable energy deployments.

(*Continued*)

Table 6.1 (Continued)

Sub-criteria of jobs related to sustainable energies		
Subcriterion	*References*	*Comments*
Employment creation	(Ricaurte, 2015; Majid, 2020)	Typically, job creation is a key priority. Total employment is a key economic indicator of the health of a region or country.
Addition to workplace diversity	(Osorio Londono, 2017)	Employment diversity implies that for a healthy society, different types of jobs must be created and coexist with each other.
Labor availability	(Pilipczuk, 2020; Majid, 2020)	Adequate trained manpower is needed for the generation and distribution of the target renewable energy.
Poverty alleviation	(Majid, 2020; Cuesta et al., 2020)	Developing countries need renewable energy-based projects that can also alleviate poverty.
Production/ manufacturing sector employment	(Merritt & Flores, 2024)	Employment growth in the manufacturing sector is a good indicator of employment and long-term industrial growth.

Health and safety sub-criteria related to sustainable energies		
Subcriterion	*References*	*Comments*
Security	(Brodny & Tutak, 2021; Axon & Darton, 2021)	Consideration of the long-term socio-economic benefits of maintaining a healthy society should play a role in assessing the impact of any form of renewable energy.
Dangerous health effects (accidents)	(Chotchoungchatchai et al., 2020)	
Investment in the health of society (indirect)		

Sub-criteria on the development of local infrastructure for sustainable energies		
Subcriterion	*References*	*Comments*
Infrastructure development/ improvement	(Pandey, 2020; Brüser, 2022)	Infrastructure is the basic structure necessary for the functioning of a society and typically includes roads, water supply, sewage, electricity and communications.
Related industry support.	(Lowitzsch et al., 2020)	Related to the development of economic and technological clusters for focused industrial growth. This subcriterion was recommended by the experts.

Sub-criteria on policies related to sustainable energy		
Subcriterion	*References*	*Comments*
Security	(Axon & Darton, 2021)	Policies are moving away from lowest cost sourcing toward portfolio-based sourcing for energy security and avoiding supply disruptions.

National energy independence	(Van de Graaf & Sovacool, 2020)	The EU biodiesel program and the US renewable fuels program (Energy Independence and Security Act, 2007) are examples of replacement policies designed to improve energy security.
Funding Options/ Government Support	(Brüser, 2022; Van de Graaf & Sovacool, 2020)	Certain countries (e.g. Canada) require partial local sourcing of renewable energy equipment for feed-in tariffs to apply.
Integration/ replacement of existing plants	(Arent, 2020)	Integrated energy planning is needed to reliably meet energy demands.

Sub-criteria on regulation/deregulation of energy markets

Subcriterion	*References*	*Comments*
Energy price controls/rate structure.	(Lu et al., 2020; Inês et al., 2020)	Price controls also often reduce or erode the operating and profit margins of energy companies, forcing them to cut spending on the investments necessary to meet demand or to operate at a loss, causing the sector to deteriorate.
Subsidies (tax credits, tax exemptions etc.). Incentives	(Qadir et al., 2021)	To the extent that they encourage the consumption of fossil fuels, energy subsidies also increase greenhouse gas emissions and pollution.
carbon tax	(Qadir et al., 2021; Lu et al., 2020)	Carbon credits are a method of offsetting carbon dioxide (CO_2) emissions, which allow both companies and individuals to reduce the impact of their carbon footprint.

Sub-criteria on the public/governmental R&D framework in relation to sustainable energies

Subcriterion	*References*	*Comments*
Government laboratories R&D	(Majid, 2020; Khan et al., 2020)	
Technology transfer	(Ferreira et al., 2020)	

Jobs related to sustainable energy

Employment is a crucial consideration for any government or society. Employment generates economic well-being for individuals and society in general. Politicians and statesmen know that job creation and sustained employment lead to a satisfied voting public, while the opposite has a highly negative effect: the population clearly expresses its discontent and demands reforms. Employment not only refers to total employment but also includes sub-criteria such as job creation, poverty alleviation, attention to specific types of employment and manufacturing jobs, and ensures that the workforce is adequately trained for the new economy. It should be noted that the manufacturing sector is vital for employment, providing productivity growth, high-quality jobs and long-term economic stability. Local or national manufacturing is also critical to the United States of America (USA) economy, as a large portion of international trade is in manufactured goods. It is also mainly responsible for the growing deficit of USA due to the importation of manufactured goods (Sheikh et al., 2016). Renewable energy has the potential to play an essential role in meeting the employment criterion. The sub-criteria related to employment are indicated in Table 6.1. However, it is essential to highlight that the main jobs generated by deploying renewable energies, whether direct or indirect, correspond to their production, installation, maintenance and support phases.

Health and security

To safeguard health and safety, governments and society must protect the safety, health and well-being of individuals, communities and the workplace. Health and safety include public safety, workplace safety and preventing or alleviating dangerous long-term health effects. Overall, it should also be an investment in the long-term health of society. Renewable energy must also consider the sub-criteria that makeup health and safety during the production, operation or energy production of energy source equipment and during the decommissioning and disposal of equipment at the end of its useful life. The primary health and safety sub-criteria are listed in Table 6.1.

Local infrastructure development

Infrastructure is the basic structure necessary for the functioning of a society and typically includes roads, water supply, sewage, electricity and communications. Local infrastructure development is commonly accepted as a critical sub-criterion of economic growth. The beneficial impact of this is felt immediately during development in terms of direct and indirect jobs with the multiplier effect of supporting industries. Infrastructure development also has a long-term benefit for the locality and the region, which consists of infrastructure improvements and the promotion of related industries and it allows the region to improve productivity and quality of life, as shown in Table 6.1.

Political perspective

Many nations have realized that dependence on fossil fuels has significant negative implications concerning energy supply and climate change. Renewable energy technologies are beginning to play an essential role in the social and economic development of communities, regions and nations. Politicians and governments are considering the growing economic benefits of the renewable energy industry. This industry increases employment and business opportunities, creates essential federal and state tax revenues and helps revitalize distressed communities. Strong government policies and incentives that favor deploying renewable energy are part of the political perspective. By evaluating this perspective, the impact of criteria such as policies can better understand electricity market regulation (or deregulation), national R&D financing, compliance with codes and standards and the perception of electricity companies and electrical services. The following criteria have been identified from the political perspective:

- Policies
- Regulation/deregulation of energy markets
- Public/government R&D framework
- Perception/position of public service companies
- Security

Sustainable energy policies

Renewable energy policies are usually at the national or local level and can mark the success or failure of a renewable energy source. Policy sub-criteria include security, support for renewable energy and energy efficiency (such as feed-in tariffs (FIT) and renewable portfolio standards (RPS)), national energy independence (from fossil fuels) and financing options with government backing, local sourcing, stipulated five- or ten-year plans for renewable energy or energy efficiency, workforce training in new energy sources and integration or replacement of existing power plants.

Regulation/deregulation of energy markets

Electric energy markets are changing a political process combining deregulation and specific aspects of regulation. This new paradigm is affecting the generation and distribution of traditional energy based on fossil fuels and renewable energy. Regulation of energy markets may include sub-criteria such as RPS, which require clear renewable energy targets, FIT to benefit consumers supplying reverse energy to the grid, metering net (with the meter reading of energy received and supplied by the consumer), multiple types of incentives, energy price controls through tariff structures (and this is a widespread form of FIT), subsidies (such as tax credits, tax breaks etc.), carbon tax (as a penalty for carbon dioxide pollution), cap and trade (also known as "emissions trading" or "pollution credits" to allow big polluters to buy credits) (Table 6.1; Sheikh et al., 2016).

Public/government R&D framework

The government can play an essential role in accelerating the Perception/position of utilities and sub-criteria for developing and implementing renewable energy technologies by funding research and providing a supporting framework for research and development (R&D). For example, in the United States, most national laboratories have implemented some form of renewable energy R&D for decades, especially the National Renewable Energy Laboratory (NREL). This criterion mainly consists of three aspects or sub-criteria: Support from national government laboratories, increased technology transfer activity to the private sector and the execution of a strategic technology plan or roadmap (Table 6.1).

References

Arent, D., Engel-Cox, J., Logan, J., Zhou, E., Ericson, S., Anderson, K., & Ruth, M. (2020). *Next Generation renewables and, separately, energy system transformation, and related topics* (CRADA CRD-14–557 Final Report) (No. NREL/TP-6A50–76744). National Renewable Energy Lab. (NREL). chrome-extension://efaidnbmnnnibpcajpcglclefindmkaj/https://www.nrel.gov/docs/fy20osti/76744.pdf

Axon, C.J., & Darton, R.C. (2021). Sustainability and risk—A review of energy security. *Sustainable Production and Consumption*, *27*, 1195–1204. https://doi.org/10.1016/j.spc.2021.01.018 http://www.spentamexico.org/v15-n1/A4.15(1)40-51.pdf

BESUN Energy. (January 10, 2024). *Advantages of photovoltaic energy*. https://besunenergy.com/energia-fotovoltaica-ventajas-y-desventajas/

Brodny, J., & Tutak, M. (2021). The comparative assessment of sustainable energy security in the Visegrad countries: A 10-year perspective. *Journal of Cleaner Production*, (317), 1–18. https://doi.org/10.1016/j.jclepro.2021.128427

Bruni, S. (2014). *A new series on energy innovation, geothermal energy*. Inter-American Development Bank. https://publications.iadb.org/en/geothermal-energy-sustainable-source-power

Brüser, M.L. (2022). *Economic Viability of Contracting Models for Financing and Operating Sustainable Energy Infrastructure in Multi-Storey Residential Buildings* (Doctoral dissertation, Wien University).

Bryant, S.T., Straker, K., & Wrigley, C. (2020). Designing our sustainable energy future: A shock doctrine for energy. *Energy Policy*, (147), 111914. https://doi.org/10.1016/j.enpol.2020.111914

Chotchoungchatchai, S., Marshall, A.I., Witthayapipopsakul, W., Panichkriangkrai, W., Patcharanarumol, W., & Tangcharoensathien, V. (2020). Primary health care and sustainable development goals. *Bulletin of the World Health Organization*, *98*(11), 792–800. http://dx.doi.org/10.2471/BLT.19.245613

Chuang, F., Manley, E., & Petersen, A. (2020). The role of worldviews in the governance of sustainable mobility. *Proceedings of the National Academy of Sciences*, *117*(8), 4034–4042. https://doi.org/10.1073/pnas.1916936117

Cuesta, M.A., Castillo-Calzadilla, T., & Borges, C.E. (2020). A critical analysis on hybrid renewable energy modeling tools: An emerging opportunity to include social indicators to optimize systems in small communities. *Renewable and Sustainable Energy Reviews*, *122*, 109691. https://doi.org/10.1016/j.rser.2019.109691

Daza Vargas, M.A. (2023). *Hydroelectric Projects and Their Contribution to the Energy Generation Matrix in Colombia* (Master's thesis in Administration, EAFIT University).

de Sena, L., Ferreira, P., & Braga, A. (2016). Social acceptance of wind and solar power in the Brazilian electricity system. *Environment, Development and Sustainability*, *18*, 1457–1476. https://doi.org/10.1007/s10668-016-9772-0

Ferreira, J.J., Fernandes, C.I., & Ferreira, F.A. (2020). Technology transfer, climate change mitigation, and environmental patent impact on sustainability and economic growth: A comparison of European countries. *Technological Forecasting and Social Change*, *150*, 119770. https://doi.org/10.1016/j.techfore.2019.119770

Garces, Y., Henao, V., Gómez, D., López, Á., & Toro, N. (2021). Social impact of renewable energy systems: Solar energy system in vulnerable community case study. *Bulletin of Electrical Engineering and Informatics*, *10*, 2337–2344. https://doi.org/10.11591/eei.v10i5.3149

Global Solar Atlas. (2024). World Bank Group, Energy Sector Management Assistance Program (ESMAP). *SOLARGIS*. https://globalsolaratlas.info/map

IEA. (2021). Hydropower data explorer. *IEA*. www.iea.org/data-and-statistics/data-tools/hydropower-data-explorer

Inês, C., Guilherme, P.L., Esther, M.G., Swantje, G., Stephen, H., & Lars, H. (2020). Regulatory challenges and opportunities for collective renewable energy prosumers in the EU. *Energy Policy*, *138*, 1–11. https://doi.org/10.1016/j.enpol.2019.111212

Ioannidis, R., & Koutsoyiannis, D. (2020). A review of land use, visibility and public perception of renewable energy in the context of landscape impact. *Applied Energy*, *276*, 115367. https://doi.org/10.1016/j.apenergy.2020.115367

IRENA. (2023). Renewable power generation costs in 2022. *International Renewable Energy Agency, Abu Dhabi*. www.irena.org/Data/View-data-by-topic/Capacity-and-Generation/Country-Rankings

ISA. (2022). Annual report 2022. *International Solar Alliance*.

Khan, S.A.R., Zhang, Y., Kumar, A., Zavadskas, E., & Streimikiene, D. (2020). Measuring the impact of renewable energy, public health expenditure, logistics, and environmental performance on sustainable economic growth. *Sustainable Development*, *28*(4), 833–843. https://doi.org/10.1002/sd.2034

Krouse, P. (2011). Charles Brush used wind power in house 120 years ago: Cleveland innovations. *Advance Local Media*. www.cleveland.com/metro/2011/08/charles_brush_used_wind_power.html

Letcher, T. (Ed.). (2023). *Wind energy engineering: A handbook for onshore and offshore wind turbines*. Elsevier.

Liming, D. (2012). *Careers in geothermal energy*. Green Jobs.

Lowitzsch, J., Hoicka, C.E., & van Tulder, F.J. (2020). Renewable energy communities under the 2019 European Clean Energy Package—Governance model for the energy clusters of the future? *Renewable and Sustainable Energy Reviews*, *122*, 1–13. https://doi.org/10.1016/j.rser.2019.109489

Lu, Y., Khan, Z.A., Alvarez-Alvarado, M.S., Zhang, Y., Huang, Z., & Imran, M. (2020). A critical review of sustainable energy policies for the promotion of renewable energy sources. *Sustainability*, *12*(12), 5078. https://doi.org/10.3390/su12125078

Lubowiecki-Vikuk, A., Dąbrowska, A., & Machnik, A. (2021). Responsible consumer and lifestyle: Sustainability insights. *Sustainable Production and Consumption*, *25*, 91–101. https://doi.org/10.1016/j.spc.2020.08.007

Majid, M. (2020). Renewable energy for sustainable development in India: Current status, future prospects, challenges, employment, and investment opportunities. *Energy, Sustainability and Society*, *10*(1), 1–36. https://doi.org/10.1186/s13705-019-0232-1

Merritt, H., & Flores, J.C.V. (2024). China's leadership in solar photovoltaics and its impact on international solar panel trade. *Mexico and the Pacific Basin*, *13*(37), 39–65.

Moreno Jiménez, D. (2022). *Identification of Environmental Impacts Produced by Hydroelectric Plants* (Bachelor's thesis, Universidad de América Foundation).

Office of Energy Efficiency & Renewable Energy. (2023). *Wind turbines: The bigger, the better*. United States Department of Energy. https://www.energy.gov/eere/articles/wind-turbines-bigger-better

Omenge, P., Obwoyere, G., Eshiamwata, G., Makindi, S., & Nathwani, J. (2020). Environmental and social impact assessment procedural steps that underpin conflict identification: Reference to renewable energy resource development in Kenya. *International Journal of Energy Production and Management*, *5*(2), 157–174. https://doi.org/10.2495/EQ-V5-N2-157-174

Osorio Londono, I. (2017). *Environmental, Social and Economic Impacts of Small Hydroelectric Plants (SHP) in Antioquia* (Doctoral dissertation, EAFIT University).

Our World in Data. (2024, January 5). *Modern renewable energy generation by source*. https://ourworldindata.org/grapher/modern-renewable-prod

Palacio-Villa, M.A., Blessent, D., López-Sánchez, J., & Moreno, D. (2020). Enhanced geothermal systems: Case study review and analysis. *Geology Bulletin*, *42*(1), 101–118.

Pandey, V. (2020). Energy infrastructure for sustainable development. In W. Leal Filho, A. Azul, L. Brandli, A. Lange Salvia, & T. Wall (Eds.), *Affordable and clean energy: Encyclopedia of the UN sustainable development goals*. Springer. https://doi.org/10.1007/978-3-319-71057-0_77-1

Pilipczuk, O. (2020). Sustainable smart cities and energy management: The labor market perspective. *Energies*, *13*(22), 6084. https://doi.org/10.3390/en13226084

Qadir, S.A., Al-Motairi, H., Tahir, F., & Al-Fagih, L. (2021). Incentives and strategies for financing the renewable energy transition: A review. *Energy Reports*, *7*, 3590–3606. https://doi.org/10.1016/j.egyr.2021.06.041

Reed, S.P., Trelles, S.A., & Hirirart, G. (April–June 2010). Water energy. *Science*, 52–61.

Ricaurte, P. (2015). Analysis of non-conventional renewable energies (NCRE), current situation and production costs with emphasis on the most common types of generation: Photovoltaic solar energy, hydroelectric energy, wind energy and biomass. *University: San Francisco de Quito*, *1*, 21–79.

Sánchez-Pantoja, N., Vidal, R., & Pastor, M.C. (2018). Aesthetic impact of solar energy systems. *Renewable and Sustainable Energy Reviews*, *98*, 227–238.

Sheikh, N.J., Kocaoglu, D.F., & Lutzenhiser, L. (2016). Social and political impacts of renewable energy: Literature review. *Technological Forecasting and Social Change*, *108*, 102–110.

Siemens. (2024). SIEMENS. *Gamesa renewable energy*. www.siemensgamesa.com/es-es

Soeiro, S., & Dias, M.F. (2020). Renewable energy community and the European energy market: Main motivations. *Heliyon*, *6*(7), 1–6. https://doi.org/10.1016/j.heliyon.2020.e04511

Solarama. (2019). *History of the solar panel: Its origins and evolution*. https://solarama.mx/blog/historia-del-panel-solar/

Spain. (2024). Geothermal energy in the world. *Government of Spain*. Ministry of Science and Innovation of Spain. Geological and Mining Institute of Spain. www.igme.es/geotermia/la%20geotermia%20en%20el%20mundo.htm#:~:text=Los%20primeros%20intentos%20de%20producci%C3%B3n,en%20el%20yacimiento%20de%20Landarello

Statista. (2023). Weighted average cost of installed offshore wind energy worldwide from 2010 to 2022. *Statista*. www.statista.com/statistics/506756/weighted-average-installed-cost-for-offshore-wind-power-worldwide/

Torres Sibille, A.D.C. (2011). *Visual Impact Assessment of Human Interventions on the Landscape: The Case of Wind Farms and Solar Power Plants* (Doctoral dissertation, Universitat Politecnica de Valencia).

Unidad de Planeación Minero Energética. (2015). Atlas del Potencial Hidroenergético de Colombia. *Government of Colombia*.https://www1.upme.gov.co/Paginas/Primer-Atlas-hidroenergetico-revela-gran-potencial-en-Colombia.aspx

Van de Graaf, T., & Sovacool, B.K. (2020). *Global energy politics.* John Wiley & Sons.

WINDExchange. (2024). *Production Tax Credit and Investment Tax Credit for wind energy.* U.S. Department of Energy's Wind Energy Technologies Office. https://windexchange.energy.gov/projects/tax-credits

World Bank. (2016). Geothermal energy: An expensive but attractive option for Latin America. *World Bank Group.* www.bancomundial.org/es/news/feature/2016/08/16/energia-geotermica-america-latina-ventajas-retos

Wu, J., Xiao, J., Hou, J., Sun, W., Li, P., & Lyu, X. (2023). A multi-criteria methodology for wind energy resource assessment and development at an intercontinental level: Facing low-carbon energy transition. *IET Renewable Power Generation, 17*(2), 480–494.

7 Decent work, knowledge management and sustainability in a technology-based company

A case study

María Catalina Rangel-León, Abraham Olivares-Arriaga and Sergio Cano-Andrade

Introduction

Nowadays, business practices oriented toward decent work, knowledge management and sustainability are especially relevant because of their impact on corporate social responsibility (CSR), attraction and retention of talent, innovation and competitiveness, regulatory compliance and reputation, business resilience and access to markets and conscious customers (Zobel de Ayala & Tan, 2021; Davenport & Mittal, 2023). These business practices currently represent some of the main challenges of the business sector of a country (Audretsch et al., 2019).

The business sector plays a fundamental role in the economic growth of a country through the creation of jobs, encouragement of innovation and technological development, contribution to tax revenues, encouragement of international trade, improvement of the quality of life and encouragement of entrepreneurship and CSR (Stam & Van de Ven, 2021). However, it is the technology-based companies (TBCs) that generate the biggest impact by stimulating the economy (Acs et al., 2017; Cowell et al., 2018; Audretsch et al., 2019) because: they remain at the forefront of innovation by investing in research and development (R&D) to create novel products or services, which provides them with competitive advantages in global markets (Motoyama & Knowlton, 2017); they experience an exponential growth due to their ability to rise rapidly (Andries & Debackere, 2006); they require highly qualified workers in areas such as programming, engineering and design (Bliemel et al., 2019); they can more easily export digital products and services in sectors such as information technologies (Mathisen & Rasmussen, 2019); they increase economic resilience because they are less prone to global economic fluctuations and, thus, can offer a long-term stability (Malecki, 2018); they arise from R&D processes focused on finding sustainable and environmentally friendly solutions, which allows to direct their efforts toward objectives such as sustainability and environmental responsibility (Mack & Mayer, 2016); and

DOI: 10.4324/9781003465058-7

finally, the presence of startups and TBC bring investment, talent and collaborations, creating a good environment for innovation and entrepreneurship (Wright et al., 2017; Stam & Van de Ven, 2021).

Thus, the study of TBC is gaining importance due to its relevance in the generation of employment, increase in sales, added value, and dynamics of innovation (Spigel, 2017; Vedula & Fitza, 2019). TBC high productivity and capacity to generate knowledge are the main reasons for their study. The knowledge generated is applied in the company's processes, products, and employees. Thus, the employees, with relatively small capital, can produce a greater quantity of goods with higher added value (Alarcón & Díaz, 2016; Spigel, 2017; Drover et al., 2017; Corsi et al., 2017).

The purpose of this study is to contribute, based on empirical research, to the knowledge about TBC, particularly about the practices that these companies carry out to contribute to the creation of decent work and the impacts of their knowledge management processes on sustainability.

A review of the literature related to TBC, decent work, knowledge management, and their points of convergence with sustainability is presented in the following paragraphs.

Technology-based companies

Technology-based companies are knowledge-intensive companies that are creators of technology and drivers of innovation. Their main asset is a series of technological capabilities, such as skills, knowledge, and people's experiences, which are used to operate existing production systems as well as to generate novel and innovative products, processes, and services (Motoyama & Knowlton, 2017). Andries and Debackere (2006) point out that these capabilities are the result of events where the companies invest in knowledge-based assets. These capabilities are developed by the company on a day-to-day basis and are the result of their R&D activities, patent registration, product design, production engineering, quality control, personnel training, and interactions with external technological collaborators and specialists. All these knowledge-based assets, together with the financial structure of the company, business strategy and alliances with other companies or universities, allow the company to master new technologies and innovate in new products and processes (Onetti et al., 2012).

In addition, it is observed that TBCs rely on taking advantage of the business opportunities that result from new technological developments. Thus, it is understood that, although every company has a technological base with which it works, not every company can be denominated as a TBC, because the use of new technology is required and this technology must generate new business opportunities in the market (Storey & Tether, 1998; Onetti et al., 2012).

Decent work

Decent work is directly related to the goal of people to fulfill their aspirations while they are still working. It is the opportunity for personnel to access productive employment that offers a fair income, social protection, workplace security, better perspectives for individual development, social integration, and the freedom to express their opinions, organize in labor groups, participate in decisions that affect their personal lives and those of their families, and have access to the same opportunities and treatment (International Labor Organization, 2008).

The United Nations plays a key role in promoting decent work by the creation of international standards and the implementation of programs to "promote sustained, inclusive, and sustainable economic growth, full and productive employment, and decent work for all" (United Nations, 2015). The latter is based on the values of freedom, equity, security and human dignity. It is important to notice the formation of the International Labor Organization, the development of the 2030 agenda for sustainable development, the Sustainable Development Goal 8 corresponding to decent work and economic growth, the global alliance for decent work and the United Nations Program for Development (Frey, 2018).

A series of categories for the study of decent work in TBC can be found in the literature, such as: (1) equity in access and promotion, where equal opportunities for employment and professional advancement are examined, without discrimination based on gender, race, age or other characteristics (Sen, 2021; Nogues & Tremblay, 2022; Zuboff, 2023); (2) compensation and benefits, which evaluates equity in compensation, as well as the availability of benefits such as health insurance, stock options and other incentives (Wood et al., 2019); (3) balance between work and personal life, which analyzes the ability employees to achieve a healthy balance between work and personal responsibilities, considering work flexibility and leave policies (Veen et al., 2020; Nogues & Tremblay, 2022); (4) participation in decision-making, which examines whether employees have the opportunity to participate in decision-making within the company, including corporate governance practices and feedback mechanisms (Nogues & Tremblay, 2022); (5) continuous professional development, which considers learning and development opportunities throughout the professional career, including continuous training and access to resources that encourage professional growth (Nogues & Tremblay, 2022); (6) organizational culture and work environment, which analyzes a business culture in terms of inclusion, respect and creating an environment that promotes diversity and collaboration (Ruggie, 2008, 2020); (7) job security and working conditions, which allows evaluating job stability, job security and the physical and psychological conditions of the working environment (Wood et al., 2019; Veen et al.,

2020); (8) ethical use of technology, which considers whether the company uses technologies in an ethical and responsible manner, avoiding practices that may have negative impacts on its employees or the society (Wood et al., 2019; Veen et al., 2020); (9) social and environmental impact, where the company's commitment to socially responsible and sustainable practices is evaluated, including its impact on the community and the environment (Wood et al., 2019; Wood & Lehdonvirta, 2023); (10) collective negotiation and social dialogue, which analyzes the existence of channels for collective negotiation and social dialogue, allowing employees to participate in decision-making and express their concerns (Locke et al., 2023).

Knowledge management

Drucker (1998, 2012) addressed the importance of knowledge management in organizations, highlighting how knowledge is a key strategic resource and how organizations must learn to manage it effectively to remain competitive.

Davenport and Prusak (1998a) proposed that knowledge management consists of the acquisition, development and use of the capability to transform knowledge into actions and, therefore, results. They highlight not only the importance of acquiring and developing knowledge but also the importance of using it effectively to achieve results in the organizational context, involving processes and practices for capturing, storing, sharing and applying knowledge within an organization, with the goal of improving performance and decision making.

In addition, Nonaka and Takeuchi (2021) introduced the concept of conversion of knowledge, highlighting the importance of socialization, externalization, combination and internalization in the process of creation and management of knowledge.

Several categories to study decent work in TBC can be found in the literature. Regarding the study of knowledge management in TBC, these categories are (1) technological innovation, which corresponds to the company's ability to generate technological innovation through effective knowledge management, including the use of new technologies and the creation of novel solutions (Davenport, 1993; Tsui et al., 2000; Benbya et al., 2020; Davenport and Mittal, 2023; Alavi et al., 2024); (2) collaboration and networks of knowledge, which allow the identification of how technology companies promote internal and external collaboration, creating knowledge that help the exchange of ideas and experiences (Davenport et al., 2020); (3) management of tacit knowledge, which is based on the experiences and skills of a person (Alavi & Leidner, 2001; Pollach, 2022); (4) continuous learning, such as the company's ability to learn from its experiences, successes and failures and apply that knowledge to improve processes and get better results (Davenport & Mittal, 2023); (5) innovative organizational culture, such as the importance to develop an organizational culture that encourages innovation and experimentation (Zobel de Ayala & Tan, 2021); (6) information technologies (IT) and collaboration platforms, which study how information technologies, including collaboration platforms, knowledge management systems and analytical tools, can support effective knowledge management (Hu & Hui, 2012); (7) transfer of knowledge and research and development (R&D), such as the way in which R&D within the company contributes to the generation of knowledge and how that knowledge is transferred to the rest of the organization (Davenport & Mittal, 2023); (8) protection and management of intellectual property, which studying how companies protect and manage their intellectual property, making sure that valuable knowledge is preserved and used strategically (Tsui et al., 2000); and (9) organizational resilience, such as the company's ability to quickly adapt to changes, learn from these changes and adjust its strategies and processes accordingly (Davenport & Prusak, 1997; Dragicevic et al., 2019; Zobel de Ayala & Tan, 2021).

Sustainability of decent work and knowledge management

The scientific literature on the sustainability of decent work and knowledge management in TBC addresses various important dimensions, some of which are (1) environmental impact, which analyzes the environmental impact of the company's operations, as well as initiatives to reduce the ecological footprint (Davenport & Prusak, 1998b; Drucker, 1998, 2012); (2) social responsibility, which evaluates the company's contribution to social well-being, including community initiatives, philanthropy and actions to address social problems (Elkington, 1997; Pollach, 2015, 2022); (3) R&D, where efforts and investments destined for the research and development of new technologies are studied (Rebentisch & Prusak, 2017); (4) use of sustainable technologies, where it is studied how technology companies use more sustainable and environmentally friendly technologies (Nonaka & Takeuchi, 2021); (5) ethical practices, analyzing the company's ethical practices, including transparency in decision-making and integrity in business relationships (Nonaka et al., 2021; Pollach, 2022); and (6) regulatory compliance, which considers compliance with labor, ethical and environmental laws and regulations (Nonaka et al., 2018).

Methodology

The research strategy used in this work is the case of study (Yin, 1989) with a qualitative approach and an ethnographic design (Hernández-Sampieri & Mendoza, 2018) that allows to answer the question: What are the practices that a technology-based company uses to contribute to the creation of decent work and its practices for sustainability, which are obtained from knowledge management processes?

The sampling units for the research, according to Lofland et al. (2022) are organizations, groups and people.

The units of analysis correspond to practices, processes and episodes. The practices refer to the routine activities of the collaborators of the TBC; the processes correspond to activities, tasks and actions that take place and have taken place successively or simultaneously in the company, subject to analysis. The episodes correspond to outstanding events in institutions such as technology parks, government institutions that promote innovation and entrepreneurship, public research centers and higher education institutions.

The determining factor for the selection of the case of study is the nature of the phenomenon under analysis. The research of the present work focuses on a TBC located on the state of Guanajuato, Mexico, dedicated to offer scientific, technological and professional services in the market of biotechnology and bioengineering, using biology systems and metabolic engineering applied to different biological systems. In addition, the TBC focuses on the design of processes for developing crops and fermentation of biofuels and biopolymers. It has 15 years of experience in the market and an average of 40 permanent and temporary employees.

The interest in focusing the study on this company is because of the importance of TBC for the economy of the regions, particularly in the state of Guanajuato, Mexico, which in 2020 generated a gross domestic product (GDP) of 650,175 million pesos; thus, becoming the sixth best contributor state to Mexico's economy (INEGI, 2020). In addition, the company under study belongs to the group of 482 companies that have "*RENIECYT*" (CONACYT, 2019), according to information obtained from the List of Current Science and Technology Institutions and Companies by Sector, Federative Entity 2018 (CONACYT, 2019), having the characteristics to be considered a TBC and maintaining an active participation in projects with high schools and universities, public research centers, technology parks, government institutions and municipal, state and national business sectors.

The type of sample used is chosen because of convenience and typical cases (Battaglia et al., 2008), looking for richness, depth and quality of the information.

The sample size corresponds to a technology-based company. A focus group, integrated by four employees, is studied. Interviews are conducted with the owner of a technology park, a researcher at a public research center, the person in charge of the link-up office of a university, a government official in the area of innovation and entrepreneurship and the person in charge of projects in a biofuels company that has been a client of the subject under study. The data collection period is August–November 2023.

In-depth interviews, focus groups and participant observation are used as data collection techniques (Vasilachis de Gialdino, 2009). Interview scripts are developed using a matrix of authors, where three categories of analysis such as decent work, knowledge management and sustainability are determined, from which 25 dimensions are derived. Table 7.1 shows the matrix of authors used for the analysis.

A general narrative is used as a strategy for the analysis of the data collected. The units of analysis, categories formed by open and axial coding,

Table 7.1 Matrix of authors considered for the study

Category	*Dimension*	*Reference*
Decent Work	Equity in access and promotion	Sen (2021); Nogues and Tremblay (2022) and Zuboff (2023)
	Compensation and benefits	Wood et al. (2019)
	Work-personal life balance	Veen et al. (2020) and Nogues and Tremblay (2022)
	Participation in decision-making	Nogues and Tremblay (2022)
	Continuous professional development	Nogues and Tremblay (2022)
	Organizational culture and work environment	Ruggie (2008, 2020)
	Job security and working conditions	Wood et al. (2019) and Veen et al. (2020)
	Ethical use of technology	Wood et al. (2019) and Veen et al. (2020)
	Social and environmental impact	Wood et al. (2019) andWood and Lehdonvirta (2023)
	Collective negotiation and social dialogue	Locke et al. (2023)
Knowledge Management	Technological innovation	Davenport (1993); Tsui et al. (2000); Benbya et al. (2020); Davenport and Mittal (2023) and Alavi et al. (2024)
	Collaboration and knowledge networks	Davenport et al. (2020)
	Management of tacit knowledge	Alavi and Leidner (2001) and Pollach (2022)
	Continuous learning	Davenport and Mittal (2023)
	Innovative organizational culture	Zobel de Ayala and Tan (2021)
	Information technologies (IT) and collaboration platforms	Hu and Hui (2012)
	Transfer of R&D knowledge	Davenport and Mittal (2023)
	Protection and management of intellectual property	Tsui et al. (2000)
	Organizational agility	Davenport and Prusak (1997); Dragicevic et al. (2019) and Zobel de Ayala and Tan (2021)
Sustainability	Environmental impact	Davenport and Prusak (1998b) and Drucker (1998, 2012)
	Social responsibility	Elkington (1997) and Pollach (2015, 2022)
	Research and development	Rebentisch and Prusak (2017)
	Adoption of sustainable technologies	Nonaka and Takeuchi (2021)
	Ethical practices	Nonaka et al. (2021) and Pollach (2022)
	Regulatory compliance	Nonaka et al. (2018)

Source: Own elaboration

topics and emerging patterns of the data are considered for the analysis. This analysis is developed through detailed descriptions and the presentation of personal experiences, which are compared with the theory of the construction of meanings. ATLAS.ti version 7 software is used as a tool for the analysis, where a hermeneutic unit is developed by means of line-by-line open coding. This hermeneutic unit allows to link and merge codes, achieving an axial coding of the data collected by means of the development of categories, topics and families of codes. This is possible due to the saturation of the codes during the analysis and their subsequent support with theory (Weitzman & Miles, 1995).

Results

The findings obtained from the study are classified into three families of codes and correspond to decent work, knowledge management and sustainability. A total of 41 codes are derived from these families. Figure 7.1 shows a summary of the practices implemented by the company under study with respect to the consideration of decent work, knowledge management and sustainability.

Decent work

As part of the encouragement and application of decent work in the company under study, there are observed practices such as inclusive hiring policies, where skills and competencies are considered instead of focusing on

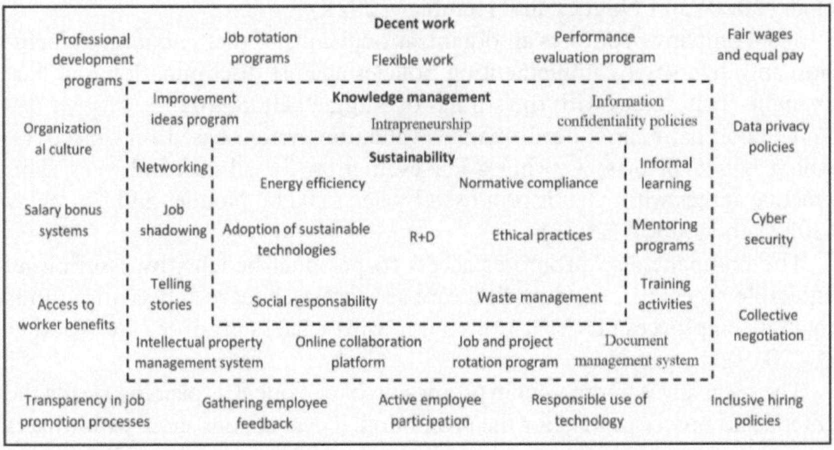

Figure 7.1 Practices implemented by the company under study with respect to the consideration of decent work, knowledge management and sustainability.

gender, race, sexual orientation or other personal characteristics, which coincides with the studies of Sen (2021); Nogues and Tremblay (2022) and Zuboff (2023) regarding the support of decent work.

Another practice observed is the implementation of professional development programs such as internal training programs, which are optional or mandatory. Another practice observed is the implementation of giving economic incentives to employees that take professional development programs outside the company. These practices coincide with what is reported by Nogues and Tremblay (2022) as practices that promote decent work in companies.

Another practice observed is the rotation of tasks, so that employees gain experience in different areas of the company; thus, increasing their skills and knowledge, which is related to the results reported by Nogues and Tremblay (2022).

Another practice observed is the implementation of a program of fair salary and equal payment, which offers clear policies of remuneration and promotion to its employees, which agrees with what is proposed by Wood et al. (2019).

Another practice observed is the implementation of a bonus systems based on performance and achievement of objectives, to recognize and reward the effort and dedication of its employees, which agrees with what is reported by Wood et al. (2019) as a practice that encourages decent work.

The company also has as a practice offering flexible work options to its employees, such as flexible work hours and home office. This practice allows its employees to avoid sending emails outside of working hours as well as taking additional days off, which improves the balance between work and personal life, regardless of gender. This agrees with what is reported by Veen et al. (2020) and Nogues and Tremblay (2022).

The company promotes an organizational culture that encourages inclusion and diversity by implementing policies against discrimination and harassment. This agrees with the studies of Ruggie (2008, 2020).

The company has a performance evaluation system based on objectives, which is free of bias, assuring a fair evaluation for all its employees. This practice agrees with what is proposed by Sen (2021); Nogues and Tremblay (2022) and Zuboff (2023).

The company also promotes access to personal benefits by assuring an equitable access to major medical care services, sick leave and savings funds to all its employees. These actions agree with what is proposed by Wood et al. (2019).

The company is transparent in promotion of personnel, explaining clearly the criteria and processes used for the promotion. These actions agree with what is studied by Sen (2021); Nogues and Tremblay (2022) and Zuboff (2023).

The company applies surveys twice a year to collect the opinions of its employees on various aspects of work, organizational culture and internal policies. The participation of employees is encouraged by including them in important projects so they can contribute with their knowledge and perspectives from the inception to the implementation of the project. This agrees with what is suggested by Nogues and Tremblay (2022) as types of practices.

The company is involved in community initiatives that promote equal opportunities and improve the quality of life of people in the community. These initiatives agree with what is studied by Wood et al. (2019) and Wood and Lehdonvirta (2023).

The company implements data privacy policies to protect personal information of its employees and follows the privacy regulations. The company also has a cybersecurity program that encourages the responsible use of technology and protects the company from cyber-attacks. In addition, the company encourages technological ethics and cybersecurity, this is related to what is proposed by Wood et al. (2019) and Veen, et al. (2020).

Finally, the company implements programs for collective negotiation based on policies that respect the freedom for the formation of unions and labor associations and promotes a policy of no retaliation. This coincides with what is proposed by Locke et al. (2023).

Knowledge management

As part of the actions implemented by the company under study to promote knowledge management, it is observed that Microsoft Teams is used as an online collaboration platform to ease the communication and share information between working teams. In addition, the company has a Dropbox Business license as a document management system to store and organize information efficiently. Both practices coincide with what is studied by Davenport (1993); Tsui et al. (2000); Davenport et al. (2020); Benbya et al. (2020); Davenport and Mittal (2023) and Alavi et al. (2024).

The company uses social networks to encourage the collaboration and the exchange of experiences; however, the company does not have strategies to encourage its employees to use actively these social networks. The employees who participate in the social networks do it by their own initiative.

The company implements mentoring programs between its employees, which helps the transfer of knowledge between more experienced employees and those who are in the early stages of their careers. Both activities coincide with what is studied by Alavi and Leidner (2001); Davenport et al. (2020) and Pollach (2022).

The company implements an improvement ideas program to encourage the presentation of innovative ideas and active participation in continuous improvement projects. This coincides with what is proposed by Davenport and Mittal (2023).

The company has an intellectual property management system to protect its innovations and developments. This coincides with what is proposed by Hu and Hui (2012).

The company has a weekly lunch day with the purpose of having internal networking and an informal learning event, where all the employees are encouraged to interact with each other. This strategy that coincides with what is proposed by Davenport et al. (2020).

The company implements training activities to encourage the collaboration between teams from different areas, promoting interdisciplinary learning. In addition, the company has a job and project rotation program so that its employees acquire a variety of experiences and tacit knowledge in different areas of the company. Both practices coincide with what is proposed by Alavi and Leidner (2001) and Pollach (2022).

The company encourages the communication of success and failure events within the company, where employees share their experiences so that others can learn from these past events. In addition, the company promotes job shadowing and cross-training with the figures of research assistant and intern, where the employees are motivated to observe closely to and learn how their superiors develop their daily responsibilities and tasks. This is in agreement with what is proposed by Davenport and Mittal (2023).

The company has a regular feedback and evaluation processes by means of its performance evaluation program, so that employees receive information about their current performance and areas for improvement. The company promotes a culture that values continuous learning and experimentation, be means of a remuneration program and a succession planning initiative: These two actions coincide with what is proposed by Davenport and Mittal (2023).

The company encourages intrapreneurship by motivating its employees to plan and start their own companies, looking that these new companies are similar or complementary to the TBC. This action agrees with what is proposed by Davenport and Prusak (1997); Dragicevic et al. (2019) and Zobel de Ayala and Tan (2021) as a knowledge management practice.

The company has a project policy which requires a complete and a rigorous documentation of research and development results, ensuring that the information is clearly recorded and easily accessible to all the employees. Finally, the company promotes the responsible use of information and its detailed registration by means of confidentiality policies. This action agrees with what is proposed by Tsui et al. (2000).

Sustainability

The company implements actions to promote sustainability, which is a result of knowledge management processes and decent work practices. These actions are oriented toward energy efficiency by means of the implementation of technologies and practices that reduce energy consumption and the existence of policies to turn off unused lights and devices. In addition, the company has a program for the management of biological and solid wastes that result from the processes and electronic wastes from unused equipment. These practices agree with what is proposed by Davenport and Prusak (1998b) and Drucker (1998, 2012).

Finally, the company has practices related to social responsibility, research and development, adoption of sustainable technologies, ethical practices and regulatory compliance. These practices agree with what is described in the previous sections of knowledge management and decent work.

Conclusion

This chapter presented the analysis of the practices implemented by a technology-based company to contribute to the creation of decent work, the creation of knowledge and its management and the sustainability of its daily activities. The existence of different practices related to each of the these three dimensions were observed, such as (1) with respect to decent work: equity in access and promotion, compensation and benefits, work-life balance, participation in decision-making, continuous professional development, organizational culture and work environment, job security and working conditions, ethical use of technology, social and environmental impact, collective negotiations and social dialogue; (2) with respect to knowledge management: technological innovation, collaboration and knowledge networks, management of tacit knowledge, continuous learning, innovative organizational culture, information technologies and collaboration platforms, transfer of knowledge obtained by means of research and development, protection and application of intellectual property and organizational agility; (3) with respect to sustainability: social responsibility, research and development, implementation of sustainable technologies, ethical practices and regulatory compliance.

As future research, it is suggested the analysis of the reasons why technology-based companies implement these practices. In addition, it is suggested to study the practices implemented toward decent work, knowledge management and sustainability, of the people associated with knowledge-intensive companies, such as clients, suppliers, higher education institutions, technology parks, research centers and offices dedicated to the transfer of knowledge and technology.

References

Acs, Z., Stam, E., Audretsch, D., & O'Connor, A. (2017). The lineages of the entrepreneurial ecosystem approach. *Small Business Economics*, *49*(1), 1–10. https://doi.org/10.1007/s11187-017-9864-8

Alarcón, M., & Díaz, C. (2016). La empresa de base tecnológica y su contribución a la economía mexicana en el periodo 2004–2009. *Contaduría y administración*, *61*(1), 106–126. https://doi.org/10.1016/j.cya.2015.09.004

Alavi, M., & Leidner, D.E. (2001). Knowledge management and knowledge management systems: Conceptual foundations and research issues. *MIS Quarterly*, 107–136. https://doi.org/10.2307/3250961

Alavi, M., Leidner, D.E., & Mousavi, R. (2024). Knowledge management perspective of generative artificial intelligence. *Journal of the Association for Information Systems*, *25*(1), 1. https://doi.org/10.17705/1jais.00859

Andries, P., & Debackere, K. (2006). Adaptation in new technology-based ventures: Insights at the company level. *International Journal of Management Reviews*, *8*(2), 91–112.

Audretsch, D., Cunningham, J., Kuratko, D., Lehmann, E., & Menter, M. (2019). Entrepreneurial ecosystems: Economic, technological, and societal impacts. *The Journal of Technology Transfer*, *44*(2), 313–325. https://doi.org/10.1007/s10961-018-9690-4

Battaglia, M., Sampling, N., & Lavrakas, P. (2008). *Encyclopedia of survey research methods*. Publication date.

Benbya, H., Davenport, T.H., & Pachidi, S. (2020). Artificial intelligence in organizations: Current state and future opportunities. *MIS Quarterly Executive*, *19*(4). http://dx.doi.org/10.2139/ssrn.3741983

Bliemel, M., Flores, R., De Klerk, S., & Miles, M. (2019). Accelerators as start-up infrastructure for entrepreneurial clusters. *Entrepreneurship & Regional Development*, *31*(1–2), 133–149. https://doi.org/10.1080/08985626.2018.1537152

CONACYT. (24 de octubre de 2019). Listado de instituciones y empresas de ciencia y tecnología vigentes por sector, entidad federativa 2018 [Archivo Excel]. *Registro de Instituciones y Empresas de Ciencia y Tecnología (RENIECYT)*. https://datos.gob.mx/busca/dataset/registro-de-instituciones-y-empresas-de-ciencia-y-tecnologia-reniecyt/resource/cd5ad407-5e12-4f02-a514-bb901fdd6012

Corsi, C., Prencipe, A., Rodríguez-Gulías, M., Fernández-López, S., & Rodeiro-Pazos, D. (2017). The effect of parent university on firm growth: An analysis of the Spanish and Italian USOs. *Journal of Management Development*, *36*(2), 233–249. https://doi.org/10.1108/JMD-06-2016-0108

Cowell, M., Lyon-Hill, S., & Tate, S. (2018). It takes all kinds: Understanding diverse entrepreneurial ecosystems. *Journal of Enterprising Communities: People and Places in the Global Economy*, *12*(2), 178–198. https://doi.org/10.1108/JEC-08-2017-0064

Davenport, T.H. (1993). *Process innovation: Reengineering work through information technology*. Harvard Business Press.

Davenport, T.H., Godfrey, A.B., & Redman, T.C. (2020). To fight pandemics, we need better data. *MIT Sloan Management Review*, *62*(1), 1–4.

Davenport, T.H., & Mittal, N. (2023). How companies can prepare for the coming "AI-first" world. *Strategy & Leadership*, *51*(1), 26–30. https://doi.org/10.1108/SL-11-2022-0107

Davenport, T.H., & Prusak, L. (1997). *Information ecology: Mastering the information and knowledge environment*. Oxford University Press.

Davenport, T.H., & Prusak, L. (1998a). Learn how valuable knowledge is acquired, created, bought and bartered. *The Australian Library Journal*, *47*(3), 268–272. https://doi.org/10.1080/00049670.1998.10755852

Davenport, T.H., & Prusak, L. (1998b). *Working knowledge: How organizations manage what they know*. Harvard Business Press.

Dragicevic, N., Ullrich, A., Tsui, E., & Gronau, N. (2019). A conceptual model of knowledge dynamics in the industry 4.0 smart grid scenario. *Knowledge Management Research & Practice*, *18*(2), 199–213. https://doi.org/10.1080/14778238.2019.1633893

Drover, W., Busenitz, L., Matusik, S., Townsend, D., Anglin, A., & Dushnitsky, G. (2017). A review and road map of entrepreneurial equity financing research: Venture capital, corporate venture capital, angel investment, crowdfunding, and accelerators. *Journal of Management*, *43*(6), 1820–1853. https://doi.org/10.1177/014920631769058

Drucker, P. (1998). The discipline of innovation. *Harvard Business Review*, *76*(6), 149–157.

Drucker, P. (2012). *Management*. Routledge.

Elkington, J. (1997). The triple bottom line. *Environmental Management: Readings and Cases*, *2*, 49–66.

Frey, D. (2018). Economic growth, full employment and decent work: The means and ends in SDG 8. In *The sustainable development goals and human rights* (pp. 122–142). Routledge. https://doi.org/10.4324/9781351024303

Hernández-Sampieri, R., & Mendoza, C. (2018). *Metodología de la investigación. Las rutas cuantitativa, cualitativa y mixta*. Editorial McGraw Hill.

Hu, P.J.H., & Hui, W. (2012). Examining the role of learning engagement in technology-mediated learning and its effects on learning effectiveness and satisfaction. *Decision Support Systems*, *53*(4), 782–792. https://doi.org/10.1016/j.dss.2012.05.014

INEGI. (2020). Banco de información económica. *Cuentas Nacionales, Producto Interno Bruto por Entidad Federativa, base 2013, Guanajuato*. www.inegi.org.mx/app/indicadores/?tm=0#D482254

International Labor Organization. (2008). Decent work: Some strategic challenges ahead. *International Labour Conference, 97th Session, Report of the Director-General*. International Labour Office.

Locke, R.M., Armstrong, B., Schaab-Rozbicki, S., & Young, G. (2023). Supply chains and working conditions during the long pandemic: Lessons for a new moral political economy? *Dædalus*, *152*(1), 131–142. https://doi.org/10.1162/daed_a_01970

Lofland, J., Snow, D., Anderson, L., & Lofland, L.H. (2022). *Analyzing social settings: A guide to qualitative observation and analysis*. Waveland Press.

Mack, E., & Mayer, H. (2016). The evolutionary dynamics of entrepreneurial ecosystems. *Urban Studies*, *53*(10), 2118–2133. https://doi.org/10.1177/0042098015586547

Malecki, E. (2018). Entrepreneurship and entrepreneurial ecosystems. *Geography Compass*, *12*(3), 1–21. https://doi.org/10.1111/gec3.12359

Mathisen, M., & Rasmussen, E. (2019). The development, growth, and performance of university spin-offs: A critical review. *The Journal of Technology Transfer*, *44*(6), 1891–1938. https://doi.org/10.1007/s10961-018-09714-9

Motoyama, Y., & Knowlton, K. (2017). Examining the connections within the startup ecosystem: A case study of St. Louis. *Entrepreneurship Research Journal*, *7*(1), 3–23. https://doi.org/10.1515/erj-2016-0011

Nogues, S., & Tremblay, D.G. (2022). Managers' views about employed carers' well-being: A qualitative study in Quebec. *Wellbeing, Space and Society*, *3*, 100096. https://doi.org/10.1016/j.wss.2022.100096

Nonaka, I., Nishihara, A., & Kawada, H. (2018). Knowledge-based management theory. In *knowledge creation in public administrations: Innovative government in southeast Asia and Japan* (pp. 1–21). https://doi.org/10.1007/978-3-319-57478-3_1

Nonaka, I., & Takeuchi, H. (2021). Humanizing strategy. *Long Range Planning*, *54*(4), 1–11. https://doi.org/10.1016/j.lrp.2021.102070
Nonaka, I., Takeuchi, H., & Uno, K. (2021). Reconceptualizing tacit knowing: A phenomenological perspective. *Kindai Management Review/The Institute for Creative Management and Innovation, Kinki University*, *9*, 22–34.
Onetti, A., Zucchella, A., Jones, M., & McDougall-Covin, P. (2012). Internationalization, innovation, and entrepreneurship: Business models for new technology-based firms. *Journal of Management & Governance*, *16*(3), 337–368. https://doi.org/10.1007/s10997-010-9154-1
Pollach, I. (2015). Strategic corporate social responsibility: The struggle for legitimacy and reputation. *International Journal of Business Governance and Ethics*, *10*(1), 57–75. https://doi.org/10.1504/IJBGE.2015.068685
Pollach, I. (2022). The diffusion of management fads: A popularization perspective. *Journal of Management History*, *28*(2), 284–302. https://doi.org/10.1108/JMH-11-2020-0072
Rebentisch, E., & Prusak, L. (2017). *Integrating program management and systems engineering: Methods, tools, and organizational systems for improving performance.* John Wiley & Sons.
Ruggie, J. (2008). Protect, respect and remedy: A framework for business and human rights. *Innovations: Technology, Governance, Globalization*, *3*(2), 189–212.
Ruggie, J. (2020). The social construction of the UN guiding principles on business and human rights. In *Research handbook on human rights and business* (pp. 63–86). Edward Elgar Publishing. https://doi.org/10.4337/9781786436405.00009
Sen, A. (2021). *Nuevo examen de la desigualdad.* Comercial Grupo ANAYA, SA.
Spigel, B. (2017). The relational organization of entrepreneurial ecosystems. *Entrepreneurship Theory and Practice*, *41*(1), 49–72. https://doi.org/10.1111/etap.12167
Stam, E., & Van de Ven, A. (2021). Entrepreneurial ecosystem elements. *Small Business Economics*, *56*(2), 809–832. https://doi.org/10.1007/s11187-019-00270-6
Storey, D., & Tether, B. (1998). New technology-based firms in the European Union: An introduction. *Research Policy*, *26*(9), 933–946.
Tsui, E., Garner, B.J., & Staab, S. (2000). The role of artificial intelligence in knowledge management. *Knowledge Based Systems*, *13*(5), 235–239.
United Nations. (2015). Transforming our world: The 2030 agenda for sustainable development. *Resolution adopted by the General Assembly on 25 September 2015 (A/RES/70/1). 69th Session of UN General Assembly.* United Nations. www.un.org/ga/search/view_doc.asp?symbol=A/RES/70/1&Lang=E
Vasilachis de Gialdino, I. (2009). Los fundamentos ontológicos y epistemológicos de la investigación cualitativa. *Forum Qualitative Sozialforschung/Forum: Qualitative Social Research*, *10*(2).
Vedula, S., & Fitza, M. (2019). Regional recipes: A configurational analysis of the regional entrepreneurial ecosystem for US venture capital-backed startups. *Strategy Science*, *4*(1), 4–24. https://doi.org/10.1287/stsc.2019.0076
Veen, A., Kaine, S., Goods, C., & Barratt, T. (2020). The "gigification" of work in the 21st century. In Holland, P., & Brewster, C. (Eds.), *Contemporary work and the future of employment in developed countries* (pp. 15–32). Routledge.
Weitzman, E., & Miles, M. (1995). *Computer programs for qualitative data analysis.* Sage.
Wood, A.J., Graham, M., Lehdonvirta, V., & Hjorth, I. (2019). Good gig, bad gig: Autonomy and algorithmic control in the global gig economy. *Work, Employment and Society*, *33*(1), 56–75. https://doi.org/10.1177/0950017018785616

Wood, A.J., & Lehdonvirta, V. (2023). Platforms disrupting reputation: Precarity and recognition struggles in the remote gig economy. *Sociology*, *57*(5), 999–1016. https://doi.org/10.1177/00380385221126804
Wright, M., Siegel, D., & Mustar, P. (2017). An emerging ecosystem for student start-ups. *The Journal of Technology Transfer*, *42*(4), 909–922. https://doi.org/10.1007/s10961-017-9558-z
Yin, R. (1989). *Case study research: Design and methods, applied social research methods series*. Sage.
Zobel de Ayala, J., & Tan, C. (2021). Balancing social impact and business outcomes in turbulent times. *Asian Management Insights (Singapore Management University)*, *8*(1), 6–9. https://ink.library.smu.edu.sg/ami/145
Zuboff, S. (2023). The age of surveillance capitalism. In *Social theory re-wired* (pp. 203–213). Routledge.

8 Management strategies for transitioning from conventional industries to green and low-carbon production systems

Noé Aguilar-Rivera

Introduction

Nowadays, research on agro-industrial plants has increased worldwide and there is more evidence about the crops, handling, processing and final disposal of their products and by-products. In this respect, the decarbonization of agriculture, industry and logistics is a complex problem and the solutions will require interdisciplinary collaboration between various fields combined with innovation, the involvement of stakeholders and regulatory, legislative and even a lot of infrastructure and financial incentives.

Furthermore, the development of innovation-based industrial systems for the transition to sustainable nature systems and low-carbon green technologies is one of the main challenges for industrial competitiveness. However, issues as corporate social responsibility (CSR) and the development of low-carbon manufacturing, conversion or transformation processes are still in their early stages mainly in developing countries and regions where the socioeconomic dependence on the agricultural sector is high. Besides, the GHG generation is even higher than the rest of the world, because they have a low rate of technological innovation to transform integrally with zero waste these raw materials into high-value-added products for highly differentiated markets and the participation of policymakers, researchers, stakeholders and involve the entire society and inhabitants in a green transition is still disjointed without understanding the interconnectedness of growth and sustainability.

In relation to the above, the systematic application of the United Nations' 2030 Agenda for Sustainable Development Goals (SDGs) number 9, "build resilient infrastructure, promote inclusive and sustainable industrialization and foster innovation" should be part of the transformation of conventional agro-industries and agribusiness. These productive systems could contribute in social, economic, environmental, infrastructural and institutional aspects to new technologies aiming at achieving higher quality and increased value and facilitating green manufacturing with high efficiency in all processes of

DOI: 10.4324/9781003465058-8

the value chain (input production, agro-ecological farming stage, transport and logistics, industrial transformation, waste management and conversion and target markets) to improve the contribution to society and the environment. (Leal Filho et al., 2022)

However, industrial activity is limited by several constraints to carry out their corporate social responsibility, therefore, investments, technologies and infrastructures are needed to assist in the implementation of SDG 9 considering:

1. Planning and the provision of resources
2. Significantly raising industry's share of GDP
3. Substantially increasing the expenditure for scientific research and development as a proportion of GDP
4. Increasing access to mobile networks.
5. Developing infrastructure

Notwithstanding, for the application of green technologies and achieving a reconversion in agriculture, logistics, manufacturing, industry, biorefineries and the generation of low-carbon products, infrastructure (SDG 9 industry, innovation and infrastructure), either directly or indirectly, influence all 17 of the SDGs, including 121 of the 169 targets (72%) and 68% are influenced by multiple infrastructure sectors. Therefore, it is fundamental to achieving the SDGs for energy management, water, waste management, transport and telecommunications, population growth, urbanization, economic development, climate change and infrastructure deterioration (Thacker et al., 2019) to develop green, durable, biodegradable and eco-friendly products for a sustainable future (Bradu et al., 2022).

Gilbert et al. (2022) carried out an extensive review of the complexity and the role of infrastructure systems in achieving sustainability.

For instance, every organization, company or productive sector (agriculture, industry, market) has a strategy to maximize comparative and competitive advantages through strategic planning to evaluate how to achieve objectives, improve economic and environmental indicators and develop within the uncertainty of the markets. The goal of achieving greater competitive advantage can be achieved through a variety of strategies, such as green innovation, which is currently one of the biggest challenges in the achievement of the best company performance (Farida & Setiawan, 2022).

Innovation and management strategies

Pattinson et al. (2023) defined the *Green innovation* for achieving low-carbon industries as the scheme by means of which the companies can achieve a multi-value approach to direct strategies to address the challenge of environmental sustainability while potential opportunities are exploited with new products and services, processes, business models and markets that reduces or eliminates environmental impact with a positive impact on the economy and wider society balancing people, planet and profit with the participation of policymakers, stakeholders, entrepreneurs, growers, academics and practitioners

Therefore, *green innovation is hardware or software innovation related to green products or processes, including innovation in technologies in energy saving, pollution prevention, waste recycling, green product design, or corporate environmental management* (Chen, 2011).

The potential of the introduction, integration and adoption of green technologies in developing countries highlighted the transformative potential of agriculture, agroecology, renewable energy, energy-efficient practices and sustainable infrastructure in promoting economic growth while mitigating environmental impacts (Yeboah, 2023).

In this regard, manufacturing companies and the agricultural sector should share the objective of "doing the same things but better" (Mosgaard & Kristensen, 2023).

According to Shahzad et al. (2022), a large number of various organizations in the production sector have adopted green innovation and environmentally friendly practices in production stages, organizational structure, the management or business models, quality improvement and hardware or software as key component to mitigate the negative consequences of traditional growth models based on the green revolution and industrial revolution, significantly reduce adverse effects on the environment and ensure a competitive advantage to manufacture environmentally friendly products by minimizing resource utilization and waste generation to achieve sustainable development.

In this sense, the productive sector of conventional technologies faces important challenges such as investment in the transition to green technologies and innovation to be competitive in the market, on the other hand, the quality of inputs, processes, services and products requires measurement standards that consider numerous controllable and non-controllable factors which affect the risk of failures and the overall quality. Therefore, the challenge of incorporating green technologies leads to identifying strategies and opportunities that foster economic growth and social welfare while promoting resilient infrastructure, inclusive and sustainable industrialization and green innovation contributing to a more sustainable future for regions and countries.

Sahoo et al. (2023) concluded that for green innovation in firms, the acquisition of green-based knowledge by workers and entrepreneurs can improve green knowledge management, green technological innovation activities and environmental performance, thereby generating practical ideas that enable firm managers to focus on planning, budgeting resources to implement effective green innovations that can contribute to improving firms' environmental performance, production, profitability, their CSR and the welfare of the population.

Climate change, reduction of ecosystemic services and resource depletion from nature and mineral and fossil sources are deeply impacting the activities of society favoring the emergence of new needs and evolutionary trends in the industry. New approaches such as circular economy (CE), green technologies, Agriculture 4.0 and Industry 4.0 will be a priority in addressing the challenges of humanity.

The CE refers to a shift from the traditional linear production and consumption "end-of-life" mode to a circular one with reducing, reusing, recycling and recovering materials in production/distribution and consumption processes Industry 4.0 focuses on developing intelligent factories and products, entailing opportunities for enhanced performance for production activities, organizational strategies, business models and skills digital technologies (DTs), such as the Internet of Things (IoT), big data analytics (BDA) and additive manufacturing (AM), have been recognized as fundamental tools for the Industry 4.0 transition (Neri et al., 2023).

Kannan et al. (2024) concluded that with the evolution of green technology, smart waste management, manufacturing enterprises, diversified industry, biorefineries and social processes, Industry 4.0 (I4.0) aims to increase interconnectivity and smart automation for traditional processes based on agricultural raw materials and non-renewable resources (oil, coal, gas, minerals) and new ones with a largely digital focus based on smart technology.

Consequently, it is necessary to achieve SDG 9 the application of various frameworks for the development of generic indicators for agribusiness; such as SWOT analysis, PESTLE and Competitiveness Diamond; life cycle assessment tools in its components of social, cost, environmental and so forth; calculation of ecological footprint in its components water, energy and carbon; and also explore the possibility of obtaining certifications such as those of the International Organization for Standardization (ISO) for processes, products and impacts among others.

Bag et al. (2021) discussed how the green innovation has a major impact on the adoption of circular economy strategies 3Rs (re-use, recycling and remanufacturing), 5Rs (refuse, reduce, reuse, repurpose and recycle) and 10Rs of circular economy (R0 Refuse, Rl Reduce, R2 Resell, Reuse, R3 Repair, R4 Refurbish Referring, R5 Remanufacture, R6 Re-purpose, R7 Recycling, R8 Recovery and R9 Rethink).

Nonetheless, Khan and Abonyi (2022) concluded that for the industrial and manufacturing sector, it is preferable to apply the 6Rs framework of rethink, refuse, reduce, reuse, repair and recycle of the circular economy because they relate to the objective of achieving a low carbon and zero emission industrial sector about sustainability, cleaner production and the application of green technologies and innovations.

Kurita et al. (2023) mentioned that the successful implementation of the circular economy in industry should consider four stages: decision-making; capacity and training; sustainable practices; and green supply chain.

Nevertheless, green innovation is a complex task that establishes the synergy between green product innovation and green process innovation in the manufacturing and production process while reducing pollution and carbon emissions and improving environmental performance to achieve zero carbon and increase the number of CSR. In other words, the integration of sustainability into the business strategy and keeping an open-to-dialogue attitude with the firms' stakeholders (Ogiemwonyi et al., 2023; Ruiz-Blanco et al., 2022).

In connection with the foregoing, Divanoğlu and Taş (2022) and Wahjoedi (2020) concluded that there are numerous strategic planning tools to apply in different types of companies or businesses, one of them being *The 8D methodology* as a systematic problem-solving mostly in the automotive industry but with potential for application in other production sectors involves teams working together to solve problems, using a structured eight steps approach to help focus on defects *(D1) Team Formation, (D2) Problem Description, (D3) Immediate Action, (D4) Identification of Root Causes, (D5) Action Plan, (D6) Measuring of Effectiveness, (D7) Prevent Recurrence, (D8) Congratulate the Team to*

1. Understand the problem by clarifying the problem.
2. Choose the right problem-solving tools that can help solve the problem.
3. Stick to the chosen method of work and use this tool in the right way.

Therefore, with a cumulative amount of frames for the transition to a *green economy with renewable energy highly efficient, sustainable agriculture, application of frame of circular economy practices, eco-friendly initiatives and green jobs* Smol (2022) suggests the formulation of a green deal or strategy where all social actors and companies agree to create a clean and green economy by applying pro-environmental solutions at all stages of production (agriculture, industries, logistics, markets, political decisions etc.), taking into account the three aspirations of sustainable development—the well-being of people, the environment and economic sustainability by applying Green Deal Strategies (GDSs).

Consequently, the transition from conventional industries to green companies presents several limiting factors. The most urgent of these are the creation of knowledge, training and capacity building in various related frameworks such as cleaner production, international quality and environmental certifications; the development of energy-systems based on biomass;

water treatment and reuse; improvement or creation of sustainable infrastructure and so forth; and the substitution of raw materials with a high ecological footprint for greener ones. In connection with the foregoing, reconverting agricultural production systems using various tools, such as spatial modeling and precision agriculture, to locate the places within the territory with the greatest agro-ecological aptitude for production and therefore use fewer inputs such as fossil energy, agrochemicals, water and civil and process infrastructure and so forth. Therefore, strategies based on Agriculture 4.0 are fundamental for this transition.

Analysis of edaphoclimatic suitability of coffee *(Coffea arabica)* in Mexico for the transition to a green agroindustry

Climate change, as an agricultural constraint, poses major stress on all ecosystems (natural and agroecosystems), with severe risks to productivity, profitability, and physical well-being, including prosperity, welfare, poverty eradication and employment, food, energy, water availability, and health (Fuso Nerini et al., 2019).

Agricultural systems commodity-producing agribusinesses and social-ecological systems (SES) are affected by a variety of externalities and the combined impact of multiple anthropogenic stressors so they must reorganize their business models, value chain and production systems with green strategies and innovations and the goals of sustainable development to improve their environmental performance in order to minimize the risks of climate change in a global economy (Awan et al., 2022).

Coffee is one of the most traded commodities in the world, next to petroleum, and is the second most consumed beverage after water. Due to its typical flavor, aroma, color, and beneficial health effects, its market has grown regularly for several decades, with periods of extreme growth or decline due to a number of factors resulting from complex social-ecological systems with low biodiversity conservation in coffee fields, a large number of stakeholders in the value chain, grain quality, overproduction, volatile prices, climate change, political and economic factors, and sustainability issues.

During processing after harvest, several by-products are generated from cherries such as skin, pulp, mucilage, parchment, silverskin and immature / defective coffee beans. Around 50% of coffee fruit is discarded, despite the existence of green technology for their conversion into high value-added products due to their particular properties such as antioxidant, anti-inflammatory, antimicrobial, anti-aging, anti-cancer, anti-cellulite and sunscreen and not just discarded into the environment polluting it due to the compounds present such as caffeine, tannins, cellulose and other polysaccharides and so forth. dos Santos et al. (2021) reported a detailed description of the applications of the by-products and their biological activity.

Besides, Zhao et al. (2023) conducted a review of the physicochemical characterization of Spent coffee grounds and current and potential applications of this highly valuable by-product and Banu et al. (2020) showed the technological possibilities for the establishment of biorefineries for this by-product of beverage production.

Hu et al. (2023) proposed several technologies for the treatment and production of bioactive compounds of coffee pulp.

Coffee sustainability

Coffee production in 2023/24 was 178.0 million 60-kg bags and the consumption was 177.0 million bags. *Coffea arabica* (Arabica) and *Coffea canephora* (Robusta) are the two coffee species that are commercially produced. At the global level, people consume 102.2 million 60-kg bags (57.4%) of Arabica and the remaining 75.8 million 60-kg bags (42.6%) of Robusta.

The outlooks for coffee year 2023/24 establish that worldwide coffee consumption to grow by 2.2% to 178.0 million 60-kg bags in coffee-producing countries (CPCs) and non-producing countries to make the biggest contribution to the overall increase (https://icocoffee.org/documents/cy2023-24/Coffee_Report_and_Outlook_December_2023_ICO.pdf).

Coffee production worldwide has been carried out with take-make-use-dispose manufacturing systems without considering the product life cycle and utilization of waste, by-products and circular production models. Therefore, for coffee producers, it is essential to create knowledge on green practices on farms to carry out agricultural innovation that includes changes in management practices, processes and equipment to produce environmentally friendly products that meet ecological objectives with economic benefits with specialized coffees in niche markets (da Silva et al., 2023).

According to Samoggia and Riedel (2018), the quality of coffee is the result of environmental, biological, climatic, human and cultural factors, which allow the expression, development and conservation of the physical-chemical characteristics of coffee until the moment of its transformation and consumption.

The act of drinking coffee means more than simply consuming a beverage, it is about pleasure, experience, lifestyle and social status. This change in consumer behavior has been possible due to three approaches that currently characterize coffee as a consumer product: pleasure, health and sustainability.

Therefore, the consumption of specialty or high-quality coffee has grown rapidly in recent years, one of its key attributes is its origin, that is to say, the coffee growing region where it was cultivated and processed, generally placed in the same markets: Fairtrade, sustainable, organic and gourmet also known as premium coffee, for which consumers are willing to pay higher prices, however for coffee to be of high quality; in addition to its organoleptic properties (aroma, body, acidity, bitterness and fineness), it must represent benefits for the producer.

In the last decade, consumers have become more sensitive to the socio-economic difficulties of farmers mainly in developing countries, are interested in health and food safety and recognize that the expansion of the agricultural frontier, climate change and other socio-ecological factors constitute a threat to global biodiversity, so that several agricultural initiatives have been popularized in the form of public policies and academic studies have been disseminated that search for the sustainability of coffee through the application of various multidisciplinary methodological tools (Hidalgo et al., 2023).

Application of SDG 9 to the sustainability of coffee production in Mexico

Knowledge management and green innovations have been successful in their implementation in the productive sector as in the case of the coffee agroindustry. Coffee growers could be protagonists of the production process and value chain, to improve their welfare and at the same time contribute to the economic and environmental development of their local, regional and international environment, since most of the world's production is carried out by micro- and small-scale producers. In addition, competitiveness is increased through the identification of factors, models and tools for knowledge management and the application of innovations in the coffee value chain. Concerning the above, Cisneros (2024) concluded that knowledge management and innovations, mainly of an ecological nature, could increase agricultural development, improve environmental conditions and increase the quality of life of growers through sustainable agricultural development.

In this regard, the implementation de la Circular Economy (CE) has focused on great businesses and multinational corporations; however, the participation of small and medium-sized enterprises (SMEs) toward circularity is increasing, as in the case of coffee production that both transform sectors are presented (Ferasso et al., 2023).

The review of Kim et al. (2023) commented the Nature Futures Framework (NFF) applied in modeling socio-ecological systems as coffee to support decision-making must be carried out considering three value perspectives: Nature for Nature, Nature for Society and Nature as Culture to develop modeling in three perspectives: *(i) multiple value perspectives on nature as a state space where pathways improving nature toward a frontier can be represented; (ii) mutually reinforcing key feedbacks of social-ecological systems that are important for nature conservation and human well-being; and (iii) indicators of multiple knowledge systems describing the evolution of complex social-ecological dynamics.*

Elsawah et al. (2019) concluded that for research by modeling socio-environmental systems (SES), it is necessary to consider the complex interactions between the nature-environment relationship, that is, socioeconomic, technological and environmental or nature (biophysical, ecological, environmental) systems. For the success of the above objective, eight grand interdisciplinary challenges for future generations of models and modeling were developed:

1. *Bridging epistemologies across disciplines*
2. *Integrated treatment of modeling uncertainty*
3. *Combining qualitative and quantitative methods and data sources*
4. *Dealing with scales and scaling*
5. *Capturing systemic changes in SES*
6. *Integrating the human dimension*
7. *Elevating the adoption of SES models and impacts on policy*
8. *Leveraging new data types and sources*

Leveraging new data types and sources

Coffee in Mexico is one of the main agro-industries, with a high social impact since most of them are small family farms. According to the Mexican government, coffee is a strategic crop; its production employs more than 515,000 producers, of which 310,000 cultivate at least one hectare, with 85% of the population being indigenous; located in 15 states and 480 municipalities. Five states account for 94.2% of production: Chiapas contributes 41.3%, Veracruz, 24.4%, Puebla 15.8%, Oaxaca 8.2%, Guerrero 4.5% and other states 5.9%. In 2023, Mexico had a harvested area of 653,225.08 ha producing 1,056,388.26 tons of cherry coffee (https://nube.siap.gob.mx/avance_agricola/), which faces challenges as a socio-ecological system since it contributes 0.66 % to the national agricultural GDP (www.gob.mx/cms/uploads/attachment/file/256426/B_sico-Caf_.pdf) in addition to the recurrent affectations by pests and the impact of land use change, extreme weather events and climate change (Ramírez-León et al., 2023; Castillo et al., 2020).

In Mexico, coffee growing is considered a fundamental strategic activity, because it allows the integration of productive chains, the generation of foreign exchange and employment, it is the subsistence factor for many small producers and around 30 indigenous groups and, more recently, of enormous ecological relevance, since more than 90% of the area cultivated with coffee is under diversified shade, which contributes to the conservation of biodiversity and as a provider of vital environmental services to society. Notwithstanding its relevance, the coffee sector has been immersed in recurrent crises due to the fall in prices in the international market (Agostini et al., 2020).

Therefore, these environmental and geopolitical externalities directly affect the profitability of the crop and the environmental services of coffee plantations, making it necessary to employ green technologies, biodiversity management and local knowledge to direct production toward sustainable management, particularly in the regions with the greatest agroecological potential (Ruiz-García et al., 2021).

For this purpose, a spatial modeling tool called the Maximum Entropy (MaxEnt) algorithm was used to identify and quantify the agroecological suitable zones for coffee production, highlighting the regions with ideal potential for the species according to Jiménez et al. (2023) and Short, Jr. et al. (2023).

We used data on the geographic coordinates of the states with coffee crops in Mexico, which were obtained from the National Geostatistical Framework (INEGI, 2015). Table 8.1 presents the states of the Mexican Republic and the absolute and percentage frequency of the number of geographic coordinate records. In total, coffee points were used for the spatial analysis.

The modeling of edaphoclimatic or agroecological suitability was carried out using 19 climatic layers and one topographic (altitude) layer, at a resolution of 30 arcseconds, which is equivalent to ≈1 km^2 at the equatorial level (Hijmans et al., 2005). The information corresponding to each cell of

Table 8.1 Data on coffee crops in Mexico used in the analysis

State	*Absolute frequency (%)*	*Percentage frequency (%)*
Campeche	2	0.2
Chiapas	239	24.5
Colima	3	0.3
Guanajuato	17	1.7
Guerrero	72	7.4
Hidalgo	1	0.1
Jalisco	168	17.2
México	8	0.8
Michoacán	65	6.7
Nayarit	21	2.1
Puebla	243	24.9
Querétaro	3	0.3
Quintana Roo	6	0.6
Tamaulipas	4	0.4
Tlaxcala	1	0.1
Veracruz	117	12.0
Yucatán	4	0.4
Zacatecas	3	0.3

each layer represents the environmental values interpolated from observed data from 1950 to 2000 without considering climate change scenarios. These layers were scaled to the extreme coordinates: Northern boundary 33°, Southern boundary 14°; Eastern boundary –86° and Western boundary –119°, to ensure the inclusion of the Mexican territory. Likewise, nine layers of Mexican soil properties at a scale of 1:1,000,000 were used (Cruz-Cárdenas et al., 2014).

The MaxEnt software (Phillips & Dudík, 2008) was used for the modeling, which is based on the theory of maximum entropy, whose geospatial database determines the environmental variables that intersect at the georeference point of the crop presence and from this, estimates the average probability for each environmental variable that intersects at each of the points of crop presence (geographic coordinates), considered in the analysis (Maceda et al., 2023).

As a first action, a preliminary run was carried out to select the climatic variables that have the greatest agroecological importance for the biological development of coffee cultivation in Mexico. The 29 variables (environmental, topographic and soil variables) of the model were used. In a second run, those who did not contribute any information to the agroecological model for coffee cultivation were discriminated against, which led to a more accurate interpretation of the results (Soberon & Peterson, 2005).

The agroecological suitability model obtained was evaluated with the values of the area under the curve (AUC > 0.9), which characterizes the performance of the agroecological gradient as a function of crop presence (Phillips et al., 2006). The model corresponds to a graphical output (map) showing the ability to discriminate a presence (sensitivity) versus the ability to discriminate an absence (specificity; Phillips et al., 2004). The scale of the map indicates the probability of coincidence of environmental conditions suitable for crop development. The sharp color (white) determines the best environmental conditions for the agroecological development of the crop, and as the color gradient becomes more intense (black), the probability of the presence of suitable environmental conditions for the development of the coffee crop decreases.

The model determined the environmental variables of greatest importance for the agroecological development of the coffee crop, in a logistic prediction output format (Merow et al., 2013). To validate the model, the Jackknife statistical test configured in MaxEnt was applied to calculate the relative importance of each variable to the model, which shows the most important agroecological requirements (Jiménez et al., 2023; Phillips et al., 2006).

Additionally, the fraction of the predicted area of the total study area described by the crop occurrence data in the states of the Mexican Republic was calculated, using for this purpose a binomial test of omission with its respective statistical significance of the prediction (Elith & Leathwick, 2009).

Figure 8.1 represents the edaphoclimatic suitability for coffee in Mexico. This map represents the zones with high agroecological development potential for the crop in the Mexican territory. The gray-white color within the polygon indicates the high agroecological potential of the territory (probability >70%), which meets the conditions for the development of the crop, and as the color gradient turns to black, it indicates a low probability (<70%), which is an indicator that these areas do not meet the agroecological conditions necessary for the development of the crop, being these areas of low potential.

The regions with high agroecological potential are in the Mexican southeast and the Pacific coast. The evaluation of the coffee agroecological model, according to the AUC, determined a reliability value of 0.935, that is, there was a 93.5% adjustment between the sensitivity of the omission rate and the specificity of the area predicted in the model (Figure 8.2).

The gray line represents the level of fit of the model derived from the data collected from the coffee. Besides, the black line represents the ideal model fit.

Table 8.2 shows the relative importance values of the variables that explain the model of the edaphoclimatic vocation of coffee. Of the 29 variables evaluated, only 10 variables contributed to the model, which determine the edaphoclimatic conditions that should be a priority for the development of the crop.

The most important environmental variables for crop establishment and for optimizing agroecological crop management are related to the level of

Figure 8.1 Agroecological zoning of coffee in Mexico, using the maximum entropy spatial model.

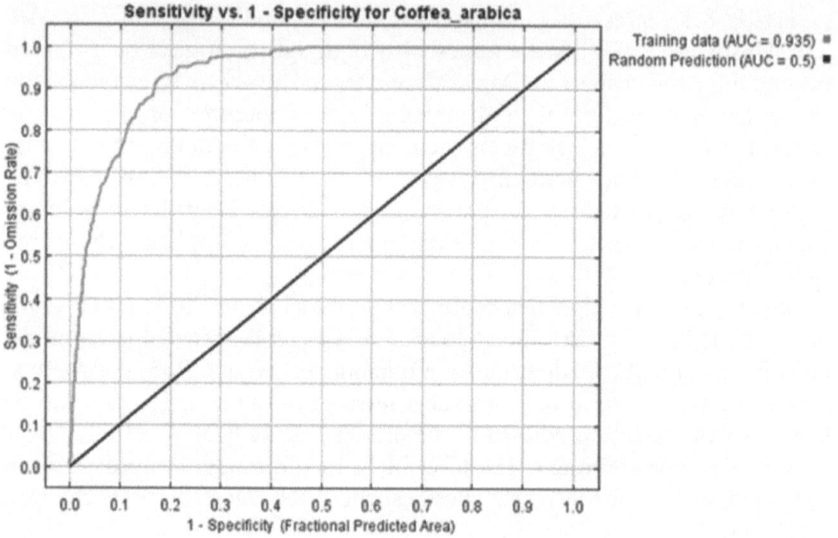

Figure 8.2 Evaluation curve of the edaphoclimatic suitability model for coffee in Mexico.

Table 8.2 Variables of edaphoclimatic or agroecological importance for coffee cultivation

Temperature	*Significance (%)*	*Precipitation*	*Significance (%)*	*Soil*	*Significance (%)*
BIO7 Temperature annual range (°C)	29.9	BIO12 Annual precipitation (mm)	28.9	pH	2.1
BIO5 Max temperature of the warmest month (°C)	4.9	BIO14 Precipitation of the driest month (mm)	17.5		
BIO9 Mean temperature of the driest quarter (°C)	3.3	BIO11 Mean temperature of the coldest quarter (mm)	5.6		
BIO8 Mean temperature of the wettest quarter (°C)	2.7	BIO17 Precipitation of the driest quarter (mm)	2.7		
		BIO15 Precipitation seasonality (CV)	1.6		
		BIO16 Precipitation of the wettest quarter (mm)	0.8		

annual precipitation and temperature. Besides, the Jackknife test corroborated the relative importance of each variable when each variable was not excluded in the model when it was evaluated independently and when all variables were evaluated (Figure 8.3).

Jackknife test for the relative importance of individual environmental variables, which are represented by the darkness bars. The gray bars represent the information manifested by the variables when they are removed from this test. Concerning the above, the smaller the size of the bar of the variable that represents the information the more informative it is. The last bar shows the information expressed by the whole set of variables.

Table 8.3 shows the fraction of the predicted area for the cumulative thresholds, which correspond to the omission rates of the prediction model.

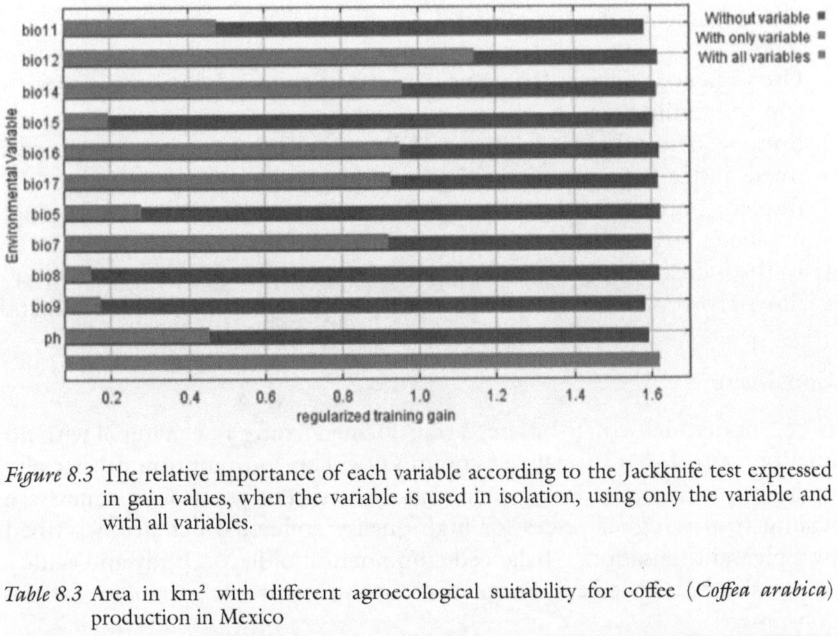

Figure 8.3 The relative importance of each variable according to the Jackknife test expressed in gain values, when the variable is used in isolation, using only the variable and with all variables.

Table 8.3 Area in km² with different agroecological suitability for coffee (*Coffea arabica*) production in Mexico

Cumulative range	*Logistic requirement*	*Fraction of predicted area*	*P value*	*Area in km²*
1	0.022	0.43	0.007	844.52
5	0.92	0.291	0.024	571.52
10	0.153	0.218	0.048	428.15
0.665	0.014	0.467	0.000	917.18
15.544	0.206	0.167	0.097*	327.99
19.758	0.246	0.138	0.138*	271.03
14.730	0.198	0.174	0.076*	341.74
1.334	0.030	0.405	0.007	795.42
11.886	0.171	0.199	0.069*	390.84

* Not significant

In the search for alternatives to improve the cultivation of coffee and the growing demand for "sustainable" products by consumers globally, new opportunities arise in niche markets for certified production, being organic the most important, so the application of agroecological zoning through the Maxent method allowed establishing the regions in Mexico with greater productive potential and less environmental impact by consuming less inputs such as infrastructure development, water, land, energy, agrochemicals and so forth.

In this regard, organic coffee, as the most profitable option, is produced sustainably with the environment (soil, flora, fauna, water and air) without the use of agrochemicals and through a certification process to offer high-quality products. Likewise, these coffees must comply with two criteria: Environmental protection and social justice to represent a value-added and differentiated product and even compete in select markets in other countries with key characteristics:

1. Use organic fertilizers (compost) instead of chemical fertilizers to maintain soil fertility.
2. Employ nature-based solutions (NBs) to control diseases, pests and weeds instead of synthetic pesticides and herbicides.
3. Implementing soil conservation practices such as contour planting, implementing cover crops and using shade trees.
4. In the industrial sector, apply circular economy principles for the conversion of by-products (husk, pulp, mucilage, spent grains) into bioproducts.

Conclusion

In recent decades, coffee has been transformed from a raw material with no quality control to a specialized commodity. The consumption of specialty or high-quality coffee has grown rapidly in recent years. Consumers are willing to pay higher prices for high-quality coffees, which are described by a pleasant sensation, a balanced combination of flavor, body and acidity in the absence of defects. Flavor is the most important parameter for the consumer.

The factors that determine the quality of coffee begin with the agroecological variables of production or pre-harvest that are grouped into genetic, topographical, climatological, edaphic, socio-economic and human, another important aspect of quality is the sustainability of the crop. To guarantee the quality of coffee, governments have issued legislative measures, mandates and public policies known as Quality Standards, which are a set of specifications that coffee producers must comply with to establish the specifications and characteristics that coffee must present to guarantee the aspects of environmental management, safety, innocuousness and commercial information to achieve effective consumer protection, as well as establish clear criteria for its adequate commercialization and sustainability.

In this work, the main frameworks and technologies applied to the sustainability of the industrial sector based on agricultural raw materials were discussed. The application of the Maxent method, as a management tool, allowed us to demonstrate its application to redirect and increase coffee production with agroecological bases, maximizing its quality. However, other sustainability analysis tools should be considered in future work to allow stakeholders to obtain the best decision-making directed through green innovation to ensure the efficient use of materials and the reduction of pollutants to promote less environmental impacts.

References

Agostini, M.R., Bitencourt, C.C., & Vieira, L.M. (2020). Social innovation in Mexican coffee production: filling "institutional voids". *International Review of Applied Economics*, *34*(5), 607–625. https://doi.org/10.1080/02692171.2019.1638351

Awan, U., Sroufe, R., & Bozan, K. (2022). Designing value chains for industry 4.0 and a circular economy: A review of the literature. *Sustainability*, *14*(12), 7084. https://doi.org/10.3390/su14127084

Bag, S., Gupta, S., & Kumar, S. (2021). Industry 4.0 adoption and 10R advance manufacturing capabilities for sustainable development. *International Journal of Production Economics*, *231*, 107844. https://doi.org/10.1016/j.ijpe.2020.107844

Banu, J.R., Kavitha, S., Kannah, R.Y., Kumar, M.D., Atabani, A.E., & Kumar, G. (2020). Biorefinery of spent coffee grounds waste: Viable pathway towards circular bioeconomy. *Bioresource Technology*, *302*, 122821. https://doi.org/10.1016/j.biortech.2020.122821

Bradu, P., Biswas, A., Nair, C., Sreevalsakumar, S., Patil, M., Kannampuzha, S., & Gopalakrishnan, A.V. (2022). Recent advances in green technology and Industrial Revolution 4.0 for a sustainable future. *Environmental Science and Pollution Research*, 1–32. https://doi.org/10.1007/s11356-022-20024-4

Castillo, N.E.T., Melchor-Martínez, E.M., Sierra, J.S.O., Ramirez-Mendoza, R.A., Parra-Saldívar, R., & Iqbal, H.M. (2020). Impact of climate change and early development of coffee rust—An overview of control strategies to preserve organic cultivars in Mexico. *Science of the Total Environment*, *738*, 140225. https://doi.org/10.1016/j.scitotenv.2020.140225

Chen, Y.S. (2011). Green organizational identity: Sources and consequence. *Management Decision*, *49*(3), 384–404. https://doi.org/10.1108/00251741111120761

Cisneros, J.R.A. (2024). Towards a knowledge management system for the strengthening of coffee production: A case study in the Panama Canal Basin, Panamá Oeste province. *Green Technologies and Sustainability*, *2*(1), 100056. https://doi.org/10.1016/j.grets.2023.100056

Cruz-Cárdenas, G., López-Mata, L., Ortiz-Solorio, C.A., Villaseñor, J.L., Ortiz, E., Silva, J.T., & Estrada-Godoy, F. (2014). Interpolation of Mexican soil properties at a scale of 1: 1,000,000. *Geoderma*, *213*, 29–35.

da Silva, A.R., Cirani, C.B.S., Serra, F.A.R., Pigola, A., da Costa, P.R., Scafuto, I.C., . . . Mazieri, M.R. (2023). Determining factors on green innovation adoption: An empirical study in Brazilian agribusiness firms. *Sustainability*, *15*(7), 6266. https://doi.org/10.3390/su15076266

Divanoğlu, S.U., & Taş, Ü. (2022). Application of 8D methodology: An approach to reduce failures in automotive industry. *Engineering Failure Analysis, 134*, 106019. https://doi.org/10.1016/j.engfailanal.2021.106019

dos Santos, É.M., de Macedo, L.M., Tundisi, L.L., Ataide, J.A., Camargo, G.A., Alves, R.C., & Mazzola, P.G. (2021). Coffee by-products in topical formulations: A review. *Trends in Food Science & Technology, 111*, 280–291. https://doi.org/10.1016/j.tifs.2021.02.064

Elith, J., & Leathwick, J. R. (2009). Species distribution models: Ecological explanation and prediction across space and time. *Annual Review of Ecology, Evolution, and Systematics, 40*, 677–697. https://doi.org/10.1146/annurev.ecolsys.110308.120159

Elsawah, S., Filatova, T., Jakeman, A.J., Kettner, A.J., Zellner, M.L., Athanasiadis, I.N., & Lade, S.J. (2019). Eight grand challenges in socio-environmental systems modeling. *Socio-Environmental Systems Modelling, 2*. https://doi.org/10.18174/sesmo.2020a16226

Farida, I., & Setiawan, D. (2022). Business strategies and competitive advantage: The role of performance and innovation. *Journal of Open Innovation: Technology, Market, and Complexity, 8*(3), 163. https://doi.org/10.3390/joitmc8030163

Ferasso, M., Tortato, U., & Ikram, M. (2023). Mapping the circular economy in the small and medium-sized enterprises field: An exploratory network analysis. *Cleaner and Responsible Consumption, 11*, 100149. https://doi.org/10.1016/j.clrc.2023.100149

Fuso Nerini, F., Sovacool, B., Hughes, N., Cozzi, L., Cosgrave, E., Howells, M., . . . Milligan, B. (2019). Connecting climate action with other Sustainable Development Goals. *Nature Sustainability, 2*(8), 674–680. https://doi.org/10.1038/s41893-019-0334-y

Gilbert, M.R., Eakin, H., & McPhearson, T. (2022). The role of infrastructure in societal transformations. *Current Opinion in Environmental Sustainability, 57*(C). https://doi.org/10.1016/j.cosust.2022.101207

Hidalgo, F., Quiñones-Ruiz, X.F., Birkenberg, A., Daum, T., Bosch, C., Hirsch, P., & Birner, R. (2023). Digitalization, sustainability, and coffee: Opportunities and challenges for agricultural development. *Agricultural Systems, 208*, 103660. https://doi.org/10.1016/j.agsy.2023.103660

Hijmans, R. J., Cameron, S. E., Parra, J. L., Jones, P. G., & Jarvis, A. (2005). Very high resolution interpolated climate surfaces for global land areas. *International Journal of Climatology: A Journal of the Royal Meteorological Society, 25*(15), 1965–1978. https://doi.org/10.1002/joc.1276

Hu, S., Gil-Ramírez, A., Martín-Trueba, M., Benítez, V., Aguilera, Y., & Martín-Cabrejas, M.A. (2023). Valorization of coffee pulp as bioactive food ingredient by sustainable extraction methodologies. *Current Research in Food Science*, 100475. https://doi.org/10.1016/j.crfs.2023.100475

INEGI. (2015). *Catálogo Único de Claves de Áreas Geoestadísticas Estatales, Municipales y Localidades—consulta y descarga.* www.inegi.org.mx/geo/contenidos/geoestadistica/catalogoclaves.aspx

Jiménez, A.A., Marceleño Flores, S.M.L., González, O.N., & Vilchez, F.F. (2023). Potential coffee distribution in a Central-Western Region of Mexico. *Ecologies, 4*(2), 269–287. https://doi.org/10.3390/ecologies4020018

Kannan, D., Khademolqorani, S., Janatyan, N., & Alavi, S. (2024). Smart waste management 4.0: The transition from a systematic review to an integrated framework. *Waste Management, 174*, 1–14. https://doi.org/10.1016/j.wasman.2023.08.041

Khan, A.A., & Abonyi, J. (2022). Simulation of sustainable manufacturing solutions: Tools for enabling circular economy. *Sustainability*, *14*(15), 9796. https://doi.org/10.3390/su14159796

Kim, H., Peterson, G.D., Cheung, W.W., Ferrier, S., Alkemade, R., Arneth, A., . . . Pereira, H.M. (2023). Towards a better future for biodiversity and people: Modelling nature futures. *Global Environmental Change*, *82*, 102681. https://doi.org/10.1016/j.gloenvcha.2023.102681

Kurita, A.E., Espuny, M., Campos, T.L.R., Kazançoğlu, Y., Kandsamy, J., & de Oliveira, O.J. (2023). Drivers for circular economy development: Making businesses more environmentally friendly. *Environmental Science and Pollution Research*, 1–18. https://doi.org/10.1007/s11356-023-28048-0

Leal Filho, W., Vidal, D.G., Chen, C., Petrova, M., Dinis, M.A.P., Yang, P., & Neiva, S. (2022). An assessment of requirements in investments, new technologies, and infrastructures to achieve the SDGs. *Environmental Sciences Europe*, *34*(1), 1–17. https://doi.org/10.1186/s12302-022-00629-9

Maceda, A., Delgado-Alvarado, A., Salazar-Rojas, V.M., & Herrera-Cabrera, B.E. (2023). Vanilla planifolia Andrews (Orchidaceae): Labellum variation and potential distribution in Hidalgo, Mexico. *Diversity*, *15*(5), 678. https://doi.org/10.3390/d15050678

Merow, C., Smith, M.J., & Silander, J.A. (2013). A practical guide to MaxEnt for modeling species' distributions: What it does, and why inputs and settings matter. *Ecography*, *36*(10), 1058–1069. https://doi.org/10.1111/j.1600-0587.2013.07872.x

Mosgaard, M.A., & Kristensen, H.S. (2023). From certified environmental management to certified SDG management: New sustainability perceptions and practices. *Sustainable Futures*, *6*, 100144. https://doi.org/10.1016/j.sftr.2023.100144

Neri, A., Negri, M., Cagno, E., Franzò, S., Kumar, V., Lampertico, T., & Bassani, C. A. (2023). The role of digital technologies in supporting the implementation of circular economy practices by industrial small and medium enterprises. *Business Strategy and the Environment*, *32*(7), 4693–4718. https://doi.org/10.1002/bse.3388

Ogiemwonyi, O., Alam, M.N., Hago, I.E., Azizan, N.A., Hashim, F., & Hossain, M.S. (2023). Green innovation behaviour: Impact of industry 4.0 and open innovation. *Heliyon*, *9*. https://doi.org/10.1016/j.heliyon.2023.e16524

Pattinson, S., Damij, N., El Maalouf, N., Bazi, S., Elsahn, Z., Hilliard, R., & Cunningham, J.A. (2023). Building green innovation networks for people, planet, and profit: A multi-level, multi-value approach. *Industrial Marketing Management*, *115*, 408–420. https://doi.org/10.1016/j.indmarman.2023.10.016

Phillips, S.J., Anderson, R.P., & Schapire, R.E. (2006). Maximum entropy modeling of species geographic distributions. *Ecological Modelling*, *190*(3), 231–259. https://doi.org/10.1016/j.ecolmodel.2005.03.026

Phillips, S.J., & Dudík, M. (2008). Modeling of species distributions with Maxent: New extensions and a comprehensive evaluation. *Ecography*, *31*(2), 161–175. https://doi.org/10.1111/j.0906-7590.2008.5203.x

Phillips, S.J., Dudík, M., & Schapire, R.E. (2004). A maximum entropy approach to species distribution modeling. *Proceedings of the Twenty-First International Conference on Machine Learning* (p. 83). ACM.

Ramírez-León, A., Avila-Foucat, V.S., & Ezzine-de-Blas, D. (2023). The historical trajectory of a coffee agri-food system: A case study in Oaxaca, Mexico. *Ambio*, 1–17. https://doi.org/10.1007/s13280-023-01893-6

Ruiz-Blanco, S., Romero, S., & Fernandez-Feijoo, B. (2022). Green, blue or black, but washing—What company characteristics determine greenwashing?

Environment, Development and Sustainability, 1–22. https://doi.org/10.1007/s10668-021-01602-x

Ruiz-García, P., Conde-Álvarez, C., Gómez-Díaz, J.D., & Monterroso-Rivas, A.I. (2021). Projections of local knowledge-based adaptation strategies of Mexican coffee farmers. *Climate*, *9*(4), 60. https://doi.org/10.3390/cli9040060

Sahoo, S., Kumar, A., & Upadhyay, A. (2023). How do green knowledge management and green technology innovation impact corporate environmental performance? Understanding the role of green knowledge acquisition. *Business Strategy and the Environment*, *32*(1), 551–569. https://doi.org/10.1002/bse.3160

Samoggia, A., & Riedel, B. (2018). Coffee consumption and purchasing behavior review: Insights for further research. *Appetite*, *129*, 70–81. https://doi.org/10.1016/j.appet.2018.07.002

Shahzad, M., Qu, Y., Rehman, S.U., & Zafar, A.U. (2022). Adoption of green innovation technology to accelerate sustainable development among manufacturing industry. *Journal of Innovation & Knowledge*, *7*(4), 100231. https://doi.org/10.1016/j.jik.2022.100231

Short, Jr., N.M., Woodward-Greene, M.J., Buser, M.D., & Roberts, D.P. (2023). Scalable knowledge management to meet global 21st century challenges in agriculture. *Land*, *12*(3), 588. https://doi.org/10.3390/land12030588

Smol, M. (2022). Is the green deal a global strategy? Revision of the green deal definitions, strategies and importance in post-COVID recovery plans in various regions of the world. *Energy Policy*, *169*, 113152. https://doi.org/10.1016/j.enpol.2022.113152

Soberon, J., & Peterson, A.T. (2005). Interpretation of models of fundamental ecological niches and species' distributional areas. *Biodiversity Informatics*, *2*, 1–10. https://doi.org/10.17161/bi.v2i0.4

Thacker, S., Adshead, D., Fay, M., Hallegatte, S., Harvey, M., Meller, H., . . . Hall, J.W. (2019). Infrastructure for sustainable development. *Nature Sustainability*, *2*(4), 324–331. https://doi.org/10.1038/s41893-019-0256-8

Wahjoedi, T. (2020). 8D methodology of problem solving. *8D Methodology of Problem Solving*. http://repository.stiemahardhika.ac.id/2495/

Yeboah, S. (2023). Balancing growth and green: Strategies for sustainable development in developing economies. *MPRA Paper*, (118180). https://econpapers.repec.org/paper/pramprapa/118180.htm

Zhao, N., Liu, Z., Yu, T., & Yan, F. (2023). Spent coffee grounds: Present and future of an environmentally friendly applications on industries-A review. *Trends in Food Science & Technology*, 104312. https://doi.org/10.1016/j.tifs.2023.104312

9 Relationship of innovative sustainable business strategies with dynamic capabilities in the apple production chain in Southern Brazil

Maria Emilia Camargo, Aprígio Teles Mascarenhas Neto, Walter Priesnitz Filho, Angela Isabel dos Santos Dullius, Beatriz Lúcia Salvador Bizotto and Angela Pellegrin Ansuj

Introduction

Innovative strategic resources refer to assets, capabilities or technologies that provide a sustainable competitive advantage through innovation. These resources are fundamental to an organization's long-term success, as they allow it to stand out in the market, anticipate or respond effectively to changes in environmental conditions and outperform the competition (Molchanova et al., 2023; Lhamby et al. 2023).

In this study, process and product innovation were innovative strategic resources. Process innovation refers to the implementation of new techniques, methods or practices that improve the efficiency, productivity and quality of an organization's internal processes, process innovation seeks to optimize the company's internal operations, while product innovation refers to the development and introduction of new products or significant improvements to existing products. This type of innovation is crucial for companies looking to stand out in the market, meet consumer needs and gain a competitive advantage.

Sustainable process innovation in the apple production chain is key to increasing efficiency, reducing costs, improving product quality and promoting sustainable practices. The apple production chain ranges from cultivation to distribution and process innovation can be applied at various stages of this cycle (Bolfe et al., 2020; Camargo et al., 2022; Kvitschal et al., 2022).

Sustainable product innovation in the apple production chain refers to the introduction of new products, significant improvements to existing products or product differentiation to meet market demands. In the apple production chain, this innovation can occur at various stages, from

DOI: 10.4324/9781003465058-9

cultivation to final distribution (Bolfe et al., 2020; Camargo et al., 2022; Kvitschal et al., 2022).

Dynamic capabilities refer to an organization's ability to adapt, integrate and reconfigure its internal resources in response to changes in the external environment. This approach highlights the importance of organizational flexibility and agility to face challenges and take advantage of opportunities in a dynamic business environment. Thus, dynamic capabilities play a fundamental role in organizations, specifically in agribusiness production chains, which is the subject of this research, because according to Aguiar et al. (2020), they contribute to the appropriation of knowledge. This study dealt with absorptive and innovative capacity.

Absorptive capacity plays an important role in the apple supply chain's ability to remain innovative, adapt to new technologies and stand out in competitive markets. Production chains that develop and cultivate a strong absorptive capacity are better placed to thrive in constantly evolving environments (Cohen & Levinthal, 1990; Grandinetti, 2016).

In this context, this article aimed to verify the influence of innovative business strategies on the dynamic capacity of the apple production chain in southern Rio Grande do Sul-Brazil.

Theoretical framework and definition of hypotheses

Innovative sustainable business strategies

Innovation refers to something newly introduced that adds social or economic value. It can manifest itself as an innovative product, advances in technology, improvements in operational processes, innovations in marketing practices or even small changes and adaptations. Its purpose is to generate economic benefits through its application (Tidd et al., 2008).

According to Schumpeter (1934), innovation plays a crucial role as a disruptive agent in the economic system and the author proposes the classification of this innovation into two types: radical and incremental.

The term "sustainable" is intrinsically related to the concept of sustainable development. According to Araújo and Mendonça (2009), sustainable development is equivalent to a rational society, the promotion of environmentally responsible industries and economic growth. A more comprehensive approach to sustainable development is based on the integration of the social, environmental and economic dimensions, constituting what is known as the sustainability tripod.

Innovations can be categorized as product, process, marketing and organizational innovation, according to Oslo Manual (OECD-Eurostat, 2005). In this study, we will deal with innovative business strategies with a focus on process and product innovation.

Innovative business strategies refer to creative and pioneering approaches adopted by organizations to stand out in competitive markets, create value for customers and drive sustainable growth. These strategies seek not only to respond to changes in the business environment but also to anticipate and lead these changes. Often, these strategies are not mutually exclusive and can be interrelated. Innovative companies generally adopt a combination of several approaches to establish a lasting competitive advantage and react effectively to transformations in the business environment (da Cruz et al., 2014).

Sustainable process innovation

Sustainable process innovation refers to the implementation of new approaches, methods or technologies in production or operational activities that seek to minimize environmental impact, promote energy efficiency and contribute to more sustainable practices. These innovations aim to meet present needs without compromising the ability of future generations to meet their own needs (Calazans & Silva, 2016; Kiperstok et al., 2002; Zogbi, 2023).

Sustainable product innovation

Sustainable product innovation refers to the creation of products that incorporate environmentally friendly features, sustainable materials, ecologically conscious manufacturing processes and ethical considerations throughout the product's life cycle. These innovations seek to meet consumer needs while minimizing negative impacts on the environment and promoting sustainable practices (Thanh et al., 2023).

It can therefore be said that sustainable innovation and green innovation are interrelated, sharing objectives and approaches that aim to reconcile economic development with environmental preservation and social responsibility. Both seek to create solutions that minimize the negative impact of human activities on the environment, promoting more ecological and socially responsible practices.

Sustainable innovation involves the creation and implementation of products, services, processes, or technologies that have a positive environmental impact, reducing the consumption of natural resources, minimizing waste and contributing to environmental sustainability. This can include the adoption of green practices such as renewable energy, recycling, energy efficiency and eco-friendly products (Ribeiro & Steiner, 2021).

Globally, sustainable innovation has evolved from the micro-company level to the macro-national level, which has an impact on the sustainable development of the company (Xiao et al., 2023; Zhang et al., 2019; Zhang et al., 2020).

Dynamic capabilities

Dynamic capabilities refer to an organization's ability to integrate, create and reconfigure its internal resources in response to rapid changes in the external environment (Tondolo et al., 2018).

Absorptive capacity

Absorptive capacity refers to an organization's ability to acquire, assimilate, transform and apply external knowledge effectively and efficiently. This concept was developed by David J. Teece, Gary Pisano and Amy Shuen in the 1990s and is fundamental to understanding how organizations manage innovation and adapt to changes in the business environment (Cohen & Levinthal, 1990; Singh et al., 2023).

Innovative capacity

Dynamic sustainable innovative capacity is the ability of an organization to adapt continuously, promoting innovation while incorporating sustainable principles and practices into all aspects of its operations. This approach seeks to integrate traditional dynamic innovative capacity with a robust commitment to environmental, social and economic sustainability.

Debates about innovative capacity have been conducted since the 1980s; however, there is still no consensus among researchers regarding its definition (Correio et al., 2013).

However, this capability refers to the organizational competence to identify new market opportunities (Neely & Hii, 1999); convert knowledge and ideas into new products (Wang & Ahmed, 2007), processes and systems (Lawson & Samson, 2001); and introduce them quickly into the market (Guan & Ma, 2003).

Relationship between innovative strategies and dynamic capabilities

The relationship between innovative strategies and dynamic capabilities is fundamental to the long-term success of organizations. Dynamic capabilities refer to a company's ability to integrate, build and reconfigure its internal resources in response to changes in the external environment. These capabilities are essential for continuous adaptation and sustainable competitive advantage. Some ways in which innovative strategies and dynamic capabilities are interlinked:

Anticipating Change—Innovative strategies often arise from the ability to anticipate and respond proactively to changes in the business environment. Dynamic capabilities allow organizations to identify emerging trends, anticipate market needs and adjust their innovation strategies accordingly (Garcia, 2017; de Almeida Guerra et al., 2016).

Continuous Learning: Dynamic capabilities involve a process of continuous learning. Innovative organizations are constantly experimenting, evaluating results and learning from successes and failures. This iterative approach is facilitated by dynamic capabilities, which allow for rapid adjustments based on feedback and accumulated experience (de Souza Gollo et al., 2023; Pérez-Rave et al., 2023).

Rapid Adaptation: Innovative strategies often require rapid and effective changes in operations and business models. Dynamic capabilities allow a company to reconfigure its resources and internal processes to adapt to new opportunities or challenges, while maintaining agility and flexibility (Huang et al., 2023).

Resource integration: Innovation often requires the effective integration of various resources, such as technology, human capital and knowledge. Dynamic capabilities enable the rapid integration and alignment of these resources to create innovative solutions that add value to the customer (Muneeb et al., 2023).

Strategic renewal: Dynamic capabilities are crucial when a company seeks strategic renewal. By seeking new directions and opportunities, the organization can reconfigure its internal capabilities to better align with new strategic goals (Ortiz-Avram et al., 2023).

Competitive Resilience: In a dynamic and volatile business environment, resilience is a key characteristic. Dynamic capabilities enable organizations to recover quickly from disruptions and maintain their competitive position, while innovative strategies help create new competitive advantages (Pertheban et al., 2023).

In short, the interaction between innovative strategies and dynamic capabilities is synergistic. Innovative strategies drive the search for new opportunities, while dynamic capabilities enable organizations to implement and sustain these innovations over time, ensuring a lasting competitive advantage.

Relationship between sustainable process innovation and absorptive capacity

Sustainable process innovation and absorptive capacity are interlinked, forming a solid foundation for organizations seeking not only to adapt to sustainable market demands but also to thrive and lead in a constantly evolving context (Aliasghar et al., 2023).

The influence of sustainable process innovation on innovative capacity can be through: Culture of Innovation; Stimulation of Creativity; Adoption of Innovative Technologies, Continuous Improvement; Integration of Stakeholders; Response to Market Trends; Development of Internal Competencies; and Sustainable competitiveness (Aliasghar et al., 2023; Teng et al., 2023).

In this context, the following hypothesis can be stated:

H_1: Sustainable process innovation has an influence on absorptive capacity.

Relationship between sustainable process innovation and innovative capacity

Sustainable process innovation can be a significant driver of an organization's innovative capacity, transforming the search for sustainable practices into a driving force for continuous innovation and improvement.

The influence of sustainable process innovation on innovative capacity can be cited as follows: innovation culture, stimulating creativity, adopting innovative technologies, continuous improvement, integrating stakeholders, responding to market trends, developing internal competencies and sustainable competitiveness (Boamah et al., 2023; Arndt et al., 2023).

Sustainable process innovation not only contributes to mitigating the environmental impacts of business operations but also plays a crucial role in boosting innovative capacity. By optimizing processes, adopting new technologies and promoting socially responsible practices, companies become not only more sustainable but also more competitive, adaptable and likely to lead in their respective sectors (Zhang et al., 2023; ul zia et al., 2023; Teng et al., 2023).

In this context, the following hypothesis can be stated:

H_2: Sustainable process innovation has an influence on innovative capacity.

Relationship between sustainable product innovation and absorptive capacity

Sustainable product innovation involves creating products that meet consumer needs in an environmentally friendly and socially responsible way. On the other hand, absorptive capacity refers to an organization's ability to acquire, assimilate, transform and exploit new external knowledge Pan et al., 2023; Dabić et al., 2023).

Thus, the following hypothesis emerges:

H_3: Sustainable product innovation has an influence on absorptive capacity.

The relationship between sustainable product innovation and innovative capacity

Sustainable product innovation not only contributes to global sustainability but also plays a crucial role in strengthening companies' innovative capacity. It requires an integrated approach, from product conception to disposal, driving the research and development of new technologies and production methods. It also meets growing consumer demands for more ethical and ecologically responsible products, providing opportunities for growth and market leadership (Afeltra et al., 2023; Cunha, 2005; de Matos Ferreira et al., 2007; Cunha, 2005; Silva et al., 2010).

In this context, the following hypothesis can be stated:

H_4: Sustainable product innovation has an influence on innovative capacity.

Based on these hypotheses, Figure 9.1 shows the theoretical model.

Methodology

To achieve the outlined objective and at the same time answer the research problem, this descriptive and quantitative study was designed based on a population made up of small and medium-sized apple producers.

Target population and measurement instrument

This study focuses on the apple production chain in the southern states of Brazil. The absorptive capacity and innovative capacity dimensions are composed of five items based on Yoo et al. (2011), sustainable process innovation and sustainable product innovation have three items each, according to Trienekens et al. (2008).

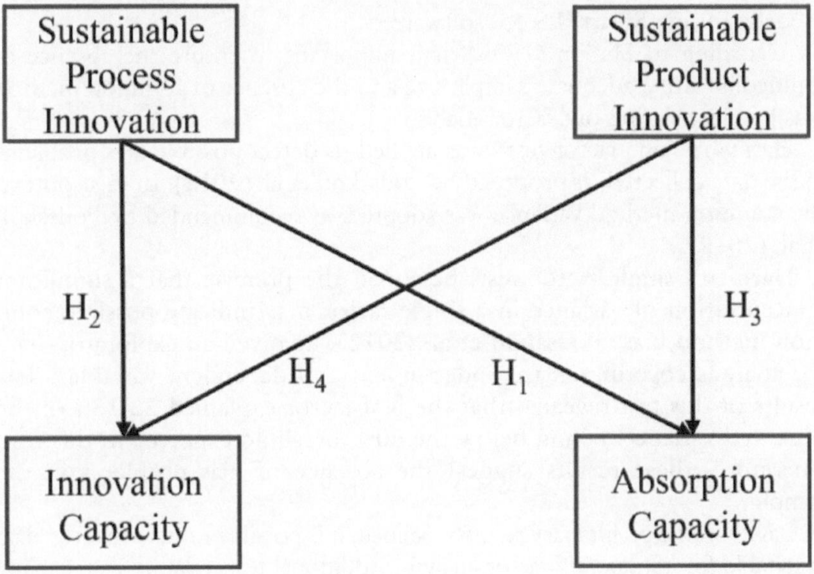

Figure 9.1 Theoretical conceptual model.

Initially, a pilot test was carried out with 20 producers participating in the apple production chain to ensure internal consistency and contextual accuracy. The initial responses indicated that the internal consistency of the constructs studied ranged from 0.77 to 0.91, in line with Hair et al. (2017), whose suggested minimum value is 0.7.

Based on the initial results of the survey, a comprehensive survey was launched on a five-point Likert scale (1 representing strongly disagree and 5 representing strongly agree), collecting data via telephone calls and e-mail, depending on the preference of the participants. In the end, 124 respondents were obtained.

To characterize the respondents in the sample, the following variables were analyzed: gender, level of education and age of the survey participants.

As for the gender of the respondents, 80% were male and 20% female. Regarding the level of education of the respondents, 40% have completed higher education, 25% have incomplete higher education, 20% have completed high school and 15% have incomplete high school.

In terms of age, 20% are aged up to 30, 50% are aged between 31 and 50 and 30% are aged 51 or over.

Statistical analysis to validate the instrument

To evaluate the data collected, a multivariate statistical approach was used using SPSS v.22 software, followed by the application of structural equation modeling using SmartPLS 4.0 software.

According to Hinkin (1995), it is important to ensure the absence of multicollinearity, adequate sample size and the absence of common method bias before carrying out factor analysis.

Harman's "one-factor test" was applied to detect possible bias problems in the data collected, as proposed by Podsakoff et al. (2012). In this context, the common method variance was adopted, as recommended by Podsakoff et al. (2012).

Harman's single-factor test, based on the premise that a significant concentration of variance in a single factor may indicate possible common method bias (Podsakoff et al., 2012), involved an exploratory factor analysis covering all the independent and dependent variables. The results of this test revealed that the first factor explained 22.13% of the observed variance, falling below the 50% threshold expected in this test. Therefore, these results suggest the absence of bias problems in the sample.

Based on the preliminary results obtained, it is possible to state that the data is suitable for conducting factor analysis. Additional tests relating to reliability and validity will be detailed in the results presentation and analysis section.

Presentation, analysis and discussion of results

Evaluation of the measurement model

The reliability (internal consistency) of the model was tested using Cronbach's alpha (α), composite reliability (ρ_c) and average variance extracted (AVE) tests, as shown in Table 9.1.

For both tests, the results range from 0 to 1, with higher values indicating greater reliability. Both coefficients must exceed 0.7 (Hair et al., 2009). Cronbach's alpha values (α) range from 0.782 to 0.944 and the composite reliability values (ρ_c) range from 0.872 to 0.964, so all the indicators met the suggested levels. To determine convergent validity, the average variance extracted (AVE) was first calculated, as also shown in Table 9.1. The values for the constructs must be greater than 0.5 to be considered satisfactory (Hair et al., 2009). According to Table 9.1, all the values exceed the threshold, indicating convergent validity of the model.

The following were used to assess the discriminant validity of the measurement model: the Fornell-Larcker criterion; the Heterotrait-Monotrait Ratio (HTMT) criterion and the cross-loading matrix (Hair et al., 2009), presented in Table 9.1.

For the F-L criterion, the square root of the AVEs is greater than the correlations of the other dimensions (r_{ij} for $i \neq j$). As for the HTMT criterion, using the bootstrapping method for 5,000 subsamples, the upper limits for 95% confidence are less than 1. The Crossed Factor Loads criterion, in which the correlation of observed variables with latent variables is measured, was met, as all original factor loads were greater than the other factor loads. As the above criteria had their assumptions confirmed, the model has convergent validity.

We can then move on to analyzing the structural model.

Evaluation of the structural model

The structural model describes the relationships between the constructs (Hair et al., 2017). The first stage is the assessment of multicollinearity, which was carried out using the Variance Inflation Factor (VIF), whose values were found to be less than 5 (Hair et al., 2017), confirming that there is no multicollinearity. The size of the f^2 effect was also checked, and if f^2 is within ($0.02 \leq f^2 \leq 0.075$), it is considered a small effect, if it is between ($0.02 \leq f^2 \leq 0.075$), medium effect ($0.075 \leq f^2 \leq 0.225$) and large effect ($f^2 > 0.225$) are shown in Table 9.2.

The values of the explanation coefficients (R^2) found for the endogenous dimensions were $R^2 = 0.381$ ($P = 0.000$) for absorptive capacity and $R^2 =$

Table 9.1 Cronbach's alpha (α), composite reliability (ρ_c) and average variance extracted (AVE), Fornell-Larcker criterion and HTMT

Dimensions			α	ρ_c	*AVE*
Absorption capacity			0.944	0.957	0.816
Innovation capacity			0.940	0.953	0.771
Sustainable process innovation			0.782	0.872	0.695
Sustainable product innovation			0.944	0.964	0.899
	$\sqrt{AVE}$	*Absorption capacity*	*Innovation capacity*	*Sustainable process innovation*	*Sustainable product innovation*
Absorption capacity	0.903	1			
Innovation capacity	0.878	0.623	1		
Sustainable process innovation	0.834	0.503	0.538	1	
Sustainable product innovation	0.948	0.562	0.679	0.498	1
UL * $(\text{HTMT})_{97.5\%}$					
Absorption capacity		1			
Innovation capacity		0.665	1		
Sustainable process innovation		0.575	0.612	1	
Sustainable product innovation		0.587	0.713	0.575	1

Source: SmartPLS from survey data (2024)

Table 9.2 Collinearity statistics (VIF), effect size, coefficient of explanation, predictive relevance and structural coefficient (β), *t*-test and *P* value

Relations	*VIF*	f^2	*Path coefficients* (*β*)	*T statistics* (|*O/STDEV*|)	*P value*
Sustainable process innovation → Absorption capacity	1.330	0.107	0.296	3.202	0.001
Sustainable process innovation → Innovation capacity	1.330	0.109	0.266	3.675	0.000
Sustainable product innovation → Absorption capacity	1.330	0.208	0.414	4.480	0.000
Sustainable product innovation → Innovation capacity	1.330	0.463	0.547	7.251	0.000
Endogenous dimensions			R^2		
			R^2	***P* value**	Q^2
Absorption capacity			0.381	0.000	0.352
Innovation capacity			0.514	0.000	0.492

Source: SmartPLS from survey data (2024)

0.514 ($P = 0.000$) for innovative capacity, shown in Table 9.2. As for the prediction values $Q^2 = 1 - (SSE/SSO)$, where: SSO = Sum of Observed Squares, SSE = Sum of Squares of Errors, the endogenous dimension Abortive Capacity presented $Q^2 = 0.352$ and Innovative Capacity $Q^2 = 0.492$.

Thus, it was found that the model is relevant, as Q^2 values are greater than zero and greater than 0.016, that is, indicators classified as moderate to strong (Chin, 2009; Hair et al., 2017).

Hypothesis testing

Structural equation modeling was used to analyze the proposed hypotheses. Table 9.2 shows the structural coefficient and *t*-test, as well as the *P* value.

The analysis of sustainable process innovation on absorption capacity showed a positive and significant impact with $\beta = 0.296$ and *P* value = 0.001, leading to the acceptance of H_1. This result is in line with the findings of (Aliasghar et al., 2023).

The analysis of sustainable process innovation on innovation capacity showed a positive and significant impact with $\beta = 0.266$ and *P* value = 0.000, leading to the acceptance of H_2. This result is in line with the findings of (Boamah et al., 2023; Arndt et al., 2023).

The analysis of sustainable product innovation on Absorption Capacity showed a positive and significant impact with $\beta = 0.414$ and *P* value = 0.000,

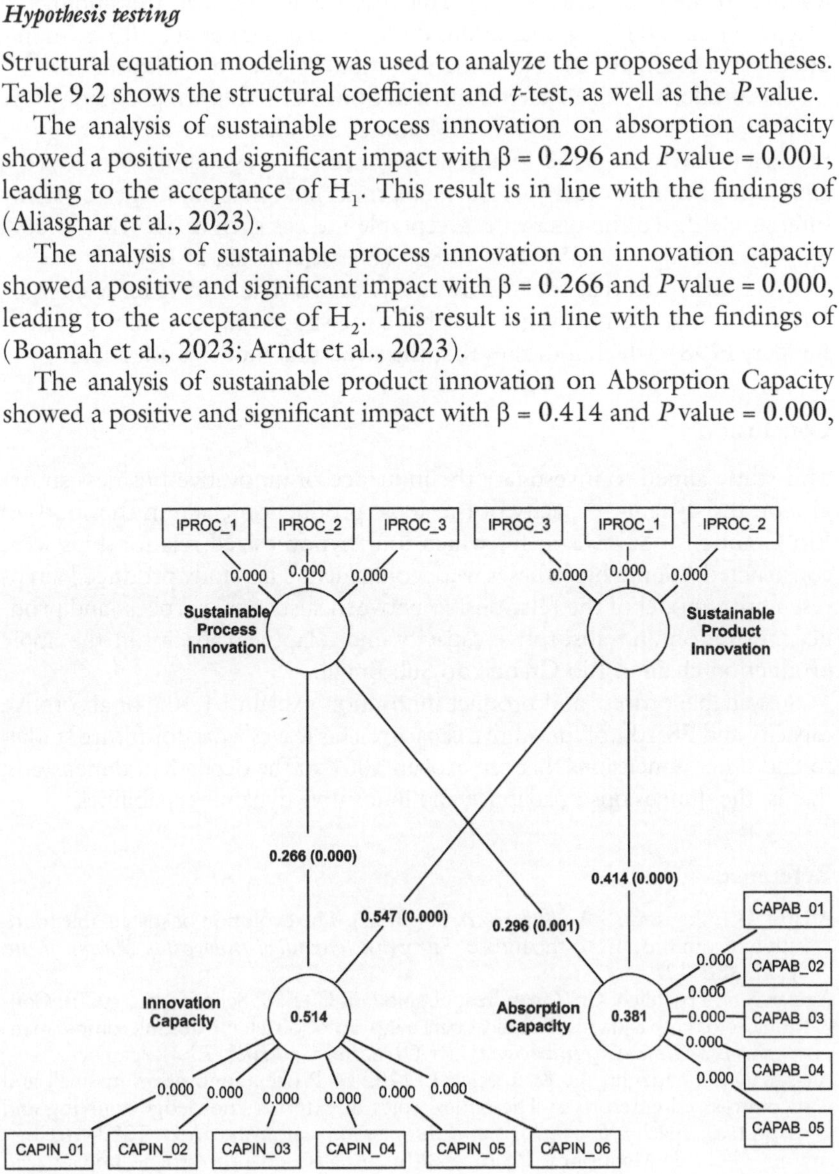

Figure 9.2 Structural model.

leading to the acceptance of H_3. This result is in line with the findings of (Pan et al., 2023; Dabić et al., 2023).

The analysis of sustainable product innovation on innovation capacity showed a positive and significant impact with $\beta = 0.547$ and *P*value = 0.000, leading to the acceptance of H_4. This result is in line with the findings of (Afeltra et al., 2023; Cunha, 2005; de Matos Ferreira et al., 2007; Cunha, 2005; Silva et al., 2010). The structural model is shown in Figure 9.2.

The model stabilized after four iterations. The following criteria were used to assess the fit of the PLS-SEM model: Standardized root mean square residual (SRMR), squared Euclidean distance (d_{ULS}), geodesic distance (d_G) and normed fit index (NFI). The results confirmed that the suggested structural model fitted the data with acceptable indices such as SRMR = 0.068, $d_{ULS} = 0.701$, $d_G = 0.735$, NFI = 0.885 (Henseler et al., 2016).

It was observed that the SRMR value was less than 0.08 (Henseler et al., 2016) and that the NFI value was above the suggested value of 0.8 (Hu & Bentler, 1998), which indicates that the structural model is adequate.

Conclusion

This study aimed to investigate the influence of innovative business strategies on the dynamic capacity of the apple production chain in the south of Rio Grande do Sul-Brazil, for which four hypothesized relationships were constructed. All the hypotheses were confirmed. This study produced a representative model of the relationship between sustainable process and product innovation and absorptive capacity and adaptive capacity in the apple production chain in Rio Grande do Sul, Brazil.

Sustainable process and product innovation explain 51.40% of absorptive capacity and 38.10% of innovative capacity. This leaves a gap for future studies to find other dimensions that can explain 100% of the dependent dimensions, that is, the dimensions of adaptive and innovative dynamic capabilities.

References

Afeltra, G., Alerasoul, S.A., & Strozzi, F. (2023). The evolution of sustainable innovation: From the past to the future. *European Journal of Innovation Management*, *26*(2), 386–421.

Aguiar, S.S., Froehlich, C., Zanandrea, G., Nodari, C.H., & Schmidt, S. (2020). Contribuição das capacidades dinâmicas para a inovação sob a lente dos microfundamentos. *Revista Gestão Organizacional (RGO), Santa Catarina*, *13*(3), set./dez.

Aliasghar, O., Sadeghi, A., & Rose, E.L. (2023). Process innovation in small-and medium-sized enterprises: The critical roles of external knowledge sourcing and absorptive capacity. *Journal of Small Business Management*, *61*(4), 1583–1610.

Araújo, G.C., & Mendonça, P.S.M. (2009). Análise do processo de implantação das normas de sustentabilidade empresarial. *Revista de Administração Mackenze*, *10*(2), 31–56.

Arndt, F., Aharonson, B., Jansen, J., Jiang, J., & Ting, C. (2023). The past and future of absorptive capacity. *Academy of Management Collections*, *2*(4), 45–59.

Boamah, F.A., Zhang, J., Shehzad, M.U., & Ahmad, M. (2023). The mediating role of social dynamics in the influence of absorptive capacity and tacit knowledge sharing on project performance. *Business Process Management Journal*, *29*(1), 240–261.

Bolfe, E.L., Barbedo, J.G.A., Massruhá, S.M.F.S., de Souza, K.X.S., & Assad, E.D. (2020). Desafios, tendências e oportunidades em agricultura digital no Brasil. *Agricultura digital: pesquisa, desenvolvimento e inovação nas cadeias produtivas*. www.alice.cnptia.embrapa.br/alice/bitstream/doc/1126283/1/LV-Agricultura-digital-2020-cap16.pdf

Calazans, L.B.B., & Silva, G. (2016). Inovação de Processo: Uma Análise em empresas com práticas sustentáveis. *Revista de Gestão Ambiental e Sustentabilidade*, *5*(2), 115–129.

Camargo, M.E., Bizotto, B.L.S., Priesnitz, M.C., dos Santos Dullius, A.I., & Gilioli, R.M. (2022). Prioridades competitivas e inovação de processo na cadeia produtiva da maçã. *Concilium*, *22*(5), 591–605.

Chin, W. W. (2009). How to write up and report PLS analyses. In *Handbook of partial least squares: Concepts, methods and applications* (pp. 655–690). Springer.

Cohen, W.M., & Levinthal, D.A. (1990). Absorptive capacity: A new perspective on learning and innovation. *Administrative Science Quarterly*, *35*(1), 128–152. https://doi.org/10.2307/2393553

Correio, M.R.W., Cabral, A.C.A., Santos, S.M., Pessoa, M.N.M., & Roldan, V.P.S. (2013). Capacidade inovativa: um estudo com empresas da indústria de vestuário do Ceará. *Gestão Contemporânea*, *10*(14), 91–118.

Cunha, N.C.V.D. (2005). *As práticas gerenciais e suas contribuições para a capacidade de inovação em empresas inovadoras* (Doctoral dissertation, Universidade de São Paulo).

Dabić, M., Posinković, T.O., Vlačić, B., & Gonçalves, R. (2023). A configurational approach to new product development performance: The role of open innovation, digital transformation and absorptive capacity. *Technological Forecasting and Social Change*, *194*, 122720.

da Cruz, M.R., Camargo, M.E., da Cruz Braz, P.H., Frey, E.H., & Frey, M.V. (2014). Estratégias para inovação na cadeia produtiva da maçã brasileira. *Proceeding of ISTI/SIMTEC*, *2*(1), 403–408.

de Almeida Guerra, R.M., Tondolo, V.A.G., & Camargo, M.E. (2016). O que (ainda) podemos aprender sobre capacidades dinâmicas. *Revista Ibero Americana de Estratégia*, *15*(1), 44–64.

de Matos Ferreira, J.J., da Encarnação Marques, C.S., & Barbosa, M.J. (2007). Relação entre inovação, capacidade inovadora e desempenho: o caso das empresas da região da beira interior. *INMR-Innovation & Management Review*, *4*(3), 117–132.

de Souza Gollo, R., da Motta, M.E.V., Camargo, M.E., Priesnitz, M.C., & Triches, D. (2023). Impacto das capacidades dinâmicas no desempenho organizacional mediadas pelos mecanismos de aprendizagem na pandemia COVID-19. *Revista de Gestão e Secretariado (Management and Administrative Professional Review)*, *14*(3), 3222–3256.

Garcia, A.E.G. (2017). A inteligência competitiva e o desenvolvimento de Capacidades Dinâmicas nas organizações. *Revista Ibero Americana de Estratégia*, *16*(1), 69–90.

Grandinetti, R. (2016). Absorptive capacity and knowledge management in small and medium enterprises. *Knowledge Management Research & Practice*, *14*(2), 159–168.

Guan, J., & Ma, N. (2003). Innovative capability and export performance of Chinese firms. *Technovation*, *23*(9), 737–747.

Hair, J. F., Black, W. C., Babin, B. J., Anderson, R. E., & Tatham, R. L. (2009). *Análise multivariada de dados*. Bookman Editora.
Hair, J.F., Hult, G.T.M., Ringle, C., & Sarstedt, M. (2017). *Partial least squares structural equation modeling (PLS-SEM)*. Sage Publications.
Henseler, J., Hubona, G., & Ray, P.A. (2016). Using PLS path modeling in new technology research: Updated guidelines. *Industrial Management & Data Systems*, *116*, 2–22. https://doi.org/10.1108/IMDS-09-2015-0382
Henseler, J., Ringle, C.M., & Sarstedt, M. (2016). Testing measurement invariance of composites using partial least squares. *International Marketing Review*, *33*(3), 405–431. https://doi.org/10.1108/IMR-09-2014-0304
Hinkin, T. (1995). A review of scale development practices in the study of organizations. *Journal of Management*, *21*(5), 967–988.
Hu, L.T., & Bentler, P.M. (1998). Fit indices in covariance structure modeling: Sensitivity to underparameterized model misspecification. *Psychological Methods*, *3*(4), 424–453. https://doi.org/10.1037/1082-989X.3.4.424
Huang, J.Y., Jiang, R., & Chang, J.Y. (2023). The effects of transformational and adaptive leadership on dynamic capabilities: Digital transformation projects. *Project Management Journal*, *54*(4), 428–446. https://doi.org/10.1177/87569728231165896
Kiperstok, A., Costa, D.P., Andrade, J.C.S., Agra Filho, S.S., & Figueroa, E. (2002). Inovação como requisito do desenvolvimento sustentável. *REAd*, *8*(6), 1–20.
Kvitschal, M.V., Couto, M., & Leite, G.B. (2022). Necessidade da diversificação de cultivares na cadeia produtiva da maçã no Brasil. *Agropecuária Catarinense*, *35*(3), 7–10.
Lawson, B., & Samson, D. (2001). Developing innovation capability in organizations: A dynamic capabilities approach. *International Journal of Innovation Management*, *5*(3), 377–400.
Lhamby, A.R., Júnior, A.N., Siluk, J., Junior, C.R.S., Carvalho, M., Nogueira, C.R.D., & Pires, V.P.K. (2023). Decision-making for efficiency and innovation in the rice production chain. *Revista de Estudos Interdisciplinares*, *5*(7), 318–350.
Molchanova, L.A., Akupiyan, O.S., Kravchenko, D.P., Pak, Z.C., & Chovgan, N.I. (October 2023). Innovative processes in the agricultural sector: Features and prospects. *AIP Conference Proceedings*, *2921*(1), AIP Publishing.
Muneeb, D., Ahmad, S.Z., Abu Bakar, A.R., & Tehseen, S. (2023). Empowering resources recombination through dynamic capabilities of an enterprise. *Journal of Enterprise Information Management*, *36*(1), 1–21.
Neely, A.D., & Hii, H.H. (1999). The innovative capacity of firms. *Report Commissioned by the Government Office for the East of England*. The Judge Institute of Management Studies.
OECD-Eurostat, O. M. (2005). *Guidelines for collecting and interpreting innovation data*. https://ec.europa.eu/eurostat/documents/3859598/5889925/OSLO-EN.PDF
Ortiz-Avram, D., Ovcharova, N., & Engelmann, A. (2023). Dynamic capabilities for sustainability: Toward a typology based on dimensions of sustainability-oriented innovation and stakeholder integration. *Business Strategy and the Environment*, 1–36. https://doi.org/10.1002/bse.3630
Pan, X., Shen, Z., Song, M., & Shu, Y. (2023). Enhancing green technology innovation through enterprise environmental governance: A life cycle perspective with moderator analysis of dynamic innovation capability. *Energy Policy*, *182*, 113773. https://doi.org/10.1016/j.enpol.2023.113773
Pérez-Rave, J.I., Guerrero, R.F., Vallina, A.S., & Echavarría, F.G. (2023). A measurement model of dynamic capabilities of the continuous improvement project and its role in the renewal of the company's products/services. *Operations Management Research*, *16*(1), 126–140.

Pertheban, T.R., Thurasamy, R., Marimuthu, A., Venkatachalam, K.R., Annamalah, S., Paraman, P., & Hoo, W.C. (2023). The impact of proactive resilience strategies on organizational performance: Role of ambidextrous and dynamic capabilities of SMEs in manufacturing sector. *Sustainability*, *15*(16), 12665.
Podsakoff, P.M., MacKenzie, S.B., & Podsakoff, N.P. (2012). Sources of method bias in social science research and recommendations on how to control it. *Annual Review of Psychology*, *63*, 539–569.
Ribeiro, O.C.D.R., & Steiner, P.J. (2021). Vantagem Competitiva Sustentável e Inovação Verde: Uma revisão sobre proposições de escalas conjuntas. *Gestão & Produção*, *28*(3), 1–20. https://doi.org/10.1590/1806-9649-2021v28e5669
Schumpeter, J. (1934). *The theory of economic development*. Harvard University Press.
Silva, M.J., Sousa, G., & Moreira, J. (2010). Actividades de inovação e a capacidade inovadora das empresas portuguesas: evidências empíricas ao nível do sector dos serviços. *Proceedings of XX Luso-Spanish Conference on Management*, Universidade da Beira Interior. (pp. 4–5). http://www.dge.ubi.pt
Singh, A.K., Jain, N.K., Sharma, M.G., & Nigam, S. (2023). Reconceptualization of absorptive capacity as potential and realized absorptive capacity for project-based organizations. *International Journal of Project Management*, *41*(2), 102449.
Teng, Z.L., Guo, C., Zhao, Q., & Mubarik, M.S. (2023). Antecedents of green process innovation adoption: An AHP analysis of China's gas sector. *Resources Policy*, *85*, 103959.
Thanh, N.D., Nga, N.T.H., & Phuong, N.T.X. (2023). Effect of new generation Ftas on sustainable product innovation: empirical evidence from Vietnamese listed textile firms. *Ingeniería Solidaria*, *19*(1), 1–24.
Tidd, J., Bessant, J., & Pavitt, K. (2008). *Gestão da inovação* (3rd ed.). Bookman.
Tondolo, V.A.G., Tondolo, R.D.R.P., Camargo, M.E., & de Almeida Guerra, R.M. (2018). Capacidades dinâmicas em organizações sem fins lucrativos: uma proposta de mensuração para o terceiro setor. *Revista Eletrônica Científica do CRA-PR-RECC*, *5*(1), 18–33.
Trienekens, J., Uffelen, R.V., Debaire, J., & Omta, O. (2008). Assessment of innovation and performance in the fruit chain: The innovation-performance matrix. *British Food Journal*, *110*(1), 98–127.
ul zia, N., Burita, L., & Yang, Y. (2023). Inter-organizational social capital of firms in developing economies and industry 4.0 readiness: The role of innovative capability and absorptive capacity. *Review of Managerial Science*, *17*(2), 661–682.
Wang, C.L., & Ahmed, P.K. (2007). Dynamic capabilities: A review and research. *International Journal of Management Reviews, Oxford*, *9*, 35–38.
Xiao, H., Al Mamun, A., Masukujjaman, M., & Yang, Q. (2023). Modelling the significance of strategic orientation on green innovation: Mediation of green dynamic capabilities. *Humanities and Social Sciences Communications*, *10*(1), 1–15.
Zhang, D., Rong, Z., & Ji, Q. (2019). Green innovation and firm performance: Evidence from listed companies in China. *Resources, Conservation and Recycling*, *144*, 48–55. https://doi.org/10.1016/j.resconrec.2019.01.023
Zhang, F., Qin, X., & Liu, L. (2020). The interaction effect between ESG and green innovation and its impact on firm value from the perspective of information disclosure. *Sustainability (Switzerland)*, *12*(6). https://doi.org/10.3390/su12051866
Zhang, Y., Sangsawang, T., & Vipahasna, P.P. (2023). Assessing factors and simulating innovation: A study of innovative capacities among data science professionals in China. *Journal of Applied Data Sciences*, *4*(3), 213–228.
Zogbi, E. (2023). *50 Estratégias para Inovações Sustentáveis*. EZ.

10 Sustainable and ecocentric change for knowledge management in the telecommunications subsector

Leonardo Andrés Carvajal Alvarez

Introduction

The economic structure of the information and communication technologies sector (ICT-S) is made up of specialties, highlighting the telecommunications subsector (TC-S) as the basis of voice, video and data services. According to Mendivelso (2018), the ICT-S value chain study specifies for the TC-S in goods: (a) communications equipment and (b) components and various goods; in production: (c) telecommunications services; on digital platforms: (d) over-the-top (OTT) services and (e) packaging of user content; in infrastructure: (f) radio spectrum, (g) fiber optics and (h) essential installations; and finally in research, development and innovation (R&D&I): the entire process. The main services of the TC-S are: fixed and mobile communications, wholesale, audiovisual, information and technology (IT), digital content, hardware and software.

Now, for Geels (2002) and Talavera (2018), transformative innovation (TI) encompasses innovations in the system that break with conventional practices, routines, forms or methods to solve problems or act, seeking a positive turn (new directionality) and stimulating modifications in different environments by impacting in the change of a socio-technical regime (STR), beginning to destabilize it. Geels (2002) defined a socio-technical system (STS) as the connections or configurations between elements (actors, technologies and institutions) necessary to fulfill a fundamental social function of a modern civilization. The stable convergence of several STSs corresponds to an STR.

For Schot and Geels (2008) and Talavera (2018), the concept of STS explains the creation, dissemination and consumption of technology, entailing a co-evolutionary process where social functions are key for innovations to penetrate society. In reference to Geels' conceptual framework of STS transformations, the following must be taken into account: (a) systems themselves (resources and infrastructure); (b) actors involved; (c) standards, laws and policies; (d) interactions, complementarities and interdependencies

DOI: 10.4324/9781003465058-10

between sectors; (e) competition and selection processes; and (f) user and market practices. From this position, we can then speak of the STS of the TC-S within the STR of the ICT-S.

For its part, the coronavirus pandemic (COVID-19) caused a global crisis that tested the socio-economic mechanism, which remains in force in the long term as anticipated by Aniorte (2020), reflected by Stangl (2020) with his projections of economic growth and analyzed by Sevilla (2020). Only now is the uncertainty being overcome by being able to measure the real repercussions. Due to the epidemic, the world was oriented toward the search for global solutions in all sectors while telecommunications services supported business, institutional and personal communications, keeping businesses and markets active. Today, great challenges are faced that lead to discussing the status quo, taking accelerated actions, creating and reconfiguring processes to transform what was not so important before.

Contrary to the past, currently all types of actions in favor of progress are not justified, which is why countries have been regulating certain technological-environmental practices. The STS of the TC-S, which behaves as a network of interdependent relationships, must be located in an "ecocentric" rather than an anthropocentric vision.[1] The new paradigm relates TC-S to nature.[2] To survive in competition and take advantage of the opportunities generated by facing the challenges due to COVID-19, in Geels' framework, the subsector must maintain a respectful and protective ecosystem dynamic balance. Its actions in the digital ecosystem are limited to not affecting human beings, living beings or the environment. Its business viability demands strategic actions for sustainable and ecocentric change, with activities and resources related to these opportunities (adjustments to the STS).

Mora and González (2018) affirm that *knowledge (or "know-how") and its management* are increasingly relevant in industries. Consistent with Zabala (2012), the acceptance of the value of knowledge as an asset and greater competitive advantage is crucial in the global market and hence the importance of identifying and expanding strategies to manage it. This leads companies[3] in the subsector to have to assume and adapt their internal structures and knowledge assets[4] to improve conditions, highlighting the people, processes and technologies (Escobar, 2009) that constantly move, participating in the flow of knowledge, making possible the development of solutions that satisfy users, productivity or any variable that generates operational value (Mora & González, 2018).

Sustainable telecommunications subsector

The guidelines that characterize the TC-S can be identified (Aniorte, 2020; Inter-American Telecommunications Commission [CITEL], 2020; Andean Development Corporation [CAF], 2020a, 2020b; García, 2020; Meya,

2020) as an industry that supports the information and knowledge society, to establish new rules and face the social and economic situation. From the perspective of Schot and Steinmueller (cited by ISET, 2024), the crisis due to COVID-19 requires an analysis framework to respond to the challenges by scenarios, promote and take advantage of opportunities for changes that may be permanent. A "just transition" process is sought (Swilling cited by ISET, 2024) corresponding to incremental innovations that can become radical, with a well-being result assured in "superior sustainability". Innovating is imperative to advance the fulfillment of the indicators of the 2030 Agenda of the United Nations (UN) that contains the Sustainable Development Goals (SDGs) (La Rábida Observatory [LRO], 2021), with telecommunications being a tool for this.

All human activity, the pace of progress and lifestyle leave a mark on the Earth, positive or negative and the "impact on the environment" can result in extreme changes. Telecommunications have a paradox related to energy efficiency, the use of physical and channel resources. While recent wireless technologies have achieved high energy efficiency, the new 5G mobile technology, although it also offers improvement in that capacity, will require more physical infrastructure (towers and antennas) and more data capacity (because they will grow exponentially). The 5G network will be more efficient on the one hand, but less efficient on the other, consuming even more energy due to its size and density (Bravo, 2021). A sustainable and ecological initiative in the TC-S is the global Green Touch consortium,[5] an effort that brings real change (CSR Commitment, 2010; Construible, 2010; Europe Press, 2010).

"Industry 4.0" exhibits a horizon where technology constantly and vigorously reforms production and management systems. According to the World Economic Forum (WEF), one of the main factors of change and driving force in this industry is the participation of telecommunications, because it makes its benefits viable. In the Fourth Industrial Revolution, people are connected, using mobile devices with high processing and storage and accessing information and knowledge, so TC-S business managers must address several points to implement technological tools and systems: (a) awareness of the need for progress; (b) knowledge of the technological environment and success stories; (c) feasibility analysis of bringing technology to the business; (d) advice with experts; and (e) ensuring supplier adaptation to digital transformation (ICT Consumption, 2018).

A case of symbiosis between telecommunications and Industry 4.0 is the continuous growth of telephone, internet, mobile and broadband services motivated by artificial intelligence (AI). More and more operators are joining the internet of things (IoT) trend and recognizing the value of AI for the demand for higher-quality products. TC-S companies are taking advantage of the opportunities of new technologies by using their large databases, big data and data analytics to develop new goods and services that provide improved customer experience, optimization of operations and increased revenue[6] (Solomon, 2021).

Sustainability, ecocentrism and knowledge management in the TC-S

TI is inclusive, participatory, purposeful, democratic, experimental and learning. It places social and environmental well-being objectives at the center as strategic and dynamic drivers of competitiveness and development, displacing economic growth. It proposes changing STSs made up of technologies, regulations, knowledge and cultural habits (energy, health, education, telecommunications, among others) (ISET, 2024). The path to the "sustainability[7] of the TC-S" goes through "ecocentrism" and stimulating TI, which is especially useful after having suffered the effects of the emergency of a pandemic.

As long as the TC-S can satisfy the need to take advantage of the opportunities found as STS, without compromising future capacity and ensuring the balance between economic growth, environmental protection and social well-being, we can speak of "sustainable development" (Acciona, 2024). This is achieved from a global perspective guided by the 17 UN SDGs. Such objectives actively involve people, companies and countries and call for confronting the great challenges of humanity, guaranteeing equal opportunities and a better life without compromising the planet.

"Ecocentrism" interprets that man should not intervene in the evolution of the planet by exploiting it for his benefit, but rather support its evolution. As a current of thought, it supports the idea that nature is the center of everything and the supreme value, which therefore must be respected and preserved and that humans are not a superior being (Marín & Coll, 2021). The manifestation in recent years of environmentalism[8] and biocentrism[9] movements has favored and sustained the development of ecocentrism.

The so-called anthropocentric fracture (Castillo & Ceberio, 2017) and the Gaia Theory (and its disciplinary formalization, Earth Science) (Lovelock; Daily; Moore, Lemke and Loreau cited in Castillo & Ceberio, 2017) have been in good measure motivating for the "change of paradigm" from anthropocentric to ecocentric or, based on Beorlegui (2021), from a reductionism of a limiting ontological nature to deal with environmental problems to a model where the human being and his interests are not the center but part of a living planetary system.

On another topic, "knowledge can be understood as the set of information that is possessed about a concept or study and that serves to incorporate new experiences; in addition to being useful for action" (Mora & González, 2018, p. 3), being a source to design, produce and distribute new or improved goods and services, therefore, it must be managed appropriately and timely (Díaz, 2006). "Knowledge management" has gained importance in all contexts for business development and growth, given the conditions of the new economy, market globalization and modern technologies. Managing knowledge is essential, incentivized and of equal weight to the assets of companies (Escobar, 2009; González & Socarrás, 2021).

Nonaka and Takeuchi's (1995) seminal knowledge management proposal sets the tone with its four-step SECI model: Socialization (S), Externalization (E), Combination (C) and Internalization (I) (or "knowledge spiral" by rotating it from tacit to explicit and vice versa), encompassing a linear process: capture, structuring, transmission and exploitation (Mora & González, 2018), which technically enables the organization to generate new knowledge, disseminate it among its members and materialize it in products, services and systems.

Nonaka and Takeuchi (1995) and Mora and González (2018) consider knowledge management as "key to innovating" in organizations and achieving efficiencies that trigger economic benefits and higher quality intellectual capital (structural and relational). As the ability to value and take advantage of said capital to achieve objectives (Escobar, 2009), or as "management of intangible assets that generate value for the organization" (Mora & González, 2018, p. 3), it is considered "a tool strategic and for it to be implemented in an organization, there must first be a commitment from senior management evidenced with policies that promote success factors and attack barriers" (Zabaleta et al., 2016, p. 147).

Analysis of challenges and opportunities for the TC-S due to COVID-19

Digital telecommunications networks and technologies have been indispensable in human life, being more noticeable after the crisis experienced by COVID-19 in aspects such as work, health, security, education and social functioning transferred to the home, forcing companies, institutions, communities and people to seek and appropriate digital strategies and media, in principle urgently, to counteract the effects and respond to established demands. What was at stake was the ability to unite with the purpose of preserving life, while the actors had instruments such as teleworking, teleeducation, electronic commerce and others to make transactions, be in contact (social connection) and have entertainment. Thus, "the TC-S ratified its prominence" (CAF, 2020a, 2020b; CITEL, 2020; García, 2020; Meya, 2020; Pautasio, 2020; International Telecommunications Union [ITU], 2020a).

During the days of mandatory preventive isolation, the TC-S companies were providing, almost without exception, all services with high availability, without failures or pauses, many even increasing the offer in terms of capacity, to withstand the strong and growing current demand. Due to autonomous decisions or government decrees, this was normally without increasing rates for a reasonable period, helping family economic relief (Ambientum, 2020; CAF, 2020a, 2020b; CITEL, 2020; Meya, 2020; Pautasio, 2020). The above showed "more preparation than other subsectors", which led to a tacit increase in user trust in telecommunications operators.

It is possible to identify "challenges and opportunities for TC-S" that accelerate the transformation of the industry, based on existing and new processes. As MKM Partners (cited in Dano, 2020) wrote to Wall Street investors:

> We believe that the COVID-19 pandemic has accelerated society's transition to broadband and digitalization by at least a decade and that this trend will continue to advance. We see broadband access and sufficient bandwidth as increasingly fundamental human needs. We also believe that companies selling broadband solutions and network capacity will see accelerated business trends, compared to before the crisis (n.p.).

Post-COVID-19, the STS of the TC-S faces multiple "challenges" in the world that are described classified in "seven scenarios". From there, "four factors" or "lines of strategic action" are identified on which "sustainable opportunities" are generated (Aniorte, 2020; CAF, 2020a, 2020b; CITEL, 2020; García, 2020; Meya, 2020; Molina et al., 2020). These scenarios and factors are listed in table 10.1. The correlation of challenges and opportunities occurs through such lines of strategic action, which is schematized in figure 10.1.

Table 10.1 Scenarios and factors for STS of the TC-S post-COVID-19

STS OF THE TC-S POST-COVID-19			
Scenarios			
1) Corporate Social Responsibility (CSR)		2) Actions against market reduction	
3) Services adaptation capacity		4) Changes and growth of services	
5) Digital transformation		6) Business sustainability	
7) Business dynamism			
Factors or lines of strategic action			
1) User base		2) Digital service channel	
3) Networks		4) Operations	

Source: Author

Figure 10.1 Correlation of challenges and sustainable opportunities for STS of the TC-S at a global level post-COVID-19.

Source: Author.

Corporate social responsibility (CSR) challenges for the TC-S

- The TC-S is appreciated as fundamental for all social and economic activities, so its companies, especially operators, are expected to always intervene quickly, dynamically and safely to guarantee the continuity of services and collaborate to counteract the risks, effects of any crisis, activating the mechanisms for recovery.
- For the government sector, it has always been a priority to work as a team with telecommunications companies, first of all with the operators, in order to protect the actors, above all users and the companies themselves.
- Historically, the TC-S has been an instrument of the financial markets whose value increases during periods of crisis, economic recession, prevention or fear of market risk, its analysis being a reference for interpreting the development.

Due to the above, it is mandatory to present a business brand image and a speech in line with expectations, which grants confidence and places the subsector as decisive, responsible and committed at all times and circumstances. This has been reflected in decisions and actions such as: (a) expand the offer in availability and features without additional costs (for example, in bandwidth with higher speeds and without traffic limits); (b) strengthen operational and technical capacity, basically in network maintenance processes; (c) manage portability and configuration changes and user installations; (d) share customer and supplier databases with the government and support agencies, without affecting confidentiality, to manage crises; and (e) acquire equipment and elements for the permanent health management of collaborators.

Challenges of actions against market reduction for the TC-S

- Fortunately, the TC-S was little affected by the crisis; however, development plans, programs and projects were temporarily limited. A reduction in investment due to the recession, not seen since the beginning of 2008, could have compromised the possibility of growth.
- The subsector has not been immune to the risk of unemployment, so the collaboration of governments is expected with measures that encourage the maintenance of collaborator plants. Microeconomic and macroeconomic agreements are also necessary between governments and companies in the sector to achieve balance and achieve planned objectives.
- The global recession caused customer contract cancellations and non-performing loans to increase and revenues to decrease, although demand grew, resulting in rates having to be reduced or not increased. Still, the retained users sustained the business. All of this represented serious difficulties for the subsector, affecting the profitability margin, which forced costs and expenses to be reduced.

Given the problem in the countries of lack of consolidation (low quantity, capacity and coverage) of telecommunications networks, commonly broadband and fixed and mobile applications, it was and continues to be forced to resort to cooperation between operators to share system infrastructure resources. of transmission. Such a path risks the dynamics and regularity with which network infrastructures have been expanding in the era of the Fourth Industrial Revolution (Industry 4.0), among them for 5G technology and hyperconnectivity. In any case, the temporary non-investment created an accumulated fund of economic resources for the opportune moment of the projects, which must be carried out to reaffirm the availability, continuity and robustness strategies of telecommunications, something crucial to respond to the increase in demand, face crisis situations of any proportion, withstand effects on the market and network tension and thus guarantee the future.

Services adaptation capacity's challenges for the TC-S

- Telecommunications networks supported and continue to do so, the growing load due to demand for services, features and traffic, with some exceptions of degradation. It is imperative to strengthen and scale the infrastructure to continue assimilating it with a guarantee of continuity in bandwidth, connection immediacy (latency) and multi-threaded execution (concurrency).
- The characteristics of remote communications have practically not changed, but the urgency that was had to implement teleworking, teleeducation, telemedicine, online government and electronic banking, among others, added to the general inexperience, did have an impact on security that was transmitted to the business of TC-S companies, forcing them to carry out risk analysis and action plans to resist.
- The reserves and controls of governments toward service providers will be increasingly greater to verify and guarantee technological operation. It is possible that there will be infrastructure replacements and improvements, calls for optimization and even sanctions, as well as the appearance of new competitors in the market and even the withdrawal of many of the small ones.

From all this, it is necessary to develop strategies and actions for the resilience of networks (an example is the Global Network Resiliency Platform—GNRP) (ITU, 2020b). Here, governments and multinational technology providers play a leading role in putting pressure to correct shortcomings and scale infrastructure to have excess capacity, which is transcendental in the context when the crisis passes. The main problems with telecommunications networks during the COVID-19 epidemic occurred in mobile voice services, streaming OTT (such as video on demand—VOD), customer service (call and contact centers) and online commerce, with the market having been saturated. functioning of digital care channels, especially in official and health entities, despite the stability of digital platforms based on internet protocol (IP).

Challenges of changes and growth of services for the TC-S

- As a consequence of the growth in demand and the fundamental nature of telecommunications services, technological development plans and associated improvements have been intensifying and accelerating. Governments and regulatory bodies continue to promote TC-S, while the financial sector provides investment options at low interest rates.
- Technological development points toward the expansion of fiber optic and satellite systems for voice, video and data transport and the implementation of 5G and hyperconnectivity networks, seeking to expand urban and rural broadband coverage and fixed and mobile applications, reaching unserved areas to overcome limitations due to lack of consolidation.
- During COVID-19, there was no certainty about the future conditions and behavior of users and markets (acquisition, abandonment,

cancellation and portability), so operators that provided services for free or without increasing rates had to warn of the need to capitalize on this, in the short term, with an increase in subscribers or extension of current contracts, to prevent these provisional measures from being perceived as established or becoming part of the panorama.

So, with the modification of the characteristics of digital consumption in organizations and homes, turned toward the internet and online activities with unconventional multimedia applications, the demand and momentum for Industry 4.0 services will continue to grow: cloud computing, big data, data analytics, cybersecurity, IoT, AI, hyperconnectivity, digital manufacturing (3D printing), robotics, automation, virtual and augmented reality and so forth, opening up to multiple possibilities and spaces in the markets for specialization and emergence of niche suppliers, which will bring more dynamism to the subsector and therefore to the ICT-S.

Digital transformation challenges for the TC-S

- Everything seems to be turning toward the internet with online and virtual activities, which had a stellar and even ecstatic moment during the active period of COVID-19. Even though there is some lack of knowledge among ordinary people, with forced or planned learning processes, the trend is for organizational operations to become completely digitalized.
- Organizations must carry out digitalization using proven models that largely deliver results of autonomous operations and self-supported services, available in real time and virtualized. To achieve this, telecommunications companies, mainly service operators, are the necessary allies.
- The primary objective of TC-S companies is to be closer, know users and the market better and segment communication channels. They must quickly use Industry 4.0 technologies such as big data, data analytics, process integration, vertical and horizontal integration and other traditional ones such as business intelligence and digital marketing to implement, scale and improve digital systems for care and delivery services. capture (call and contact centers).

The differentiation of key and support activities enables the reorganization or modification of structures and collaborator plants and the incorporation of new models such as hypertext organization (with business to consumer—B2C, business to business—B2B, business to employee—B2E and employee to employee—E2E platforms), achieving learning, high performance, simplification of support processes and systems. Those companies in the subsector with greater digital maturity reacted more effectively to the crisis and continue to advance in this aspect, being better qualified and recognized. Digital transformation, although it does not ensure income or profitability of the business, is not an alternative but an obligation.

The workforce and people in general must be trained and acquire conceptual and technical skills for sufficient technological preparation to facilitate coupling with digital processes in all fields and applications.

Business sustainability challenges for the TC-S

- The TC-S, by its very essence, is apparently very sure of its permanence as STS and part of the STR of the ICT-S, but it will present some changes. The telecommunications business will continue and will continue to experience the corresponding life cycle stages for its technologies, goods and services.
- Due to the crisis, the subsector has experienced a cycle of recession characterized by temporary limitation of investments, cancellation of contracts or abandonment of services (not by choice but due to economic circumstances or organizational inactivity), reduction in income and profitability and tension in its cash flow, despite the increase in demand. Contraction and deflation for the business are then potentially feasible, in the short and medium term.
- Private investment funds and individual investors will appear and there will be reactivated and new merger, acquisition and alliance agreements to make viable and capitalize telecommunications companies (primarily operators) with resource needs for cash flow and projects. Companies, in most cases, will specialize in content or infrastructure services, and in a few others, they will bring them together as the same provider.

Indeed, for telecommunications services, new marketing and commercialization strategies and projects will be required with more flexible, segmented, personalized and low-priced offers to attract, retain and build loyalty for business and home users. As these services are commodity and there is homogeneity of the offer, the rate factor has been the main parameter of customer decisions, but it will probably be displaced by the quality and safety factors. Some goods and services must be redefined, and efforts must be made for users of fixed and mobile services to expand their services (channels, bandwidth and plans) and affirm the contracting of convergent services, and those who are in prepaid to migrate to postpaid.

Business dynamism challenges for the TC-S

- In the short term, the TC-S has to resolve the evident problems by acting with speed and agility. It must demonstrate activity, movement and innovation, as well as changes that make transformation possible. In other words, it must energize the business to anticipate the effects, both adverse and favorable, brought by the health and socio-economic crisis due to COVID-19 and maintain the leadership and competitive strategic position it holds.
- Assessing the conditions and behaviors of the actors involved, a push is envisioned that moves the development of digitalization in processes

and markets forward, in the latter starting in specialized niches of users and suppliers based on business relationships and measurement of forces, then addressing to higher niches until they permeate the entire society.
- With the identification and classification of actions for the exploitation of opportunities resulting from the process of socio-technical change, it is expected to establish a dynamism that leads to the digital transformation of the TC-S and project it toward all types of users.

Telecommunications companies must address the strategic lines of action that generate opportunities: the user base, the digital service channel, networks and operations. Above all, they must realize the social responsibility that concerns them as part of society, as they are providers of services (and suppliers of goods on many occasions) that are truly essential for the functioning of all economic sectors and citizens, making activities and community life are getting better and better.

Opportunities for the TC-S

In this order of ideas, Table 10.1 presents the "opportunities" for the TC-S due to COVID-19, by factors or lines of strategic action identified (Aniorte, 2020; CAF, 2020a, 2020b; CITEL, 2020; García, 2020; Meya, 2020; Molina et al., 2020). These opportunities manifest themselves from the challenges previously classified and described by scenarios.

Analysis results within the framework of STS transformations

According to Geels (2002) and Geels and Schot (2007), for the TI process, from the "multilevel perspective (MLP)" and in terms of transitions, results are obtained for the three levels of analytical concepts (technological niches, STR and landscape). First, "technological niches" form the micro level where radical innovations originate. There is maximum prominence for the social groups of users and markets that will be able to benefit from the proposed changes that materialize in the TC-S. These groups have affinities, interact and are interdependent (specialized niches), corresponding to a wide range of economic and social sectors (government, health, education, manufacturing, commerce, services, households) since they all require telecommunications services for their activities, tasks or purposes.

From the sustainable opportunities presented for the TC-S arise, in terms of "solution approaches", the novelties or "radical responses" demanded for the present and the post-crisis future and which are tested in specialized niches, such as: (1) strengthening the network and systems infrastructure; (2) consolidation of own or third-party technological infrastructure; (3) independence of the content components and technological infrastructure; (4) use of Industry 4.0 technologies; (5) conversion of the digital service channel; and (6) development of a new brand for the market (CAF, 2020a, 2020b; CITEL, 2020; Meya, 2020).

Table 10.2 Sustainable opportunities for the STS of the TC-S due to COVID-19

SUSTAINABLE OPPORTUNITIES (ADJUSTMENTS TO THE STS OF THE TC-S)	
Factor 1: User base	*Factor 2: Digital service channel*
Keys: *Customer orientation.* *Orientation to new trends in use and behavior.* ***Aim:*** *Avoid its decrease and guarantee a minimum portfolio.* • Market segmentation based on usage trends and post-crisis behavior. • Technical strategies for convergent and disaggregated products (goods and services). • Offer and price strategies for specific segments. • Customization of solutions tailored to user needs. • Effective, flexible and adaptable user retention models due to intention to abandon or cancel contracts. • Strengthening the digitalization offer, integrated value-added products (goods and services) (cloud computing, B2B, teleworking, cybersecurity, etc.). • Horizontal and/or vertical integration with strategic allies for the needs of the offer and the evolution of services.	***Keys:*** *Expansion and optimization for user acquisition and retention.* *Quick and efficient business transformation.* ***Aim:*** *Continue efforts in its development.* • Assignment of short-term goals to evaluate performance. • Optimization of operation through analysis of performance tests. • Conversion toward the digital channel as the main channel for comprehensive care, with policies, strategies, specific plans and immediate solutions (e.g. to prevent abandonment or contract cancellations). • Support of conventional channels through websites, social networks and CSR communication channels. • Support and expansion of corporate strategic communication actions (media). • Strengthening logistics processes toward users and the market in general.
Factor 3: Networks	**Factor 4: Operations**
Keys: *Resilient service.* ***Aim:*** *Guarantee quality, safety and availability.* • Strengthening strategies, projects, technologies and processes for implementation, adaptation, expansion and operation of infrastructure. • Restructuring of infrastructure consolidation, expansion and improvement plans, optimizing costs and maximizing investments. • Identification and management of strategic technology suppliers, evaluating the acceptable level of dependency. • Strengthening (technological, functional and coverage) of transportation networks. • Expansion and improvement of coverage and technology of user networks (last mile and end customer network), including terminal equipment and wired and wireless access. • Quality assurance, infrastructure robustness and spectrum management. • Provision of security and availability in all user segments.	***Keys:*** *Digitization.* *Redefinition and automation of processes and interrelationships.* ***Aim:*** *Simplify and digitize tasks.* • Significant decrease in human participation and simplification of service channels (digital and conventional). • Development of objective and efficient processes to provide quick and early responses to cases such as complaints, queries, billing, portfolio management, etc. • Significant increase in the digitalization of technical activities, real-time infrastructure management (equipment, supervision and maintenance processes, incident response, network and equipment reconfiguration and others) and administration activities in general. • Simplification based on process automation and collaborative interrelationships, mainly in critical cases and those with high execution volume.

Source: Author

Based on the expectations created with its "niche opportunities", the subsector is pursuing strategies to attract attention, achieve legitimate government protection, inter-institutional support and direction of learning processes, constituting what Schot and Geels (2008) propose as "Strategic Management of Niches (SMN)", which in this particular is annexing the two particular types of innovations that Talavera (2018) highlights as "socially desirable innovations that serve long-term objectives, such as sustainability; and radical transformations, which face a discrepancy with respect to existing infrastructure, user practices or regulations" (n.p.).

Second, the "STR" constitutes the intermediate level, which in this case accounts for the stability of the STS of the TC-S. The interaction processes in specialized niches will continue to be very dynamic, providing actors with an environment of mutual help and collaboration, but also of high competition and critical negotiations. The combination of both situations allows for constant learning, which in essence is a win-win for everyone. At this level, it is expected that the socio-technical practices raised will continue, being alternative consumption experiences for niche social groups. However, the niche innovations achieved are not expected to become regimes.

The ways in which telecommunications companies provide services to users are susceptible to positive changes, which makes them available for innovation. "The TC-S can be transformed towards a more sustainable environment", engaging the seven scenarios and the four factors. Following Schot and Geels (2008), operators are gaining experience with a certain degree of success, at the niche level, with their reconfigured and new services which could rapidly position themselves as mature innovations and spread toward higher levels to reach the divergent evolutionary paths that the theory speaks of, impacting until they become sources of sustainable changes in the STS of the TC-S, which as an important part of the STR of the ICT-S incubates its destabilization as a regime.

The transformation process, being complex, does not occur in the long term as is typical but rather accelerated in the medium term, depending on the actions of all actors[10] in the regime. The truth is that, due to the crisis caused by the coronavirus, the TC-S experimentation contributes to the transition by aligning the three required processes mentioned by Talavera (2018): "1) The articulation of expectations and visions; 2) The construction of networks of social actors; 3) Multidimensional learning processes" (n.p.). In this way, "the STS of the subsector is redistributing the epicenter of niche experimentation" in a balanced mix between technological and social aspects (concepts, visions and strategic principles), addressing the socio-technical nature of the change process.

Third, the "landscape" is the macro level, formed by an environment outside the regime and the direct influence of the actors, bringing together macroeconomic factors, cultural patterns, macrotrends and others. Unlike technological niches and STRs that function through sociological structuring, these factors have a different influence since they are not determinants by themselves, but they provide deep structural variable forces making certain actions easier to carry out than others (Geels & Schot, 2007). Normally, changes at this level occur slowly, in decades, but just as for the transformation process, in this particular case of analysis, they will have accelerated development in the medium term.

It is observed that the socio-technical change is born with new developments in niches, and that by virtue of the development articulated with processes and external influences, it impacts the STR of the ICT-S, which originally appears stable. Thus, "radical responses propose changes that begin to destabilize the regime". The new configuration takes advantage and takes the opportunity to slide through the "windows of opportunity" caused by the adjustments to the STS of the TC-S, which are, as such, sustainable opportunities. Change applies pressure to transform the landscape, whose actions in this specific case are easier to execute than if the COVID-19 crisis had not occurred. Figure 10.2 shows the results.

In the TI-driven STS reconfiguration process, "radical niche innovations may prevail", requiring strategic alignment of current and new regulations, infrastructure, user practices and technologies. Associating the concepts of Schot and Geels (2008), the inclination of niches is more toward technical issues rather than regulations, but there is consensus that all actors must support possible futures, measuring their individual risk directly proportional to the degree of the radical innovations presented. The process will be directed by technological actors through R&D&I programs and pilot projects when appropriate.

On the other hand, attention must be paid to the behavior of demand as an aspect on which the competitive development of the industry depends. There will also be a simplification of operations, leveraging and promoting "service outsourcing subsectors" (Business Process Outsourcing—BPO, Information Technology Outsourcing—ITO and Knowledge Process Outsourcing—KPO). In this matter, Díaz (2006) refers to the integration of

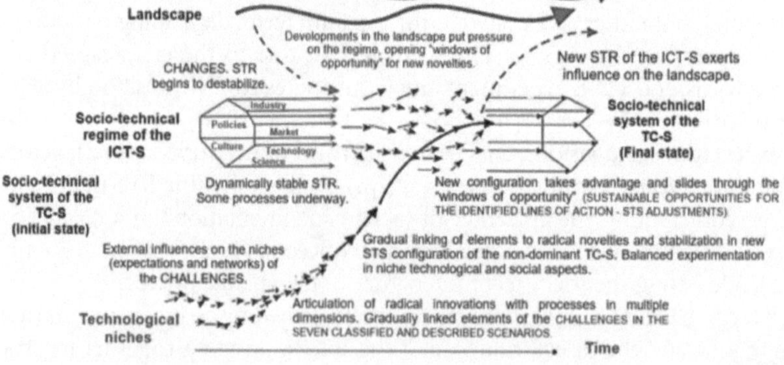

Figure 10.2 Transformative innovation (TI): Socio-technical change of the TC-S due to COVID-19 and its impact on the STR of the ICT-S.

Source: Geels (2002) and Geels and Schot (2007) with own adaptation.

applications, management, optimization of business processes and knowledge management systems.

To achieve the expected dynamism, it is crucial to identify and classify in order of importance the actions required to exploit the "windows of opportunity" that open in the process of socio-technical change, understanding that the purpose is the real "digital transformation of the TC-S". The expectation that niche innovations, consequences of COVID-19 and perhaps not yet profitable, will be important to achieve social objectives, helps motivate actors to invest time and other resources building their own niches, including governments through promotion actions and application of subsidies.

As STS, the telecommunications industry will continue to be the center of the functioning of the digital ecosystem, which it provided vital support at the height of COVID-19, uniting its members to collaborate on solutions. "The evolution of TC-S is very rapid", with innovations that clearly meet the characteristics of TI. As an order, it finds a new direction, impacts the regime to which it belongs and enables changes in the environment. These socio-technical practices are transforming the existing oligopoly and the business model with measures that promote actions that arise from challenges and opportunities.

In a complementary way, it is pertinent to specify that the human being coexists with all the other components of the planet and its development must respect nature and the ecosystem, opposing harmful practices and promoting beneficial ones. What we have is a close "coupling between evolution and environment in a self-regulated global planetary system", where living and nonliving systems have evolved together and influenced each other (Castillo & Ceberio, 2017). Well, regarding "knowledge", Díaz (2006) states that it is an asset that is enriched in advanced organizations, that ICT provides solutions for its management with various technological systems and tools and that it presents the dimensions of the knowledge structure according to their level of maturity: structured (more formal and precise) and unstructured (more informal and ambiguous). He argues:

> To be successful in the new economy, a new conceptual framework is required that refers to knowledge as a nuclear asset in organizations, not as an expense and that investments in ICT are not interpreted as a success factor in itself but as part of a broader strategy that includes social and cultural dimensions (pp. 41–42).

Applicable to TC-S, Díaz (2006) presents a "knowledge management model" with its elementary components (capture, storage, search, recovery, use and access), for which several success factors must be taken into account. However, due to the multivariate and complex nature of this type of constructs, it is advisable for TC-S companies to "design their own models" that respond to the particularities and needs detected, increasing the probability of successful implementation. In this sense, Zabaleta et al. (2016) interpret the key variables that interrelate and influence for a model supported by organizational culture oriented toward knowledge, technological infrastructure, incentive and motivation system, communication channels, among others, being in short: intellectual capital, organizational learning (basic variable for Mora & González, 2018), innovation and ICT.

Conclusion

The global crisis presented by COVID-19 triggered effects on the TC-S with a duration that is not entirely predictable, which will be present for a long time. The explosion of a more demand in quality and safety and the trend toward the consolidation of telecommunications network infrastructure requires the comprehensive, scalable and continuous development of the subsector.

Society in general will enter full digitalization sooner, requiring operating companies to have adequate and timely technological preparation, in a totally digital scenario, with products (goods and services) tailored to the needs and availability for all applications and technologies, promoting mobile services (including 5G) and promoting the deployment of new Industry 4.0 technologies.

As a derivation, there will be a few TC-S companies of significant size per country, leaving room for others of smaller size acting as service operators and/or content providers. To enable this, government regulations and regulatory bodies must be in place with effective management of policies, plans, programs, sectoral projects and public resources of a technical, tangible and intangible nature (such as the radio spectrum).

The STS of the TC-S must have a long-term strategic vision, but act effectively in the short and medium term, striving for the revealed radical responses (solution approaches), for which it has achieved the commitment of actors external to the technological niches and a learning. Thus, to comply with the socio-technical nature of the change, its experimentation in niches must continue, balancing the technological aspects with the social ones.

TC-S companies must understand the social responsibility that concerns them, as they are providers of services and suppliers of goods in many cases, which are truly essential for the functioning of all economic sectors and citizens, making activities and community life better.

Changing the paradigm, moving from an anthropocentric to an ecocentric perspective, is a real need to "build a contract that transcends society and reincorporates nature in order to recover harmony between human beings and our environment" (Castillo & Ceberio, 2017, p. 105). Ecocentric principles, in order not to generate socio-environmental damage, should be applied in all activities and industries, to which the TC-S characterized as STS is no stranger.

An ecocentric social contract for the subsector revalues nature by recognizing that: (a) it is part (ontological dimension); (b) it has knowledge belonging to a network that interacts (epistemological dimension); and (c) their behaviors and values are in harmony (ethical dimension) (Castillo & Ceberio, 2017). In the last dimension, TC-S companies must take care of resource consumption, electromagnetic and waste pollution and encourage reuse and recycling.

It is important to be aware that society must reflect on its priorities and contributions to sustainable solutions to existing problems. In this, TC-S companies are responsible for minimizing their impacts (Malfavon, 2024), responding with concrete actions, basically in the field of some of the SDGs (No. 9: Industry, innovation and infrastructure; No. 10: Reducing inequalities; No. 11: Sustainable cities and communities; No. 12: Responsible production and consumption; and No. 13: Climate action). Three examples are: (a) growth of the carbon footprint; (b) energy consumption; and (c) reduction of trips and displacements (Bravo, 2021; Malfavon, 2024).

The great challenge for man is to be more aware of being part of nature and act to interpret it and build moral values and principles with it (Castillo & Ceberio, 2017). Solutions to crises and restoration and improvement processes largely depend on the resilience of the TC-S. A multilateral program-project in this field promoted by the ITU is the new GNRP.[11] It is a unique historical moment to enhance the TC-S's contribution to change, recognizing its participation in global environmental problems and providing solutions.

The above applies to both developed and developing countries. In the latter, greater effort is required to determine the problems, size the work required and advance regulations that facilitate progress. In the reality manifested by COVID-19, the TC-S is a key agent to confront the current social and economic situation, not only limited to overcoming the effects of the crisis but also to achieving better preparation for a safer world, reliable and promising.

The importance of managing knowledge, as understood by Escobar (2009), lies in the fact that it encourages improving and facilitating the business exercise, which for TC-S companies has to do with using knowledge as a resource to face challenges and take advantage of opportunities, overcoming crises, breaking obstacles and projecting the business in a modern and innovative way, being able to establish itself as a central piece in the knowledge society.

Creating or renewing quality, value-added, differentiation and innovative goods and services with speed must be based on essential competencies. Due to the trend toward increasingly shorter product life cycles, it is a priority for TC-S companies to be assertive when executing change actions, in favor of the transformation of the industry. According to Díaz (2006), if modern process management and knowledge management practices are incorporated in the subsector, productivity and competitiveness are promoted, since knowing the processes encourages innovation and lasting competitive advantage.

Knowledge management (new management approach) is a tool with high added value and influential competitive power, which recognizes and takes advantage of human talent, as well as its relationship with the environment and its systematized contribution to the innovative process (González & Socarrás, 2021). Therefore, to achieve success in TC-S (or STS) companies and transform the ICT-S (or STR), there must be knowledge management for the execution of strategic actions for sustainable and ecocentric change articulated to the opportunities that have been described.

If as a primary orientation the nonhuman (nature and the physical environment) and the human are taken into account, based on moral principles[12] and the ethical dimension, to envision and build a prosperous future of common interest to all species in the world, independent of purely particular or utilitarian interests and reasons (Castillo & Ceberio, 2017), a sustainable and ecocentric change for knowledge management in the TC-S becomes possible.

Notes

1 Anthropocentrism considers nature as a market of resources freely available to humans, which restricts the approach to environmental problems.
2 The concept of nature refers to the material world formed spontaneously on Earth, which encompasses all physical and life phenomena, as well as the inert components resulting from processes without human intervention. It is made up of living organisms and material and mineral substances.
3 In the case of telecommunications service operators, companies are characterized by being consolidated in the market, having a large number of collaborators, having extensive geographical coverage and a recognized track record.
4 Knowledge assets arise from minimal knowledge to then structure a new one that, articulated with the existing one, is part of a whole. The following can be highlighted: databases, documents, people capabilities, routines, processes and physical space, and so on.
5 Led by Bell Labs with the participation of 58 leading members of industry, academic institutions and non-governmental organizations, in 23 countries, Green Touch is a common effort and step forward in solving the problem of the annual increase in global energy consumption in ICT, with the aim of defining challenges, identifying and creating technologies so that telecommunications networks (including the internet) are 1000 times more energy efficient within a period of five years.
6 Measurements from International Data Corporation (IDC) show that at least 63.5% of operators have invested in AI to improve infrastructure, finding positive business results and focusing on four areas: (a) network optimization, (b) preventive maintenance, (c) virtual assistants, and (d) robotic process automation.

7 From ecology, sustainability (environmental, social or economic) refers to the balance between a species and the resources of its environment. It shows how biological systems maintain productivity. This notion extends to the use of a resource without exceeding its renewal limit.

8 As an ideology, environmentalism proposes that human development must occur respecting nature and through sustainability. Production and consumption of goods and services must be done in quantity and conditions that do not conflict with the environment (waste, pollution, deforestation, loss of biodiversity, invasion and trafficking of species, global warming, drought, abusive consumption, overpopulation, disconnection social, etc.).

9 The concept of biocentrism advocates the defense of nature with a view that is limited to life, both human, plant and animal, without putting one above the other.

10 Actors have a limited capacity as agents to act independently and make free decisions because they belong to large social networks with stable and restrictive rules, typifying what is called a reversal in terms of agency.

11 The ITU GNRP is a place to share and bring together experiences, ongoing initiatives and innovative policy and regulatory measures to help ensure that communities stay connected, support each other and make the most of the power and potential of ICT to save lives.

12 The moral principles that should be protected by an ecocentric environmental ethics are: (a) responsibility, (b) caution, (c) solidarity, and (d) cooperation.

References

Acciona. (January 7, 2024). What is sustainable development? [online]. *Acciona, Business as Unusual.*

Ambientum. (April 8, 2020). Measures in telecommunications during COVID-19. [online]. *Ambientum.*

Andean Development Corporation—CAF. (2020a). *The state of digitalization in latin America in the face of the COVID-19 pandemic.* CAF.

Andean Development Corporation—CAF. (2020b). *The opportunities of digitalization in latin America in the face of COVID-19.* CAF.

Aniorte, I. (April 8, 2020). Challenges and opportunities of the telecommunications sector in the face of COVID-19. [online]. *Mobility Zone.*

Beorlegui, C. (February 24, 2021). Anthropo-centrism versus eco-centrism? [online]. *Magazine of Science, Technology and Religion—Fronteras CTR.*

Bravo, J. (December 3, 2021). Telecommunications and environment. [online]. *The Economist.*

Castillo, Y., & Ceberio, I. (2017). Towards an ecocentric contractualism. *Management and Environment*, *20*(1), 105–112. http://dx.doi.org/10.15446/ga.v20n1.64100

Construible. (January 25, 2010). The Green Touch initiative has the objective of multiplying energy efficiency by 1,000 by transforming communications networks and the internet. [Blog message]. *Construible.es, Sustainable Architecture.*

CSR Commitment. (April 13, 2010). Green Touch is committed to achieving communication networks that are 1,000 times more efficient. [Blog message]. *CSR Commitment, Custonmedia.*

Dano, M. (March 19, 2020). Could COVID-19 supercharge operators' telecom and 5G investments? *Light Reading.*

Díaz, L. (2006). Knowledge management and information and communications technology. *School of Business Administration Magazine*, (58), 41–59.

Escobar, C. (2009). *Perception on Knowledge Management in the Telecommunications Company Comcel S.A. Faculty of Economics, Business and Sustainable Development—FEEDS* (Thesis, University of La Salle).

Europe Press. (April 12, 2010). The Green initiative will multiply the energy efficiency of communication networks by a thousand. [Blog message]. *Europa Press, EPSocial, Responsible.*

García, M. (April 1, 2020). The opportunity of COVID-19 for telecommunications. [Blog message]. *Sectoral Channels. Information and Communication Technologies.*

Geels, F. (2002). Technological transitions as evolutionary reconfiguration processes: A multi-level perspective and a case-study. *Research Policy, 31*(8–9), 1257–1274. https://doi.org/10.1016/S0048-7333(02)00062-8

Geels, F., & Schot, J. (2007). Typology of sociotechnical transition pathways. *Research Policy, 36*(3), 399–417. https://doi.org/10.1016/j.respol.2007.01.003

González, B., & Socarrás, L. (2021). Open innovation based on knowledge management to be applied in telecommunications companies. *SUMMA: Disciplinary Journal in Economic and Social Sciences, 3*(2), 1–22. https://doi.org/10.47666/summa.3.2.39

ICT Consumption. (May 31, 2018). Telecommunications, engine of Industry 4.0. [Blog message]. *ICT Consumption.*

Innovation for Social and Environmental Transformation—ISET. (January 3, 2024). What is transformative innovation? [online]. *ISET.*

Inter-American Telecommunications Commission—CITEL. (2020). Communiqué—CITEL against COVID-19. *Organization of American States—OAS.*

International Telecommunications Union—ITU. (2020a). *Statement by ITU Secretary-General Houlin Zhao on the launch of a global platform to help protect telecommunications networks during the COVID-19 crisis.* ITU.

International Telecommunications Union—ITU. (2020b). *REG4COVID platform: Policy and regulatory experiences and best practices that can improve COVID-19 responses.* ITU.

La Rábida Observatory—LRO. (April 20, 2021). Innovation and transformative missions. [online]. *LRO of Sustainable Development and Climate Change for Ibero-America.*

Malfavon, M. (January 12, 2024). Sustainable telecommunications are committed to a better world. [online]. *Portfolio, Opinion.*

Marín, A., & Coll, F. (October 1, 2021). Ecocentrism. [online]. *Economipedia.*

Mendivelso, D. (2018). Study of the ICT sector. Comprehensive solution for the Emprender Fund of hosting services. [online]. *Financial Fund for Development Projects—FONADE.*

Meya, J. (2020). Challenges and opportunities of the telecommunications sector in the face of COVID-19. [online]. *NAE.*

Molina, G., Añez, J., Lloreda, C., & González, F. (2020). COVID-19: Considerations in technology, media and telecommunications. [online]. *Price Waterhouse Cooper.*

Mora, X., & González, J. (2018). Design proposal for a knowledge management project for companies supplying a telecommunications company. *Espacios Magazine, 39*(19), 2–7.

Nonaka, I., & Takeuchi, H. (1995). *The knowledge creating company: How Japanese companies create the dynamics of innovation.* Oxford University Press.

Pautasio, L. (March 27, 2020). Telecommunications have the opportunity to demonstrate their capacity in the face of COVID-19. [online]. *TeleSemana.com.*

Schot, J., & Geels, F. (2008). Strategic niche management and sustainable innovation journeys: Theory, findings, research agenda, and policy. *Technology Analysis & Strategic Management, 20*(5), 537–554. https://doi.org/10.1080/09537320802292651

Sevilla, A. (April 18, 2020). Economic recession. [Blog message]. *Economipedia.*

Solomon, G. (2021). How artificial intelligence is transforming telecommunications operators. [Blog message]. *DPL News.*

Stangl, H. (April 11, 2020). Post-pandemic economic growth. *Bakertilly.*

Talavera, M. (2018). Transformative innovation: Basic concepts and innovation frameworks. Working document. [online]. *AC Scientific and Technological Consultative Forum. Transformative Innovation Policy Consortium—TIPC.*

Zabala, M. (2012). Knowledge management in telecommunications service provider organizations. *Electronic Journal of Telematics Studies—Telématique, 11*(1), 43–68.

Zabaleta, M., Brito, L., & Garzón, M. (2016). Knowledge management model in the ICT area for a university in the Colombian Caribbean. *Lasallian Research Magazine, 13*(2), 136–150. https://doi.org/10.22507/rli.v13n2a13

11 University social responsibility: evaluation and impact on student satisfaction as an opportunity for knowledge management and sustainability

María del Consuelo Gallardo Aguilar, María Teresa de la Garza Carranza, Salustia Teresa Cano Ibarra and Mónica Servín Cervantes

Introduction

Higher education institutions have a social function by contributing to the transformation of society. The university tasks of these institutions can influence different areas of society, as they are immersed in economic, cultural, social and economic processes of development, through the dissemination of knowledge and the conduct of research, social responsibility at the university level makes sense, with higher education institutions generating positive values for society and for the institutions themselves.

Universities and higher education institutions are organizations that train people and these institutions are where most of the scientific and technological research and development of each country is carried out, thus promoting the development of higher education, including commitment to sustainability and social responsibility, as they are inherent to education as part of their social commitment.

The application of good practices and social responsibility actions within the National Technology of Mexico Celaya campus lead to changes in its structure, ways of working and, above all, in the behavior of the members of this great technological community. These changes and the way students perceive them have become the subject of this study.

This document generally describes what the National Technology of Mexico Celaya campus does in aspects of social responsibility and sustainability, and analyzes how students respond to these initiatives and the influence that social responsibility actions have and student satisfaction with the institution in its participation in sustainability actions.

DOI: 10.4324/9781003465058-11

Theoretical foundation

Social responsibility

Since the beginning of the 20th century, the concept of social responsibility, initially called social function, has existed in higher education institutions. Ojeda and Álvarez (2015) recounted how this concept has been complemented and has even been extended to the area of extension. As a task for its application, The General Assembly of the United Nations (2002) proclaimed 2004–2015 the decade of education for sustainable development and designated UNESCO as the governing body for these goals. In 2009, UNESCO clarified the need to contribute to sustainable development through education.

At the beginning of the year 2000 it was pointed out that, the term university social responsibility was constructed in Latin America, thus calling for the fair and sustainable management of university impacts, both internal and external, educational and cognitive, committing to forming not only good professionals but also good people, sensitive to the problems of others, creative in the articulation of their knowledge with the participatory development of their community (Vallaeys & Álvarez Rodríguez, 2019), which is what social responsibility really seeks in universities.

Several authors have defined university social responsibility, we highlight in this text that Barro cited in Ruíz and Soria (2009) defines university social responsibility as "policy of ethical commitment in the performance of its responsibilities by the university community through management responsible for the educational, cognitive, labour and environmental impacts that the university generates."

Ruíz and Soria (2009), in their research on social responsibility in Spanish universities, highlighted the following aspects to consider whether higher education institutions adjust to the idea of social responsibility:

a) Institutional responsibility is contemplated in the institutional philosophy or quality standards and values that govern the institution.
b) Social responsibility is integrated into the institution's strategic plan.
c) The institution organizes activities related to social responsibility.
d) The university or higher education institution carries out initiatives with socially responsible actions.
e) Two-way communication with the public or interest groups and institutions.
f) An annual report is made by the institution to society.

The National Technology of Mexico Celaya campus complies with all of the above points:

a) The vision explicitly highlights "being a technological higher education institution recognized internationally for the outstanding performance of its graduates who promote sustainable social and economic development, through innovation and research, seeking common well-being," one of the values listed is responsibility. This can be seen in its philosophy described on the website https://celaya.tecnm.mx/mision-y-vision/. Within its integrated policy for the Integrated Management System, in terms of educational organization, it assumes social responsibility considering the relevant educational, scientific and technical developments, including the quality management, environmental management, energy management and occupational health and safety system.
b) Within the 2019–2024 institutional development program, there is a project to integrate study plans and programs with an orientation toward sustainable development and inclusion, the project to promote research with a focus on inclusion, equality and sustainable development; a project to strengthen entrepreneurship with a focus on innovation and sustainability; and consolidate quality, environmental, energy, gender equality, health and safety and social responsibility management systems; additionally projects to reduce the generation of waste through prevention, reduction, recycling and reuse policies and projects for saving and using alternative and renewable energies, as well as caring for the environment.
c) There are within the National Technology of Mexico Celaya campus, more than 18 student groups that promote the carrying out of social responsibility activities, to carry out these activities the organized groups invite the entire community to join, an example is: lynces for service, culture, innovative minds in transformation, to name a few.
d) Although initiatives are taken in favor of social responsibility and sustainable development, such as the 100% single-use plastic-free program, it is not common for them to be disseminated with the explicit message of social responsibility and sustainability; this is an area opportunity for the institution.
e) Two-way communication is constant; there are linking councils for each degree program that continually meet and discuss regional problems and the need to be covered in terms of higher education and social and economic development. These councils are composed of directors and academics from the Tecnológico Nacional of Mexico Celaya campus, employers and representatives of municipal and state governments.
f) The annual accountability report is an exercise that has been conducted and disseminated publicly for several years. This document provides an account of the project progress. The projects are stipulated by the

institutional development program and the report also provides an explanation of the use of economic resources and the projects and challenges that need to be addressed.

Sustainability

Sustainable development is an idea that arises as a necessity for the social system. Lezama and Domínguez (2006) maintain that once it has been recognized that the development model of modern society has reached limits that pose problems of viability in the future, society should not continue with the same pace of exploitation of natural resources. One proposal for sustainable development is to modify the relationship between humans and nature.

For Larrouyet (2015), sustainable development is synonymous with sustainability, representing a balance that must be present in all areas of the individual, which, to date, has not occurred. Economic growth and population increase have resulted in severe environmental problems and the concept of sustainable development has emerged by reviewing this problem and proposing possible solutions so that present generations coexist without compromising the existence of future generations.

Comprehensive sustainability must occur at three levels: environmental, economic and social, in which technology plays a crucial role, given that it is related to the way society's needs to be satisfied. According to Romero (2019), green technologies are a new philosophy that integrates the adoption of measures that tend to conserve resources and reduce waste, covering a group of techniques, methods, materials and research ranging from energy generation and, the production of healthy foods to the creation of non-polluting cleaners.

Institutional processes for sustainability

Environmental problems have solutions whose initiatives emanate from the action of individuals in transformative processes, however, these initiatives are limited, so the degree of involvement of institutions, research centers, universities, government and others must be larger if what you want is to achieve greater impact, Casas et al. (2017) maintain that even individual and group initiatives can become institutional initiatives and can reach local rules or public policies.

Raising awareness about the reality that is experienced can occur through the educational work of communication and socialization of ideas and initiatives. Generally, those who cooperate, collaborate and participate are empowered and strengthen participation and decision-making for a positive transformation in relation to sustainability.

Sustainability finds its reason for being in thought and knowledge, although complexity accompanies sustainability, changing culture is the main challenge, as is widely described by Leff (2000).

The National Technology of Mexico Celaya campus has implemented measures to implement sustainable actions through basic green technology initiatives. In general, the energy-saving management system seeks to reduce energy consumption and cost through the automation of lighting in bathrooms, the change in technology in LED lighting in classrooms and hallways and the implementation of lighting in parking lots, offices and green areas with solar panels.

There are various ways to implement green technologies, Burchardt et al. (2023) say managing energy is one of them, instilling habits that save energy such as leaving the lights off when they are not necessary and taking advantage of sunlight, among others; acquire low-power computing equipment, reduce paper printing as much as possible, these measures exist at the National Technology of Mexico Celaya campus, the question is, ¿do students identify these measures? ¿Are students aware of and participating in these measures?

Methodology

The students participate in social responsibility actions within the National Technology of Mexico Celaya campus and carry out sustainable activities that promote care of the environment. The question is whether the satisfaction of these students with their teachers and, in general, with the institution is related to these actions. Under this premise, the following hypothesis is proposed.

H_1: Students' satisfaction with their teachers and their training institutions and their participation in social responsibility actions directly influence participation and actions that promote sustainability and care for the environment.

The independent variables are:

I1. Student satisfaction with the institution (ITC) and teachers.
I2. Student participation in social responsibility actions.

The dependent variable:

D1. Student participation in actions that promote sustainability.

This study was conducted using a quantitative, exploratory and transversal methodology and an electronic survey was administered to a representative sample of the student population of the National Technology of Mexico Celaya campus. The sample included 436 students out of a total of 6,796 and the responses obtained were from ten courses taught: bachelor's degree in administration, environmental engineering, biochemical engineering, electronic engineering, business management engineering, industrial engineering, mechanical engineering, mechatronics engineering, computer systems engineering and chemical engineering.

The questionnaire was taken from the model proposed by Gallardo et al. (2020) considering the following dimensions: Student participation in university activities and student satisfaction. The 21 items were answered using Likert-type scale and the answers were given by the following numbering: 1 (totally disagree), 2 (disagree), 3 (neutral), 4 (agree) and 5 (totally OK).

Descriptive analysis was carried out and derived from the factor analysis (FA), which was grouped into: (F1) institution and teachers, (F2) participation and social responsibility and (F3) Participation in sustainability actions. The items were grouped as follows:

(F1) Institution and teachers

- Everyone at the university is nice to me (TUAC).
- The staff takes my needs into account when improving teaching practices (PTCNMPD).
- I receive clear and complete information about my studies and related aspects (RICCE).
- Teachers care about student learning (PPAE).
- Teachers encourage students to engage more deeply in course topics (PMEPC).
- Teachers encourage student participation (PFPE).
- Teachers are available to provide guidance to students when needed (PDOE).
- Continuous communication occurs between teachers and students (CCPPE).
- The staff clearly seeks to stimulate the development of students' competencies (PBEDCE).

(F2) Participation and social responsibility

- I contribute to the dialogue and participate in ways to ensure that the students' interests are incorporated into the decisions of the Tecnologico (CDPAIEIDT).
- I participate in the voluntary initiatives of groups that seek to build student solidarity (PIVGCSS).
- I am committed to volunteering and social participation programs (CPVPS).

- I contributed to blood donation campaigns, in particular, or other social cause campaigns (CCDSCCS).
- I participate in sports activities that promote solidarity with the community (PADPSC).
- I feel motivated before participating in cultural outreach activities (MPAPC).
- I carry out activities in collaboration with non-governmental organizations, foundations and other entities (RACONG).

(F3) Participation in sustainability actions

- I participate in initiatives and actions that promote sustainability at school (PIAPSE).
- I voluntarily participate in initiatives that promote environmental care (PVIPCMA).
- I turn off the lights in rooms and hallways that are not being used (ALSPNU).
- I am concerned about improving the facilities of the Tecnológico and student groups (EPMITGE).
- I am motivated by diversity and cultural programs (MDPC).

Of the 436 students who responded to the questionnaire, 46.2% were women, 52.9% were men and 0.9% were non-binary. Their ages ranged between 19 and 22 years, 66.2% declared they were not working and studying and 33.8 % claimed to work and study.

Results

In the section of the questionnaire that considered the items on social responsibility, we found that, of the total sample to which the questionnaire was administered, 47.3% referred to a neutral position in relation to the participation of initiatives and actions that promote sustainability in the school, while 43.4% who reported total participation and participation in initiatives and actions that promote sustainability, the remaining 9.3% did not agree with participation in social responsibility actions.

Voluntary participation in initiatives that promote environmental care amounted to 56.6% of students, contrary to the 9.6% of students who did not participate voluntarily and another 33.8% did not support voluntary participation, responding as neutral to this question.

Energy conservation is an initiative for the application of green technology. When asked whether students turned off the lights in classrooms and hallways that were not in use, 70.8% of them agreed and totally agreed, agreement, whereas only 29.2% responded to disagree, totally disagree, or take a neutral position with this action.

Also speaking of green technologies and care for the environment in relation to fuel consumption, the students were asked if they carpooled with their classmates, this action was only supported by 30.8% of young people, 46.6% took a neutral position and 22.6% disagreed or totally disagreed, here a potential area of opportunity is identified to disseminate information about the advantages of this action as a measure of care for the environment by saving fuel.

Regarding the use of bicycles as a means of transportation to get to school, 67.7% disagreed and totally disagreed, 14.4% took a neutral position on this question and only 18% agreed or totally agreed with the realization. Of this action, there is another important area of opportunity to implement dissemination in relation to this measure that favors the implementation of green technologies and supports sustainability.

The concern for the improvement in the facilities of the National Technology of Mexico Celaya campus is reflected when questioning the young people; 73% of them expressed their concern about this aspect and only 27% responded that they did not agree or totally disagree, or assume a neutral position regarding this concern.

The contribution to dialogue and participation in incorporating them into actions and decisions in favor of the institution showed 46.3% of responses in which students agreed and in total agreement, 40.9% showed a neutral position and 12.7% expressed disagreement or were totally disagreed with this.

When asked about their motivation toward diversity and the cultural programs that are promoted and carried out at the National Technology of Mexico Celaya campus, 64.9% of the students agreed or totally agreed, 28.5% showed a neutral position and only 6.6% they are in disagreement or totally disagreed.

Participation in voluntary initiatives to build student solidarity was also an area of opportunity, as only 40.2% of students responded in agreement or totally agreed with this participation, 46.3% were neutral or indifferent to this and 13.5 % expressed their disagreement or total disagreement with these initiatives.

Regarding the commitment to volunteering and social participation programs, 42.3% of the students agreed or totally agreed, while 42.9% showed a neutral position regarding this commitment and 14.8% responded that they disagreed or totally agreed, disagree with commitment to volunteering and social participation programs.

Participation in sports activities as a way to promote solidarity in the student community was also questioned, in this aspect 41.3% took a position in favor, answering that they agreed or totally agreed with it, 41.8% answered neutrally and 16.9% they said they disagreed or totally disagreed.

Participating in cultural projection activities as something motivating is another aspect considered in the questionnaire; 51.6% of the students agreed or totally agreed with it, 38.7% did not consider this motivation for cultural projection activities as they were in a neutral position and only 8.7% showed disagreement or total disagreement with this type of activity in the institution.

Activities in collaboration with nongovernmental organizations (NGOs) were not a strong aspect among the students of the National Technology of Mexico Celaya campus; only 26.3% of the students responded to having carried out these activities, 46.1% took a neutral position and 27.6 % responded that they did not agree or totally disagreed with it. Here, another area of opportunity is identified to be addressed in terms of promoting initiatives and establishing links with NGOs to promote social responsibility activities and in favor of sustainability.

In the part of the questionnaire that presented aspects of student satisfaction in relation to the National Technology of Mexico Celaya campus, its professors and the institution in general, we have that 58.5% of the students perceived that the staff was friendly to them, 30.1% showed a neutral position and 11.4% disagreed or totally disagreed with the statement.

Knowing whether the staff considered the needs of the students to improve their teaching practices was also included in the questionnaire. Regarding this, 44.1% of the students stated that they agreed or completely agreed with this statement, 41.3% answered neutrally and 14.6% disagreed or totally disagreed with it, which is an area of opportunity to be addressed by the teaching community at the National Technology of Mexico Celaya campus.

Sixty percent of the students stated that they agreed or totally agreed to receive clear and complete information about their studies and aspects related to their studies, 31.3% responded neutrally and only 8.7% disagreed or totally disagreed with this statement. This can be considered a strong point of the institution, although it can always be improved.

Regarding whether teachers care about students' learning, 53% of young people perceived that their teachers care about this learning, 36.1% were neutral regarding this statement and only 10.9% of students did not perceive this concern for the learning.

Further, 54.6% of students agreed or totally agreed with the perception that professors motivated them to participate more deeply in the topics of their course, while 33.8% took a neutral position and 11.7% showed disagreement or total disagreement with this. In another statement about teachers' encouragement of general student participation, 61.6% of students perceived that their teachers encouraged this participation, 32.2% were neutral about it and 6.2% of young people disagreed or totally disagreed. This aspect can be considered a strength of the institution.

The students identified the availability of the teachers to give guidance to the students when necessary; 61.2% of the young people answered that they agreed or totally agreed with it, 32% were neutral and only 6.8% showed disagreement or total disagreement with it.

Another aspect that should be highlighted as a strength is the continuous communication between teachers and students, in which 58% of the students responded that they agreed or completely agreed with this, 35.6% took a neutral position and only 6.4% of the students agreed. I disagree or totally disagree with this communication.

The search to stimulate the development of skills in students was also shown to be a strong aspect, with 60.5% of students perceiving that the staff of the National Technology of Mexico Celaya campus sought the development of their skills, 30.8% expressing themselves in a neutral position and 8.7% of the students disagreed or totally disagreed with this.

Applying FA step-by-step, as suggested (Ferrando & Anguiano, 2010) the preliminary analysis was carried out on the data set using SPSS and the KMO test was .924, which indicates that the sampling was adequate. The level of significance in the Bartlett test was .000, indicating that the analysis was useful for the data collected. The communalities per item ranged from .463 to .729. By performing variable reduction through principal component analysis, three factors were obtained, as shown in Table 11.1, with the rotated component matrix.

Table 11.1 Rotated component matrix

Ítems	*1*	*2*	*3*
PMEPC	0.836		
PFPE	0.818		
CCPPEw	0.801		
PBEDCE	0.799		
PPAE	0.777		
PDOE	0.760		
PTCNMPD	0.758		
RICCE	0.755		
TUAC	0.679		
RACONG		0.826	
CPVPS		0.777	
PIVGCSS		0.733	
CCDSCCS		0.664	
MPAPC		0.576	
PADPSC		0.576	
CDPAIEIDT		0.563	0.447
ALSPNU			0.704
EPMITGE			0.634
PVIPCMA			0.588
MDPC		0.415	0.562
PIAPSE			0.536

Source: Authors' elaboration, extracted from SPSS analysis. Extraction method: principal components analysis. Rotation method: Varimax with Kaiser normalization

Table 11.2 Correlations by factor

Correlations				
		Instyprof	*Particyrs*	*Partacsust*
INSTYPROF	Pearson Correlations	1	.372*	.399*
	Sig. (bilateral)		.000	.000
	N	434	434	434
PARTICYRS	Pearson Correlations	.372*	1	.634*
	Sig. (bilateral)	.000		.000
	N	434	434	434
PARTACSUST	Pearson Correlations	.399*	.634*	1
	Sig. (bilateral)	.000	.000	
	N	434	434	434

Source: Authors' elaboration, extracted from SPSS.

* The correlation is significant at the 0.01 level (two-sided).

The adapted variables are as follows: (1 INSTYPROF) institution and teachers, (2 PARTICYRS) participation and social responsibility and (3 PARTACSUST) participation in sustainability actions. The Pearson correlation coefficient explains the relationship between these variables. The results shown in Table 11.2 were obtained.

The factors being (INSTYPROF) institution and teachers, (PARTICYRS) participation and social responsibility, (PARTACSUST) participation in sustainability actions, according to Cohen cited in Hernández et al. (2018), (F1) "Institution and teachers" have a moderate correlation in the value of .399 with (F3) "Participation in sustainability actions"; in the case of (F2) "Participation in social responsibility actions" the correlation is strong, reaching .634 with (F3) "Participation in sustainability actions."

With the above, we can say that hypothesis H_1 is met: the satisfaction of students with their teachers and their training institution and the participation they have in social responsibility actions directly influences the participation and actions that promote sustainability and environmental care.

Conclusion

The National Technology of Mexico Celaya campus has implemented a series of actions that promote social responsibility and sustainability, starting with manifesting these concepts in its organizational philosophy, implementing the management system integrated with the environmental management system, the energy, the occupational health and safety system, promoting the creation of student groups and supporting the social responsibility actions that these groups carry out, recognition for the achievement of a campus that is 100% free of single-use plastic, among other actions.

This research allowed us to identify how students perceive these actions and how they have been involved in these initiatives. It was possible to identify that communication processes are decisive for students to know the objectives and scope of social responsibility actions, sustainable on campus. Strengths were identified in the perception that students have about their satisfaction with campus staff, the availability of professors to advise students and the encouragement of professors so that students participate in different activities related to their professional training, which can be used to seek greater student participation in sustainability actions, through the implementation of measures in favor of green technologies promoted by academics.

Areas of opportunity were found, such as the low participation of students in activities with NGOs, activities that promote solidarity among the technological community, campaigns and programs for social causes. It is possible to take advantage of good communication between students and teachers, as well as the various media within the campus, carrying out awareness campaigns in favor of sustainability, social responsibility and the use of green technologies.

Derived from the factor analysis, it was found that students' satisfaction with their teachers and their training institution and their participation in social responsibility actions, directly influence the participation and actions that promote sustainability and care for the environment. This can be used to encourage social responsibility actions and motivate teachers to perform well so that they can influence the generation of initiatives and promote sustainability within the campus, thereby forming a culture that is carried to the community and other regions, seeking to expand the circle of influence of the National Technology of Mexico Celaya campus by creating a culture of social responsibility and sustainability among a greater number of people.

It is time for all educational institutions to include actions in their agendas to give collective attention to sustainability problems, which are well received by students; the challenge is to seek initiatives from individuals to bring them to the community and achieve the participation of the entire community, the community within the institutions.

Green technologies contribute to sustainable social development, ensuring long-term economic and social well-being since they preserve natural resources. Seeking sustainability through implementing green technologies is an opportunity for professional training in higher education institutions, particularly at the National Technology of Mexico Celaya campus and the challenge will be to start including this training in the community, even carrying out simple actions such as insisting on turning off lights when they are not necessary, the use of low energy consumption equipment, paper reduction and others that are already taking place in some areas of the campus, but that have not been widely communicated or the information has not had enough impact for it to be a measure adopted by the community.

References

Burchardt, H.J., Gárgano, C., & Christel, L. (2023). *¿De la sustentabilidad al desarrollo?: entre el extractivismo verde y la transformación socioambiental* (1st ed.). CLACSO. https://libreria.clacso.org/publicacion.php?p=2993&c=39

Casas, A., Torres, I., Delgado, L.A., Rangel, L.S., Torres, G.J., Cruz, A., . . . Farfán, B. (2017). Ciencia para la sustentabilidad: investigación, educación y procesos participativos. *Revista Mexicana de Biodiversidad, UNAM, 88*, 113–128. https://doi.org/10.1016/j.rmb.2017.10.003

Ferrando, P.J., & Anguiano-Carrasco, C. (2010). El análisis factorial como técnica de investigación en psicología. *Papeles del Psicólogo, 31*(1), 18–33. www.redalyc.org/pdf/778/77812441003.pdf

Gallardo, V.D., Folgado, F.J.A., Hipolito, O.F., & Valdez, J.L.E. (2020). Social responsibility attitudes and behavior's influence on university student's satisfaction. *Social Sciences, 9*(2), 1–21. https://doi.org/10.3390/socsci9020008

Hernández, L.J.D., Espinosa, C.F., Rodríguez, J.E., Chacón, R.J.G., Toloza, S.C.A., Arenas, T.M.K., . . . Bermúdez, P.V.J. (2018). Sobre el uso adecuado del coeficiente de correlación de Pearson: definición, propiedades y suposiciones. *Revista AVFT, 37*(5), 587–595. www.revistaavft.com/images/revistas/2018/avft_5_2018/25sobre_uso_adecuado_coeficiente.pdf

Larrouyet, M.C. (2015). *Desarrollo sustentable. Origen, evolución y su implementación para el cuidado del planeta.* Universidad Nacional de Quilmes, Bernal, Argentina, 1–47. http://ridaa.unq.edu.ar/handle/20.500.11807/154

Leff, E. (2000). Tiempo de sustentabilidad. *Ambiente & Sociedad, 6*(7), 5–14. https://doi.org/10.1590/S1414-753X2000000100001

Lezama, J.L., & Domínguez, J. (2006). *Medio ambiente y sustentabilidad urbana.* IIJ-UNAM, 433–459. https://archivos.juridicas.unam.mx/www/bjv/libros/6/2638/20.pdf

Ojeda, H.J.F., & Álvarez, O.D.G. (2015). Responsabilidad social en las universidades: antecedentes, trayectorias y perspectivas. *Revista COEPES, 4*(12). www.revistacoepesgto.mx/revistacoepes12/responsabilidad-social-en-las-universidades-antecedentes-trayectorias-y-perspectivas

Romero, T.I. (2019). *Factores culturales de los consumidores de tecnologías verdes en la Ciudad de México* (Tesis, IPN). http://tesis.ipn.mx/handle/123456789/31252

Ruíz, M.I.M., & Soria, I.M.M. (2009). Responsabilidad social en las universidades de España. *Revista razón y palabra, 70*, 1–22. www.redalyc.org/pdf/1995/199520478009.pdf

Vallaeys, F., & Álvarez Rodríguez, J. (2019). Hacia una definición latinoamericana de responsabilidad social universitaria. Aproximación a las preferencias conceptuales de los universitarios. *Educación XX1, 22*(1), 93–116. www.redalyc.org/articulo.oa?id=70667730006

12 Sensors and signal processing used to increase knowledge management of algae production

Luis Miguel Contreras-Medina, Diana Victoria Melo-Sabogal, Daphne Ojeda-Rodríguez and Guadalupe Esmeralda Contreras-Morales

Introduction

The CO_2 emissions have inspired investigators to search for new approaches to diminish and try to reduce the consequences of this. Microalgae have been resulting in a promising option because of their high photosynthetic efficiency, which is at least 20 times more efficient than terrestrial plants and several chemical methods to remove CO_2 from the ambient (Tamil Selvan et al., 2022). Microalgae have an important role and are responsible for 40% of global photosynthesis and produce almost 50% of atmospheric oxygen in the world (Elisabeth et al., 2021a). The biodiversity of microalgae is enormous; there are more than 50,000 different species of microalgae and only 30,000 approximately have been studied. These species offer great potential and there is a necessity for studies to exploit them (Elisabeth et al., 2021a). Also, microalgae could be used to generate biofuel, which is a green energy alternative that helps to substitute fuel and other non-renewable energy resources. Another non-less important advantage of algae is the capacity to adapt and live in several difficult environmental conditions, offering easy spaces commonly not used to grow algae and biotechnological sources of energy, food and CO_2 harvesting (Porras Reyes et al., 2024a). Also, microalgal farming is used too to produce food, medication and cosmetics (Das & Roy Chowdhury, 2023) and under stress, conditions non-ideal to microalgae, they can produce metabolites and bioactive compounds, which can be controlled and maximized by using sensors, signal processing and actuators (Elisabeth et al., 2021a). According to Das & Roy Chowdhury (2023), a network of sensors and the Internet of Things (IoT) has the potential to improve efficiently the production of biorefineries, saving money and time and allowing the monitoring and control of the biological process.

According to Javaid et al. (2021), a sensor is a device that detects changes in the environment and an electrical reaction is generated, in voltage or current form commonly, the sources of this can be light, temperature,

DOI: 10.4324/9781003465058-12

pressure, pH, humidity, movements, CO_2 variations, and so forth, and the applications of sensor are huge, going from healthcare to variables related to the growth of algae. Nowadays, there are several kinds of sensors used to monitor related variables with microalgae growth and to detect harmful species of microalgae and specific microalgae for a particular purpose; those sensors go from conventional sensors, optical sensors, amperometry sensors and to biosensors (Chin Chwan Chuong et al., 2022). Several variables need to be calculated indirectly, principally variables that need to be monitored online and are related to the physiology of algae. This demands the use of basic sensors and signal-processing techniques to infer information indirectly to phenomena related to chemical or biological functions (Havlik et al., 2022). According to Abraham (2017), signal processing condenses the measurement to extract information related to some state or variables of nature; the measurement is commonly realized by sensors, which, in a sophisticated process, can be many, making it difficult the task to extract the information. Therefore, signal processing needs to increase its capabilities to process a huge quantity of data derived from a more constant increment of the quantity of data and needs to reduce the time processing to extract valuable information as soon as possible to make a pertinent decision about a process. The growth algae process needs to be monitored to try to increase production; the variables that need to be monitored have different origins, such as physical, chemical and biological (Havlik et al., 2022).

The present work shows sensors, systems and signal processing techniques to monitor important variables related to the growth of algae and a perspective of the future of this field in terms of monitoring variables to increase algae production.

Biomass monitor of algae

Biomass is the most important variable because most products are obtained from cells and therefore, the industry of algae is procuring an increased quantity of biomass (Porras Reyes et al., 2024b). Microalgae contain abundant lipids, pigments, vitamins, proteins, essential minerals and so forth. There are several methods to measure biomass, such as dry weight, chlorophyll concentration, turbidity and absorbance, the last three fall inside the optical methods. The most common technique used in laboratories and the industry to know algae growth rate is the optical density at wavelengths of 750 and 550 nm (Porras Reyes et al., 2024b). Following are cited several works used to calculate algae biomass.

Turbidostat is a continuous culture system where adjustment of the nutrient depends on the density of biomass; the biomass is measured commonly by light transmittance (Dunham, 2010). There are few commercial options yet, but this can be built by using microcontrollers and pumps. In the following, there are some methods to measure the biomass of microalgae. A turbidostat is presented by Nguyen and Rittmann (2018). This is a low-cost system that includes an infrared-based sensor to measure turbidity connected to an Arduino with ATmega microcontroller and auxiliary boards to control the actuators. This system was able to maintain biomass concentration for all steps and can be employed to control growth rate and biomass production and by consequence to increase the production of microalgae. As can be seen, optical methods can be applied to not only monitor biomass but also monitor physiological variables, an example of this is presented in the work (Lieutaud et al., 2019), where applied Raman spectroscopy to characterize physiological kinetics of the microalgal process. In this work were acquired 35 Raman signatures for each growth day that correspond of spectral fingerprints several elements such as chlorophyll a, beta-carotene lipids and nucleic acids. These days, artificial intelligence (AI) has been used to identify the best time to harvest algae before its degradation; this is done by using a wide variety of linked sensors and modifying the growth conditions according to the result of the machine learning stage, to discover the most favorable growth parameters (Peter et al., 2023). The necessity of continuous monitoring biomass using low-cost methods has been the motivation to employ other techniques, such as RGB analysis and grayscale models, those have been used in photobioreactors with wastewater and different conditions for *Chlorella vulgaris* and was demonstrated that these techniques are very effective under controlled lighting condition, contrasting with photobioreactors installed outdoors and of different design (Salgueiro et al., 2022), the authors mentioned that the accuracy of the method could be improved by using a high-quality image sensor. The work presented by Nguyen et al. (2022) shows a complete system to monitor the density of microalgae, pH and dissolved Oxygen by using a 600 × 800 pixel camera resolution, a Raspberry pi and an Arduino nano electronic board, which, by using a predefined model, the system can be able of predict the density of microalgae, and by consequence, this is used to control de nutrient supplement and also, to determine the best time of harvest. The measurements are done by carrying water from the principal container to a small container to take all the calculus and after that, the sample taken is returned to the container. The work presented by Ratha et al. (2016) was the estimation of biomass by a moisture analyzer, which is in charge of drying the sample by using a halogen lamp generating a temperature between 40 °C and 200 °C, the time taken to dry samples of different microalgae species varies, this is an artisanal method but is used to obtain reliable estimation with the disadvantage of the time required for drying.

Temperature measurements in algae

The temperature is of great importance in many biological processes and algae growth is not the exception. There are reports that the optimum temperature for microalgae growth is between 20 °C and 25 °C. Nonetheless, this range can vary depending on the growth medium and the species to be employed (Elisabeth et al., 2021b). The measurement of temperature can be achieved by using contact and non-contact principles; contact has the disadvantage of electrical wiring, while the non-contact method is based principally on optical principles, has been used and has gained huge attention for biological and medical applications (Fallahi Chegeni et al., 2021). In the work presented by Singh and Sing (2015), differences in growth rate were demonstrated in species of algae under treatments of constant light and non-constant light; this corroborates the influence of the temperature on algae growth. Algae productivity increases when the pond temperature is up to a maximum temperature that is optimal; after that point, the increase in algae respiration and productivity is reduced (Singh & Singh, 2015). Also, in this work (Singh & Singh, 2015), it is reported that the optimal temperature of algae growth varies depending on the month of year and species, making, for example, the better range of temperature for blue-green algae from 0 °C to 20 °C.

Lipids measurement in algae

The investigation of microalgae lipids is focused principally on producing biodiesel; nonetheless, there are several limitations in producing it, such as cost production and limitations of the energy sector; because of this, lipid production has been focused too to produce lipid products for the pharmaceutical industry and the food sector which is reported to carry out benefits for the health of persons.

To increase the production of algae for biofuel applications, it is important to develop sensors able to quantify and detect lipids. Some common methods to quantify and detect lipids are gravimetry and chromatography; however, these require organic solvents and are laborious, time-consuming and costly. Optical methods proposed to solve these disadvantages have been proposed, principally those based on image quantification. The work (Jung et al., 2018) shows the identification in thermograms of lipid droplets in *Nannochloropsis oculata* cells by measuring three-dimensional refractive index distribution, demonstrating that a rapid quantification of lipid content can be achieved in individual microalgae cells by using thermography.

Other interesting works show the use of Raman micro spectroscopy for fast characterization of the composition of intracellular regions in cells; the researchers achieve quantification of the degree of unsaturation of algal lipids, which is an important parameter in green energies and the food industry, the investigators employed Raman spectral peaks related to saturated and unsaturated carbon-carbon bond lipids (Samek et al., 2010). Another method to calculate lipids is infrared spectroscopy; this method is non-invasive and can be applied to a small number of cells for real-time measurement of lipids and screening of cultures (Patel et al., 2019). Another optical method is fluorescence, which has been used to quantify lipid content during growth time, and this methodology can be used to know the best time for harvesting and by using this method, the researchers demonstrated that technology of aggregation-induced emission and fluorescent activating cell sorting (FACS) can be used to produce the double of yield, compared with the generation using natural selection (Liu et al., 2022). Another interesting method is terahertz spectroscopy to determine lipid content in *Scenedesmus obliquus* (*S. obliquus*), the researchers used PLS algorithm to model terahertz data versus lipid content of microalgae under nitrogen stress, the main contribution of this work is the correlation of terahertz characteristic peak and the lipid content calculated using gravimetry reaches 0.96, the advantage of this methodology is its suitability for industrial production or non-sophisticated laboratories that commonly require rapid at low-frequency screening and also, the constraints of using terahertz spectroscopy is less than Raman spectroscopy and the determination of lipid is easier too (Liu et al., 2022).

Signal processing in algae production

Signal processing is a crucial step in analyzing information coming from sensors, principally in nonlinear phenomena such as those occurring in microalgae cells. There is a huge quantity of signal processing algorithms that have been employed to estimate, indirectly, several variables of micro algae.

A sophisticated example of signal processing applied to algae is the use of the convolutional neural network (CNN), this has been employed using a low-cost camera to calculate density; the work (Nguyen et al., n.d.) obtained an R^2 value between density prediction and the value measured of 0.9997, which is high compared with other references. In this work, the CNN model incorporates, as inputs color images and gives, as output, the density of microalgae; the experiment was achieved utilizing the microalgal strain *Chlorella vulgaris*. The system used consists of a Raspberry board with a low-cost camera embedded in a dark box to avoid external light interference; this takes a sample of the principal container to take the images and obtain a density calculus. Another important area where signal processing has been employed is in the identification of species of microalgae. This is important because the probability of contamination is always high in closed photobioreactors. One of the principal reasons for non-successful production and for large-scale production is the contamination of microalgae bioreactor, becoming it in one of the major challenges in the field, so there are several works that have been tried to identify species of microalgae using principally cameras and AI tools such as machine learning. In the work presented by Otálora et al. (2023) were used a CNN that utilized, as input, segmented images coming from a sample culture of different species of microalgae, the CNN where trained to classify cell by its genus and where fixed classification thresholds were used to achieved the characterization of cultures.

Machine learning has increased its popularity because of the constant increment of computational capacities, which grows along the volume of data collected from different natural phenomena; the advantage of this technique is the learning obtained directly from data, allowing it to solve highly specific problems without an explicitly described program, like the learning process of humans. This technique has been used in microalgae production, for example, for pH prediction based on CNN or prediction trees, while other works use machine learning for obtaining productivity prediction; nonetheless, in the microalgae field, machine learning techniques found major applicability in microalgal classification, which avoids contamination in closed photobioreactors and also the identification of harmful microalgae, which affect the health of habitat and humans (Chong et al., 2023). Another very popular technique to process data is the deep learning method, which is used principally to detect algae and classify them according to their category. In the work shown by Abdullah et al. (2022) were used various versions of CNN based on the You Only Look Once (YOLO) model, such as YOLOv3, YOLOv4, and YOLOv5, to detect harmful algae bloom of four classes (*Cosmarium, Scenedesmus, Closterium and Spirogyra*), previously introduce the data to CNN, the information of 400 microscopic algal images were preprocessed and some results corresponding to mean average precision (mAP) of YOLOv3, YOLOv4 and YOLO v5 were 75.3%, 83% and 91%, respectively. The authors mentioned that this work is pioneering because they are applying YOLO models to detect algae and classify them from images. The justification of this work is the importance of locating harmful algae bloom because they reduce the quality of freshwater and increase the risk to the health of humans, water bodies and aquatic systems. A similar work (Yang et al., 2021) employs CNN and deep learning based on transfer learning to automatically discriminate algae and identification of damaging algae. The manuscript reports that 11 species of harmful algae and 31 species of harmless algae were compiled and transferred to 5 CNN classification CNN models (AlexNet, VGG16, GoogLeNet, ResNet50 and MobileNetV2). From the five models, GoogLeNet reach the higher recognition accuracy. These experiments support that the combination of various CNN can help successfully with the recognition of harmful algae. In another similar work, the manuscript (Gaur et al., 2023) mentioned the use of the CNN model for monitoring 15 bloom-forming algae. They used some equal and some different CNN models as previous work (MobileNet V-2, Visual Geometry Group-16 (VGG-16), AlexNet and ResNeXt-50). Also, different convolution layers with adaptative moment estimation (Adam), root-mean-square propagation (RMSprop) and rectified linear unit (ReLU) as a factor of estimation were used. The best classification accuracy was obtained using the ResNeXT-50 model; these two works support that probably the path for algae recognition and classification in open and closed systems is AI.

The necessity of constant monitoring to detect organisms that increase the risk of ecosystem function has inspired researchers, in the work presented by (Yuan et al., 2023), develop an AI chip embedded with a model, which employs the morphology of algae to achieve, in real-time, algae classification, based on Deep Neural Network (AMDNN). This signal processing method was tested on 11250 algae images, which contain the most common HAB classes in Hong Kong and reach a 99.87% of accuracy, these developments are important because it is able to realize on-line and real-time classification, and by consequence, it can be employed as early warning systems for environmental and human health risks.

Perspectives

As can be seen, microalgae have very wide industrial applications for biofuel generation, food, metabolic compounds and CO_2 capture; there are many industries that have employed bioreactors to grow microalgae for different applications and one of the principal problems is the contamination of these bioreactors and, also, to know the precise moment for harvesting, to solve these drawbacks, there is the necessity of sensors to monitor several variables involved in the process of growth to achieve online and real-time monitoring of algae, in order to indicate as soon as possible the condition of algae to help to increase the productivity.

Another important necessity is to identify different species of algae to help reduce the risk to the health of persons and ecosystems and to identify a certain variety of algae to produce certain benefits, for example, bioactive compounds, biofuel, or food. Because the characteristics used for doing the classification are highly nonlinear and, in most cases, do not follow an easily predicted pattern. AI, as a signal processing technique, has been gaining a lot of popularity. This has been used to classify between harmful and non-harmful species if algae with very good results and easy-to-use platforms have been developed to realize this classification.

It seems that with the constant scale of computing resources and the constant increase of data coming from sensors of different industries, AI could be the best signal-processing method to achieve the characterization of species of algae and to control the variables involved in algae growth to increase the production of the derived products of this organism.

References

Abdullah, A.S., Khan, Z., Hussain, A., Athar, A., & Kim, H.C. (2022). Computer vision based deep learning approach for the detection and classification of algae species using microscopic images. *Water (Switzerland)*, *14*(14). https://doi.org/10.3390/w14142219

Abraham, D.A. (2017). Chapter 11—signal processing. In T.H. Neighbors & D. Bradley (Eds.), *Applied underwater acoustics* (pp. 743–807). Elsevier. https://doi.org/10.1016/B978-0-12-811240-3.00011-4

Chin Chwan Chuong, J.J., Rahman, M., Ibrahim, N., Heng, L.Y., Tan, L.L., & Ahmad, A. (2022). Harmful microalgae detection: Biosensors versus some conventional methods. *Sensors*, *22*(9). https://doi.org/10.3390/s22093144

Chong, J.W.R., Khoo, K.S., Chew, K.W., Ting, H.-Y., & Show, P.L. (2023). Trends in digital image processing of isolated microalgae by incorporating classification algorithm. *Biotechnology Advances*, *63*, 108095. https://doi.org/10.1016/j.biotechadv.2023.108095

Das, A., & Roy Chowdhury, A. (2023). Chapter 16—Algal cultivation in the pursuit of emerging technology for sustainable development. In S.A. Bandh & F.A. Malla (Eds.), *Valorization of microalgal biomass and wastewater treatment* (pp. 357–366). Elsevier. https://doi.org/10.1016/B978-0-323-91869-5.00014-4

Dunham, M.J. (2010). Chapter 19—Experimental evolution in yeast: A practical guide. In *Methods in enzymology* (Vol. 470, pp. 487–507). Academic Press. https://doi.org/10.1016/S0076-6879(10)70019-7

Elisabeth, B., Rayen, F., & Behnam, T. (2021a). Microalgae culture quality indicators: A review. In *Critical reviews in biotechnology* (Vol. 41, Issue 4, pp. 457–473). Taylor and Francis Ltd. https://doi.org/10.1080/07388551.2020.1854672

Elisabeth, B., Rayen, F., & Behnam, T. (2021b). Microalgae culture quality indicators: A review. In *Critical reviews in biotechnology* (Vol. 41, Issue 4, pp. 457–473). Taylor and Francis Ltd. https://doi.org/10.1080/07388551.2020.1854672

Fallahi Chegeni, N., Ijadi Maghsoodi, P., Habibi, M., Zare-Behtash, H., Majles Ara, M.H., & Heydari, E. (2021). Hybrid dissolved-oxygen and temperature sensing: A nanophotonic probe for real-time monitoring of Chlorella Algae. *Sensors*, *21*(19). https://doi.org/10.3390/s21196553

Gaur, A., Pant, G., & Jalal, A.S. (2023). Comparative assessment of artificial intelligence (AI)-based algorithms for detection of harmful bloom-forming algae: An eco-environmental approach toward sustainability. *Applied Water Science*, *13*(5). https://doi.org/10.1007/s13201-023-01919-0

Havlik, I., Beutel, S., Scheper, T., & Reardon, K.F. (2022). On-line monitoring of biological parameters in microalgal bioprocesses using optical methods. *Energies*, *15*(3). https://doi.org/10.3390/en15030875

Javaid, M., Haleem, A., Rab, S., Pratap Singh, R., & Suman, R. (2021). Sensors for daily life: A review. *Sensors International*, *2*. https://doi.org/10.1016/j.sintl.2021.100121

Jung, J.H., Hong, S.J., Kim, H.B., Kim, G., Lee, M., Shin, S., . . . Park, Y.K. (2018). Label-free non-invasive quantitative measurement of lipid contents in individual microalgal cells using refractive index tomography. *Scientific Reports*, *8*(1). https://doi.org/10.1038/s41598-018-24393-0

Lieutaud, C., Assaf, A., Gonçalves, O., Wielgosz-Collin, G., & Thouand, G. (2019). Fast non-invasive monitoring of microalgal physiological stage in photobioreactors through Raman spectroscopy. *Algal Research*, *42*, 101595. https://doi.org/10.1016/j.algal.2019.101595

Liu, H., Yan, N., Wong, T.Y., Lam, H., Lam, J.W.Y., Kwok, R.T.K., . . . Tang, B.Z. (2022). Fluorescent imaging and sorting of high-lipid-content strains of green Algae by using an aggregation-induced emission Luminogen. *ACS Nano*, *16*(9), 14973–14981. https://doi.org/10.1021/acsnano.2c05976

Nguyen, B.T., & Rittmann, B.E. (2018). Low-cost optical sensor to automatically monitor and control biomass concentration in microalgal cultivation. *Algal Research*, *32*, 101–106. https://doi.org/10.1016/j.algal.2018.03.013

Nguyen, D.K., Nguyen, H.Q., Dang, H.T.T., Nguyen, V.Q., & Nguyen, L. (2022). A low-cost system for monitoring pH, dissolved oxygen and algal density in continuous culture of microalgae. *HardwareX*, *12*. https://doi.org/10.1016/j.ohx.2022.e00353

Nguyen, L., Nguyen, D.K., Nghiem, T.X., & Nguyen, T. (n.d.). Convolutional neural network regression for low-cost microalgal density estimation.

Otálora, P., Guzmán, J.L., Acién, F.G., Berenguel, M., & Reul, A. (2023). An artificial intelligence approach for identification of microalgae cultures. *New Biotechnology*, *77*, 58–67. https://doi.org/10.1016/j.nbt.2023.07.003

Patel, A., Antonopoulou, I., Enman, J., Rova, U., Christakopoulos, P., & Matsakas, L. (2019). Lipids detection and quantification in oleaginous microorganisms: An overview of the current state of the art. *BMC Chemical Engineering*, *1*(1). https://doi.org/10.1186/s42480-019-0013-9

Peter, A.P., Chew, K.W., Pandey, A., Lau, S.Y., Rajendran, S., Ting, H.Y., . . . Show, P.L. (2023). Artificial intelligence model for monitoring biomass growth in semi-batch Chlorella vulgaris cultivation. *Fuel*, *333*, 126438. https://doi.org/10.1016/j.fuel.2022.126438

Porras Reyes, L., Havlik, I., & Beutel, S. (2024a). Software sensors in the monitoring of microalgae cultivations. In *Reviews in environmental science and biotechnology*. Springer Science and Business Media B.V. https://doi.org/10.1007/s11157-023-09679-8

Porras Reyes, L., Havlik, I., & Beutel, S. (2024b). Software sensors in the monitoring of microalgae cultivations. In *Reviews in environmental science and biotechnology*. Springer Science and Business Media B.V. https://doi.org/10.1007/s11157-023-09679-8

Ratha, S.K., Rao, P.H., Govindaswamy, K., Jaswin, R.S., Lakshmidevi, R., Bhaskar, S., & Chinnasamy, S. (2016). A rapid and reliable method for estimating microalgal biomass using a moisture analyser. *Journal of Applied Phycology*, *28*(3), 1725–1734. https://doi.org/10.1007/s10811-015-0731-1

Salgueiro, J.L., Pérez, L., Sanchez, Á., Cancela, Á., & Míguez, C. (2022). Microalgal biomass quantification from the non-invasive technique of image processing through red—green—blue (RGB) analysis. *Journal of Applied Phycology*, *34*(2), 871–881. https://doi.org/10.1007/s10811-021-02634-6

Samek, O., Jonáš, A., Pilát, Z., Zemánek, P., Nedbal, L., Tríska, J., . . . Trtílek, M. (2010). Raman microspectroscopy of individual algal cells: Sensing unsaturation of storage lipids in vivo. *Sensors*, *10*(9), 8635–8651. https://doi.org/10.3390/s100908635

Singh, S.P., & Singh, P. (2015). Effect of temperature and light on the growth of algae species: A review. In *Renewable and sustainable energy reviews* (Vol. 50, pp. 431–444). Elsevier Ltd. https://doi.org/10.1016/j.rser.2015.05.024

Tamil Selvan, S., Velramar, B., Manickam Dakshinamoorthi, B., Ramamurthy, D., & Balasundram, S. (2022). Chapter 12—Microalgal adsorption of carbon dioxide: A green approach. In J.A. Malik (Ed.), *Microbes and microbial biotechnology for green remediation* (pp. 227–246). Elsevier. https://doi.org/10.1016/B978-0-323-90452-0.00014-1

Yang, M., Wang, W., Gao, Q., Zhang, L., Ji, Y., & Geng, S. (2021). Automatic recognition of harmful Algae images using multiple CNNs. *2021 International Conference on Computer Engineering and Artificial Intelligence (ICCEAI)*, 276–280. https://doi.org/10.1109/ICCEAI52939.2021.00055

Yuan, A., Wang, B., Li, J., & Lee, J.H.W. (2023). A low-cost edge AI-chip-based system for real-time algae species classification and HAB prediction. *Water Research*, *233*, 119727. https://doi.org/10.1016/j.watres.2023.119727

13 Wine tourism as a driver of knowledge management practices and the sustainability of the new rurality

Margarete Luisa Arbugeri

Introduction

The European Charter for Wine Tourism (2006) states that wine tourism is understood as the development of tourist, leisure and leisure activities dedicated to the cultural and oenological discovery of the vineyard, wine and its territory, with wine tourism being a multidimensional system resulting from the interaction of the territory, tourism and wine culture subsystems.

For its part, the Georgian Declaration on Wine Tourism highlights that wine tourism (UNWTO, 2016):

- (i) contributes to the promotion of sustainable tourism by promoting the heritage of the destination;
- (ii) generates economic and social benefits for the main actors in each destination;
- (iii) plays an important role in terms of the preservation of cultural and natural resources;
- (iv) provides unique and innovative tourism products, maximizing synergies in tourism development; and
- (v) provides an opportunity for underdeveloped tourist destinations, in most cases in rural areas.

Therefore, wine tourism is an important economic and social activity (Hojman & Hunter-Jones, 2012), since it emerges as a profitable sector, capable of generating considerable economic development (Marzo-Navarro & Pedraja-Iglesias, 2012), as well as the development of the territory through the generation of employment and wealth, thus improving the quality of life of the total population (De la Torre et al., 2012).

It may be relevant to the differentiation of a region in the tourism market (Popp & McCole, 2016), representing an increasingly significant component of the regional and rural tourism products of wine-producing countries (Bruwer, 2003).

DOI: 10.4324/9781003465058-13

From the perspective of Rodríguez et al. (2010), wine tourism creates a perfect symbiosis of the wine product with all the surroundings, allowing the tourist to enjoy a different product, discover a new place and contribute to the socio-economic development of some rural regions, promoting the sustainable development of the territory.

On the other hand, Stewart et al. (2008) consider that this type of tourism promotes wine and culture, which can often be the main attractions to visit a given region.

In this sense, wine tourism works as a means of reactivating certain rural regions and is a complementary source of economic resources linked to the wine sector (Rodríguez et al., 2010), in addition to being used by companies to promote and establish a long-term relationship with their customers (O'Neill & Charters, 2000). In this way, wine tourism involves a broad ecosystem of actors (Filopoulos & Frittella, 2019).

In Portugal, wine tourism has been gaining strength (Filopoulos & Frittella, 2019), being one of the sectors with rapid growth potential in the country (Trigo & Silva, 2022), representing an important element whose capacity to boost not only is limited to the economic dimension but also has repercussions at a social level as an enhancer of sustainable local development (Maduro et al., 2015).

By addressing the topic of sustainable wine tourism, it is not intended to explore the different views on the concept of sustainability, nor to question whether it is possible to achieve sustainability in tourist destinations. First of all and to clarify, normally when this topic is addressed, it is assumed as a tourist destination, a territory with a socio-cultural, economic and political dynamic fueled, in large part, by tourist activity.

Therefore, a territory that recognized for having a set of facilities, services and experiences of a tourist nature and that, due to this fact, presents a considerable flow of visitors. Consequently, a territory, which presupposes a structured and articulated ecosystem, is composed of a local community and a set of actors, from the public and private sectors, who act directly or indirectly in the tourism sector.

The complexity of a tourist destination is related not so much to its physical size, but mainly to the size and diversity of companies, services and people who share the same territory, whether or not they are involved in the tourist activity.

This is the scenario that makes it difficult—or even impossible—to find effective examples of sustainable tourist destinations, because, as a whole, it implies the sustainability of companies, companies, families that operate in that territory or that relate and interact with it, on a one-off or permanent basis (visitors, tourists, suppliers, among others). Despite this, it is important to develop good practices aimed at destinations that are more environmentally efficient, more dynamic and socially and economically integrated and, in political terms, more democratic, more conscious and participatory.

In this sense, it can be seen that organizations are encouraged to implement sustainable practices (Mark-Herbert et al., 2007) and sustainability is a paradigm that affects many sectors of activity due to increased pressure from stakeholders, whether for economic or political reasons (Flores, 2018).

According to Boiral et al. (2017), the pressures that exist for the conservation of biodiversity, particularly in industries whose core business is the exploitation of natural resources, reinforce the need to implement specific measures in this area and also indicate that these measures are related to ethical and environmental issues, since biodiversity conservation is increasingly considered a critical component of sustainability.

There are several instruments that have been developed to help tourist destinations move toward sustainability. Of particular note is the European System of Tourism Indicators (ETIS), developed by the European Commission, for the monitoring and sustainable management of destinations. The ETIS consists of 43 core indicators covering four key categories for effective sustainable management of the tourist destination and its monitoring. These indicators are complemented by a set of additional indicators, adjusted to the specific particularities of some destinations, related to transnational coastal, maritime, accessibility and cultural routes (European Commission, 2016).

The complexity of a tourist destination is related not so much to its physical size, but mainly to the size and diversity of companies, services and people who share the same territory, whether or not they are involved in the tourist activity.

Similar to the concept of wine tourism, the concept associated with the product of wine tourism is constantly developing and opinions are not unanimous. The tourism product is approached as a set of tangible and intangible elements, of finite duration and within an appropriate environment, which are specifically associated with each tourist (Carmichael, 2000; Olsen et al., 2007).

The interactions between existing resources and tourism resources, infrastructures and services result in the tourism product. The tourist and the location are the main factors that determine the supply and demand of this product and the tourist should be the central point of development on the supply side of wine tourism (Marzo-Navarro & Pedraja-Iglesias, 2012). Therefore, it is essential to understand what tourists are looking for and what the destination can offer and how it can do it.

For Quian et al. (2018), tourism is an integrating reflection of economic, social and cultural phenomena, which indicates that research on sustainability in wine tourism, must be comprehensive and multidimensional.

In addition, alongside visitors and all those who work in and for the tourism sector, there is also the local community, which is partly made up of families, businesses and institutions that have no connection with tourism.

When looking for references, effective examples of sustainable tourist destinations, it is very difficult to find them because, as a whole, it implies the sustainability of the businesses, companies, families that operate in that territory or that relate and interact with it, on a specific or permanent basis (visitors, tourists, suppliers, among others).

It should be noted that the good practices developed should aim at destinations that are more environmentally efficient, more dynamic and socially and economically integrated and, in political terms, more democratic, more conscious and participatory.

To help organizations and the community develop sustainable practices, international organizations have been looking for instruments that have been developed to help tourism destinations, including wine tourism, migrate to sustainability. Among the instruments are the European System of Tourism Indicators (ETIS), developed by the European Commission, for the monitoring and sustainable management of destinations.

The ETIS consists of 43 core indicators covering four key categories for effective sustainable management of the tourist destination and its monitoring. These indicators are complemented by a set of additional indicators, adjusted to the specific particularities of some destinations, related to transnational coastal, maritime, accessibility and cultural routes (European Commission, 2016). This instrument aims to communicate sustainability and transparency, being the center of the sustainability experience, seeking to identify points of contact with customers, with new methodologies for the design of services such as the sustainability accelerator in destinations and companies, aiming to respond to the 17 Sustainable Development Goals (SDGs) of the United Nations.

In other words, the wine industry has incorporated sustainability into its business strategy, since sustainable practices become not only a matter of communication but also are important actions to ensure the continuous availability of resources, sustained profitability and future growth (Graça et al., 2017).

Similarly, for González (2017), wine culture and wine tourism experiences are clearly correlated with social (socially equitable), economic (economically viable), environmental (environmentally correct) and cultural aspects of wine regions and territories. Therefore, a business in this sector, in order to be truly sustainable, must understand the environmental, social and economic effects of its activities (Barber et al., 2009).

Thus, it can be said that wine production, as well as wine tourism experiences, is clearly related to the social, economic, environmental and cultural aspects of wine regions and territories (González, 2017), so that the topic is under constant discussion and, therefore, numerous sustainability programs have been implemented in recent years (Lamastra et al., 2016; Graça et al., 2017).

According to Flores (2018), the wine industry is concerned with sustainability, since this sector faces challenges related to climate change, exposure to chemicals and availability of water and energy resources. In this sense, it seeks to analyze Wine Tourism and its developments as a driver.

Methodology

According to Dana and Dana (2005), qualitative research includes different methods: personal observation of situations, individuals and interactions, analysis of documents, as well as interviews to record testimonies.

The in-depth interview is a methodological resource that seeks to collect responses from a selected source (Duarte, 2005, p. 62). The option for an in-depth interview is related to the fact that it allows the creation of a structure to compare answers and articulate results, helping to systematize the information provided by the interviewees (Duarte, 2005, p. 65).

After the interviews, the collected information was submitted to content analysis, whose qualitative research technique is widely used (Hsieh & Shannon, 2005). Content analysis comprises a set of techniques for systematic analysis of texts and consists of the critical understanding of communication, with content analysis being used to extract information (Smith, 2000).

This type of technique allows the systematic, objective and quantitative description of the content of the communication (Marconi & Lakatos, 2003); it also allows interpreting and analyzing texts and classifying their content, allocating statements/citations to a set of categories (Flick, 2013).

This methodology is one of the most important in the social sciences, which has been used with increasing frequency by researchers (Neuendorf, 2017).

The research was carried out in 2023 and in the period from January to September, it was sought through bibliometric research to identify studies carried out in Portugal and the Algarve Region.

In October and November 2023, we sought to deepen the secondary research on Quinta dos Santos. This farm was selected for the case study due to its particularity in carrying out the activities, as well as in the relationship with the community and partners and for its accessibility.

The interviews were conducted in December 2023, with the company's chief executive officer (CEO) and commercial director as interviewees.

Along with the interviews, documents and information provided during the visit and on the website were analyzed.

Results

It can be seen that, if tourists are willing to change their habits, the organizations linked to this tourist activity and particularly wine tourism would have to reformulate their practices. The adequacy and innovation of the practices of wine tourism companies generate the ability for them to occupy a leadership position, through the defense of the culture of sustainability, much more than good environmental management, working from carbon emissions, plastic use, water consumption and food waste to work, support to the local community, responsible shopping and valuing what is authentic and genuine.

Quinta dos Santos shows concern for the environment and people (employees and the local community), highlighting aspects related to the concept of sustainability focused on the set of social and environmental criteria.

In relation to the principle of respect for nature and the environment, the personal values that are transmitted between the family are observed, where it appears that personal values and the involvement of the company's management elements are guides for the implementation of sustainable practices, with awareness of responsible behavior in relation to the environment and the use of available resources without compromising the capacity of future generations.

With regard to the implementation of sustainable practices, the company considers a strategic element the existence of commitment on the part of the management and other departments of the company, demonstrating responsible behavior.

With regard to the environmental dimension, the use of products that are not harmful to nature is highlighted, such as the non-use of phytochemical products, avoiding the waste of water by controlling its consumption, valorization of by-products, selective separation of waste, use of "encapsulated yeasts," reduction of the use of chemical products in the production process of sparkling wines.

Regarding the use of by-products, it is possible to observe that these actions refer to the concern with organic waste resulting from the process. Regarding the profitability of by-products, there is a synergy with integration into the community, such as distribution, without financial remuneration, to local residents for use in animal feed and land fertilizer.

In turn, in the social dimension, the following sustainable practices were mentioned: support for social solidarity actions and community support, for example, through corporate volunteering, donations to private institutions and donations to local populations.

As evidenced, another sustainable practice is to promote a good work environment, with opportunities for dialogue and sharing of new ideas, valuing the employee's growth.

The contribution of the voluntary work of the community and tourists in relation to the grape harvest is highlighted. Quinta dos Santos offers meals and wine to the local community that participates in the harvesting process and, for tourists who assist in harvesting and treading the grapes, taste the grape must and experience and enjoy the winemaking process. Volunteer help in winemaking is one of the activities that the Quinta has introduced in the region. Because it is a manual activity and requires very little time, it is necessary to have a group of people working at this stage of the process.

In the interviews, it was observed during the speeches that: "For us, it's a matter of quality." We always want to harvest our grapes by hand. By providing tourists and the local community with this activity, we have a group of people who are excited to be here and who get personally involved and thus, encouraging, designing conditions, it is possible to create a regional ecosystem conducive to unleashing worn-out and outdated economies to reinvent themselves, thus attracting investors, entrepreneurs and even young workers. One of the most densely populated means investing in new concepts, in new markets, in new opportunities, in an inverse parallelism to the already historic rural exodus.

Regarding the economic dimension, the interviewees mentioned the following sustainable practices: Promoting job creation, carrying out recruitment actions in the surrounding communities, providing good salary conditions, as well as developing partnerships to stimulate the local economy.

Among the sustainable practices evidenced, those related to economic and social development, business performance and environmental conservation stand out.

1. Economic and Social Development:
   a. Local suppliers in all services;
   b. Collaboration and synergies: Use of the space, at no associated cost, for the organization of local events, presentation of university projects;
   c. Staff motivation and involvement: Development of measures to reconcile personal, family and professional life: Reduction of turnover/increase of satisfaction and sense of belonging;
   d. Customer development through the provision of a stimulus to the responsible, participatory tourist, committing customers to good practices.
2. Business Performance:
   a. Project related to lodging, with a quiet environment, structures and proposals for activities designed exclusively for this segment;
   b. Creation of new products and services from the beginning of the process to the after-sales.
3. Environmental Conservation:
   a. Waste management actions and control of the use of natural resources;
   b. Conservation and enhancement of cultural heritage;
   c. Valorization of the patrimony with interpretation actions in partnership with the local business community;
   d. Health safety with the participation of the Board of Directors and employees;

e. Involvement of the local community with the awareness and involvement of the local community in recycling, tree (re)planting and cleaning activities, in the activity of collection and delivery of waste for reuse.
f. By working around this common challenge, entities, companies and governments have the potential to transform regions into more bio-sustainable territories, with bioeconomies that are more robust to international economic instabilities, fostered by a dominant economic model, very much guided by the international financial system and not very sensitive to the specificities, needs and potentialities of each region.

The development of integrated concepts of environmental quality, quality of life and economic sustainability thus gives rise to the formulation of objectives where the concepts of social, economic and territorial management are mixed. For these goals to become a reality, the responsible and efficient use of endogenous resources is essential.

Conclusion

In Portugal, wine tourism has propagated the regional development strategy, the expansion of the economic matrix of the Algarve region and a structuring part of the national strategic plan for tourism development. These actions make the wine tourism sector grow rapidly, representing a relevant activity with a driving capacity, not limited to the economic dimension but also to the social and environmental dimension, having repercussions as an enhancer of sustainable local development.

Based on the results obtained in the interviews, it was possible to conclude that there are sustainable practices framed in the three dimensions (environmental, social and economic) to be implemented and that there is a greater development in some companies, that is, according to the financial and physical resources available, companies are implementing a set of social and economic practices.

In this way, each company applies its sustainability model oriented toward the responsible and sustainable use of resources. Another fact refers to the fact that sustainability is a common concern for the company, regardless of its size.

It is necessary to develop partnerships between the business community, universities and other entities from the public and private sectors, in order to promote awareness and dissemination actions on sustainability, as well as to equip and support the promotion and training, at the national level, on the implementation of sustainable practices in the wine tourism sector with management, employees of the various departments of the companies, customers and community.

References

Barber, N., Taylor, C., & Strick, S. (2009). Wine consumers' environmental knowledge and attitudes: Influence on willingness to purchase. *International Journal Wine Research*, *1*, 59–72. https://doi.org/10.2147/IJWR.S4649

Boiral, O., & Heras-Saizarbitoria, I. (2017, February). Managing biodiversity through stakeholder involvement: Why, who, and for what initiatives? *Journal of Business Ethics*, Springer, *140*(3), 403–421. https://doi.org/10.1007/s10551-015-2668-3

Bruwer, J. (2003). South African wine routes: Some perspectives on the wine tourism industry's structural dimensions and wine tourism product. *Tourism Management*, *24*(4), 423–435. https://doi.org/10.1016/S0261-5177(02)00105-X

Carmichael, B. (2000). Um modelo matricial para atitudes e comportamentos dos residentes em uma área turística em rápida mudança. *Percorrer. Gerenciar.*, *21*, 601–611.

Dana, L., & Dana, T. (2005). Expanding the scope of methodologies used in entrepreneurship research. *International Journal of Entrepreneurship and Small Business*, *2*(1), 79–88. https://doi.org/10.1504/IJESB.2005.006071

De la Torre, G.M.V., Morales, E.F., & Castro, M.S.F. (2012). Wine tourism: An approach to good practices. Turydes. *Journal of Research in Tourism and Local Development*, *5*, 12. www.eumed.net/rev/turydes/12/tff.pdf

Duarte, J. (2005). Entrevista em profundidade. In J. Duarte & A. Barros (org.), *Métodos e técnicas de pesquisa em comunicação*. Atlas. 1, 62–83.

European Charter for Wine Tourism. (2006). *Turismo de Portugal*. www.turismodeportugal.pt/Portugu%C3%AAs/AreasAtividade/desenvolvimentoeinovacao1/EnotourismTechnical Meeting/EuropeanWineTourismCharter/Annexes/Charter%20European%20E in tourism.pdf

Filopoulos, S., & Frittella, N. (2019). *Designing Sustainable and Responsible Wine Tourism Experiences*. BIO Web of Conferences. https://doi.org/10.1051/bioconf/20191203006.

Flick, U. (2013). *Introduction to research methodology: A beginners guide*. Penso.

Flores, S.S. (2018). What is sustainability in the wine world? A cross-country analysis of wine sustainability frameworks. *Journal of Cleaner Production*, *172*(2018), 2301–2312. https://doi.org/10.1016/j.jclepro.2017.11.181

González, M.L. (2017). Wine tourism and sustainable environments. *Arbor*, *193*(785), 1–12. https://doi.org/10.3989/arbor.2017.785n3005

Graça, A.R., Simões, L., Freitas, R., Pessanha, M., & Sandeman, G. (2017). Using sustainable development actions to promote the relevance of mountain wines in export markets. *Open Agriculture*, *2*(1), 571–579. https://doi.org/10.1515/opag-2017-0060

Hojman, D.E., & Hunter-Jones, P. (2012). Wine tourism: Chilean wine regions and routes. *Journal of Business Research*, *65*(1), 13–21. https://doi.org/10.1016/j.jbusres.2011.07.009

Hsieh, H.F., & Shannon, S.E. (2005). Três abordagens para análise qualitativa de conteúdo. *Pesquisa Qualitativa em Saúde*, *15*(9), 1277–1288. https://doi.org/10.1177/1049732305276687

Lamastra, L., Balderacchi, M., Di Guardo, A., Monchiero, M., & Trevisan, M. (2016). A novel fuzzy expert system to assess the sustainability of the viticulture at the wine-estate scale. *Science of the Total Environment*, *572*(1), 724–733. https://doi.org/10.1016/j.scitotenv.2016.07.043

Maduro, A.V., Guerreiro, A., & Oliveira, A. (2015). O turismo industrial como potenciador do desenvolvimento local – estudo de caso do Museu do Vinho de Alcobaça em Portugal. *Pasos—Revista de Turismo y Patrimonio Cultural*, *13*(5), 1129–1143.

Marconi, M.A., & Lakatos, E.M. (2003). *Fundamentos de metodología científica* (5th ed.). Atlas Publishing.

Mark-Herbert, C., & Carolina, H., & Schantz, V. (2007). Communicating corporate social responsibility–Brand management. *EJBO Electronic Journal of Business Ethics and Organization Studies, 12.*

Marzo-Navarro, M., & Pedraja-Iglesias, M. (2012). Critical factors of wine tourism: Incentives and barriers from the potential tourist's perspective. *International Journal of Contemporary Hospitality Management, 24*(2), 312–334. https://doi.org/10.1108/09596111211206196

Neuendorf, K.A. (2017). *The content analysis guidebook* (2nd ed.). Sage.

Olsen, J., Thach, E., & Nowak, L. (2007). Wine for my generation: Exploring how US wine consumers are socialized to wine. *Journal of Wine Research, 18*, 1–18. https://doi.org/10.1080/09571260701526816.

O'Neill, M., & Charters, S. (2000). Service quality at the cellar door: Implications for Western Australia's developing wine tourism industry. *Managing Service Quality: An International Journal, 10*(2), 112–122. https://doi.org/10.1108/09604520010318308

Popp, L., & McCole, D. (2016). Understanding tourists' itineraries in emerging rural tourism regions: The application of paper-based itinerary mapping methodology to a wine tourism 140 region in Michigan. *Current. Issues in Tourism, 19*(10), 988–1004. https://doi.org/10.1080/13683500.2014.942259

Quian, J., Shen, H., & Law, R. (2018). Research in sustainable tourism: A longitudinal study of articles between 2008 and 2017. *Sustainability, 10*(3), 1–13. https://doi.org/10.3390/su10030590

Rodríguez, J.G., López-Guzmán, T., & Sánchez Cañizares, S.M.S. (2010). Analysis of the development of wine tourism in Spain—a case study. *Journal of Culture and Tourism, 4*(2), 51–68.

Smith, C.P. (2000). Content analysis and narrative analysis. In H.T. Reis & C.M. Judd (Eds.), *Handbook of research methods in social and personality psychology* (pp. 313–335). Cambridge University Press.

Stewart, J.W., Bramble, L., & Ziraldo, D. (2008). Key challenges in wine and culinary tourism with practical recommendations. *International Journal of Contemporary Hospitality Management, 20*(3), 303–312. https://doi.org/10.1108/09596110810866118

Trigo, A., & Silva, P. (2022). Rumos de Desenvolvimento Sustentável para o Enoturismo no Douro Vinhateiro, Portugal. *Sustentabilidade, 14*, 3949. https://doi.org/10.3390/su14073949

UNWTO. (2016). *Wine Tourism-a Growing Tourism Segment.* United Nations World Tourism Organization. PR No.: PR 16062. www.unwto.org/archive/global/press-release/2016-09-09/wine-tourism-growing-tourism-segment

United Nations (2016). *Report of the open-ended intergovernmental expert working group on indicators and terminology relating to disaster risk reduction.*

14 Assessing environmental awareness in the organizational culture and its mediating role in integrating an ecocentric paradigm into Mexican companies' knowledge management and governance systems in Guanajuato

Margarita Schmitt Revilla

Introduction

Literature review

The ecocentric paradigm and sustainability

Nowadays, governments, organizations and society face some of the most difficult challenges, being the environment one of them. If downsizing all the aspects in which the environment is being affected, the list seems endless: agriculture, forests, soil, the use of land, the food system, pollution, water, biodiversity, urbanism, chemicals, impacts and risks of climate change, energy, transport, health, inequalities, natural disasters, noise, plastic, production, consumption, waste and recycling (EEA, n.d.). Although these concerns have begun to permeate in the business world, actions toward improving socially responsible behaviors and greening their supply chains are insufficient nor is it enough the sole participation of one individual or organization but through collective consciousness (Thanh Tiep Le, 2022). A change of mindset to an ecocentric paradigm is then needed, meaning that humans should be seen as part of the whole natural system, decentering the human position in favor of the ecosystem (Allen et al., 2019). It is important to clear that ecocentric and anthropocentric standpoints value nature but differ in that ecocentrism has intrinsic value, while anthropocentrism values the quality of life which requires a protected environment (Gagnon Thompson & Barton, 1994). This attitude shifts from anthropocentric to ecocentric worldview was already studied by Gagnon Thompson and Barton in 1994 suggesting that the response to support environmental issues indeed was different between these two points of view with a tendency for apathy for the first group and pro-environment

DOI: 10.4324/9781003465058-14

attitude for the latter. Thus, raising awareness is the first step in order to construct ecological thinking through the revision of attitudes, behaviors and human habits in relation to the environment (Gagnon Thompson & Barton, 1994; Allen et al., 2019; Fios, 2019). Ideally, organizations play a key role in this shift. They are accountable as well of developing and integrating a green strategy as part of the overall strategy, making decisions based on the benefit of the natural environment (Thanh Tiep Le, 2022).

Sustainability, in turn, implies something to be sustained in the physical environment, in the form of human values and human identity (Allen et al., 2019). Thus, to sustain the ecocentric paradigm, it means to sustain nature not only in its physical environment but also at the level of human values and human identity. The multiple interpretations of ecocentric sustainability and the unanswered questions as to what, how long and in whose interest is to be sustained has led to a more superficial way of addressing it instead of truly understanding, enacting and developing an ecocentric perspective at the management level (Allen et al., 2019). Additionally, efforts in reducing the carbon footprint may not be effective due to cultural practices. Which behaviors are best to adopt in a concrete way is still unknown, although methods such as behavioral economic interventions and discounting are suggested to identify such problematic behaviors at the community and cultural level, hence, improving decision-making for environmental sustainability (Gelino et al., 2021). Nevertheless, it has been studied that knowledge management (KM) as a fundamental tool to achieve sustainability, by doing so, management may have to develop policies to train employees in how to perform according to the company's green agenda and such policies in turn should be supported by regulatory bodies (Shahzad et al., 2021).

The knowledge sharing dimension within the knowledge management strategy

Organizations require knowledge to perform successfully in such a degree that it has been found that KM is key for improved performance, competitive advantage and innovation (Si Xue, 2017). KM is a set of processes and practices that monitor, facilitate and manage the process of creation and internalization of knowledge at the individual and organizational levels (Sá Freire et al., 2021). The underlying activities implied are learning (at the individual level), retrieval, representation and structuring (at the repository level), socialization, dissemination (at the team level), identification, creation and acquisition (Straccia et al., 2023). Therefore, KM is considered a strategic tool due to its relevance throughout the organizational value chain (Sá Freire et al., 2021).

The process itself has no use if it does not constitute a means for developing competencies. It must build capacity, so the overall approach to KM should be that of a process capability strategy. In the various definitions of KM under the process-capability view identified by Kaur (2022), the main concept is that of the ability of an organization to seek and acquire new information out of existing knowledge by facilitating the flow from the outside of the company to the inside, increasing its opportunities and thus, its performance and sustained competitiveness. The nature of capability is dynamic through which the organization can truly adapt to changes.

This study focuses on the knowledges sharing (KS) dimension within the KM strategy, where acquired knowledge is shared. KS is then core to the flow of information and organizational learning (Millán et al., n.d.; Sá Freire et al., 2021; Abbas & Sağsan, 2019). Knowledge governance (KG) is also a supporting factor for companies not only in the elaboration of the governing policies and structures that focus on economic, social and environmental sustainability but also in the support of building capacity for change within the learning aspect of KS as well (Sá Freire et al., 2021). When integrating the capability dimension of KM in the KS stage, the goal is to capture and retain valuable knowledge and insights, not only from employers but also from the outside like buyers, to improve decision-making and its leadership in the industry (Neuenfeldt, 2023). Social capital and the routine of KS becomes then a need and something worth investing in as well as the governance of the generated knowledge and its learning (Huysman & Wit, 2002; Sá Freire et al., 2021).

A study conducted by Abbas and Sağsan (2019) on the different process within the KM strategy in manufacturing and service firms suggest that the KS process has a significant impact on green innovation, and corporate and social sustainable development activities. Most importantly, they found the overall KM equally important for all firm sizes. Another study by EMAS (2018) suggests that the inclusion of employees in the process of setting green standards has various positive impacts, one at the level of information exchange, which is directly related to KS, second, by raising awareness and third, by increasing employee's motivation and productivity.

The influence of knowledge governance, corporate governance and corporate social responsibility in greenwashing practices

While some organizations tend to a rather symbolical adoption of measures, which seem to constitute more of a marketing tool and less of corporate accountability for environmental performance (Heras-Saizarbitoria, 2020), other organizations have integrated green initiatives into their culture and their KM system, which has been shown to be critical in accelerating business and environmental performance ensuring green innovation and sustainable development (Wang et al., 2022). The reasons behind these two perspectives are related with the mechanisms behind KG, corporate governance

(CG) and corporate social responsibility (CSR). These three concepts are understood as KG which manages the company's activities related to knowledge (Krafft & Ravix, 2008; Cao & Xiang, 2012), CG which seeks the optimization of the company's value (Sahut et al., 2019; Krafft & Ravix, 2008) and CSR which seeks to invest in human capital, the environment and the relationship with stakeholders (Sahut et al., 2019). It is also important to notice that KG is essential to CG because it stimulates corporate development through the creation and governance of new knowledge and that CG is essential to CSR due to the board composition and ownership structure. This is what shapes the companies' policies, putting moral and economic values into play (Sahut et al., 2019; Krafft & Ravix, 2008; Cao & Xiang, 2012). In the transition to ecocentrism, close attention should be then paid on cooperation between managers and investors to bring KG, CG and CSR together to give coherence and support to the company's processes and knowledge strategy (Krafft & Ravix, 2008; Cao & Xiang, 2012).

Greenwashing is an example of the disarticulation of these components being the main drivers of markets with restricted regulations, market opportunities and low competitive pressure that favor CG low-cost interests (Yang et al., 2020). Although greenwashing is a widespread social and environmental phenomenon (Freitas Netto et al., 2020), firms may make some changes in favor of their reputation (De Jong et al., 2019) but they may also hold themselves accountable and take action to correct their negative practices and to mediate the relationship between the adoption of a green strategy and their sustainable performance (Nickerson et al., 2022; Albus & Ro, 2017; Thanh Tiep Le, 2022). However, if reputation or awareness are not sufficient to coordinate KG, CG and CSR, regulatory bodies should then intervene in order to address this lack of qualitative adoption of green standards, not only to stop the engagement in harmful behaviors but also to prevent the long-term negative impact on social welfare as well as on potential stakeholders who genuinely are willing to invest in green products (Yang et al., 2020).

Contextual background

International standards to address environmental issues

Worldwide guidelines and standards for environmentally actions have been set up for global engagement and are encouraged through governments and alliances such as the agreements from the 28th Conference of the Parties held in the United Arab Emirates signaled the "beginning of the end" of the fossil energy era and its transition to alternative sources (UNFCCC, 2022); or the 17 UN Sustainable Development Goals (SDGs) for 2030 call for "responsible, consumption and production," "sustainable cities and communities," "life on land and life below water," "climate action," "affordable and clean energy," "clean water and sanitation" and "peace, justice and strong institutions" (United Nations, 2022). Examples among international green standards are: ISO 14001 certification, which commits companies to regulatory compliance and environmental improvement (ISO, n.d.); the Global Forest Stewardship Council Certification, which seeks to ensure that products come from well-managed forests and from ecocentric family-run businesses, households, manufacturers, retailers, brands, architects, builders, artists and project developers (FSC, n.d.); and the Rainforest Alliance Seal, which addresses green practices among producers, consumers, retail and food service companies (RainforestAlliance, n.d.).

Regional and national standards

Mexico is a member of the Commission for Environmental Cooperation (CEC) of the United States-Mexico-Canada Treaty (USMCA) 2021–2025. The environmental mission of this commission is the "effective cooperation and public participation to conserve, protect and enhance the North American environment and support of sustainable development for the benefit of present and future generations" (CEC, 2021) and it is founded on six pillars: (1) clean air, land and water, (2) preventing and reducing pollution in the marine environment, (3) circular economy and sustainable materials management, (4) shared ecosystems and species, (5) resilient economies and communities and (6) effective enforcement of environmental laws. To achieve the CEC goals, solutions must be nature-based and will have to come from traditional ecological knowledge, especially coming from indigenous groups, and innovations will need to be sustainable and will have to support clean technologies and supply chains (CEC, 2021). To meet these objectives, each country determines its own certifications for businesses and organizations and in case of failure in effectively enforcing each country's environmental laws, the CEC created the Submissions on Enforcement Matters (SEM) mechanism to process it (CEC, 2023).

Mexico recognizes a variety of business labels and certificates regarding the environment, clean energy and energy efficiency, social responsibility and sustainability among which are:

- Socially Responsible Company (ESR) label. It is the main national label for social responsibility that addresses large, medium and small companies (Cajiga Calderón, n.d.).
- Environmental National Audit Program. It acknowledges industries that outperform the minimum expected indices regarding emissions, waste and water. It is cost-free so that companies do not have this matter as an excuse for not getting certified. (PROFEPA, n.d.)

- Family Responsible Company (EFR) label. It is issued by the Ministry of Labor and Social Security and acknowledges organizations that have a commitment with work-life balance, gender equity and fight against violence in the workplace (STPS, n.d.).
- Clean Transport Program (PTL). It is for transportation companies and companies that make use of transportation services. It seeks to reduce fuel consumption, operating costs and emissions; is suitable for freight, passenger, tourism and private transports (SEMARNAT, n.d.).
- 100% Neutral Carbon International Program for Latin America. It is a private initiative in Latin America that certifies companies that have plans to be net zero or have already achieved it (PI100CN, n.d.).
- NMX-R-025-SCFI-2015 Mexican standard for Employment Equality and Non-Discrimination. It is a voluntary Mexican standard that promotes best practices for gender equity, non-discrimination and equality in the workplace. It addresses all types of organizations whether large or small, private, or public, regardless of the economic sector (CONAPRED, n.d.).
- Environmental Quality label for micro-, small- and medium-sized companies, as well as rural societies that comply with applicable environmental regulations, efficient use of resources and provide services and products in a sustainable manner. This label is also cost-free (PROFEPA, 2023).
- LEED certification for green buildings. It is a US international certificate and the most famous for the field of green construction (USGBC, n.d.).
- FSC (mentioned earlier).
- ISO 14001 (mentioned earlier).
- UN SDGs (mentioned earlier). SDGs are reported by country voluntarily. The last report to the UN was published in 2021 and addresses the priority programs for 2019–2024 (Secretaría de Economía, 2021).

At the regional level, the state of Guanajuato has an environmental policy, which focuses on more ecocentric actions such as creating a green infrastructure to protect biodiversity, the designation of natural protected areas, development of water efficient and water protection mechanisms, development of electric mobility infrastructure; actions toward waste management, ecodesign and circular-economy practices, environmental education programs, a fix set of environmental standards that are compulsory for different economic sectors and it even has an environmental calendar designating several days of each month to commemorate some element of nature. It has also established the *Sustainable Land Management* policy that consists in collaborative surveillance of the environmental issues between state and local governments and it has developed an Inventory of Native Plant Species as well as a list of protected tree species, along with biodiversity studies as part of the *Strategy for the Conservation and Sustainable Use of Biodiversity of the State of Guanajuato* (SMAOT, n.d.a, n.d.b, n.d.c; CONABIO, 2015).

KM in Mexican businesses

In the case of Mexico, studies regarding KM in the business sector have different approaches that range from competitive advantage to capacity building and social responsibility. They address various sizes and sectors, that is: the relationship between KM for achieving competitive advantage in the industrial and small and medium enterprises (SME) sector (Mendoza-Arvizo & Solís-Rodríguez, 2022; Nuñez-Ramírez et al., 2020; Pinzón Castro et al., 2019; Ruiz-Corrales et al., 2022; Vásquez Sánchez & Larios-Gómez, 2021), partnerships for strategic KM and for overcoming institutional voids found in emerging economies (Becerril-Elías & Merritt, 2021; Guerrero et al., 2019), the adoption of information and communication technologies (ICT) in micro, small and medium enterprises as a means to build KM capacity toward open innovation (Alvarez-Aros et al., 2022; Bernal Jiménez & Rodriguez Ibarra, 2019; Haro & Peña, 2020; Martinez et al., 2023) and the component of social responsibility in KM. This last study focuses more on firms in the primary sector assuming they have an ecological component for sustainability, but not necessarily from the ecocentric paradigm (Lara Manjarrez, 2021; Rodríguez & López, 2021; Rodríguez-Zúñiga et al., 2019).

Only one study around ecocentrism was found addressing the underlying values around this perspective. It is a study performed around artisan family businesses in Oaxaca and Guanajuato to study how values of ecocentrism and conformity influenced entrepreneurial orientation and environmental behavior. Findings suggest that although the ecocentric value has a positive effect on entrepreneurial orientation, survival is of greater importance and thus the conformity value prevails, therefore further research should be conducted regarding sustainability within a survival venture (Sánchez-Medina, 2022).

Research objective and hypotheses

Based on the importance of businesses adopting an ecocentric paradigm, the value of KS in the organizational learning and capacity building, the somewhat adoption of environmental certifications, the role of corporate governance and corporate social responsibility regarding sustainability and the existing research opportunities in firms from emerging economies, the aim of this study is to identify the dimensions that respond to ecocentric awareness in the organizational culture of Mexican companies in the State of Guanajuato, how these dimensions relate with the ecocentric orientations within the KS dimensions and how this can potentially have an effect on sustainability, especially the SDG 16 of peace, justice and strong institutions. Independent variables such as company size, type of certifications, the economic sector and the type of administration will also be studied. Hypotheses of the study are:

H_1: Ecocentric awareness has some degree of relationship with the ecocentric practices within the KS dimensions.
H_2: Size, years of activity, the economic sector, the type of ownership, the type of administration and certifications have a positive relationship with ecocentric awareness.
H_3: Size, years of activity, the economic sector, the type of ownership, the type of administration and certifications are correlated within each other.

Methodology

An online questionnaire was designed consisting of three sections: the first section assesses the degree of ecocentric awareness of the company through a Likert scale ranging from 1 to 5. This section was based on the validated questionnaires by Gochuico (2021) and Mendis and Welmilla (2021). The second section, which is also a set of Likert scales from 1 to 5, assesses the degree of embedment of ecocentric initiatives in the knowledge sharing management model by Lee and Wong (2015) and Song et al. (2020). The third section consists of the demographic information from the participant: number of years of operations, number of years adopting a KM model, the size of the company, the sector, the type of legal constitution, the type of administration and certifications. A digital invitation was sent to companies including their consent to participate and the characteristics of the study, as well as the privacy and ethics criteria. An in-depth interview with a specialist followed the quantitative data analysis. Questions were based on the quantitative results observed.

Data analysis

A total of 49 responses were obtained ranging from micro to large companies from various sectors, in its majority independent owners in the trading sector. Specifically, 27 micro, 10 small, 3 medium and 9 large companies. Although no sensible data was asked, skepticism from potential respondents was observed when inviting them. Another observation regarding the lack of participation was the misconception from managers and business owners on ecocentrism, arguing that the topic did not apply to their activities, rather to the recycling or the primary sector. Such limited number of responses does not only affect the scope of the study but also indicate a cultural standpoint of view from companies toward empirical studies concerning their own context.

Descriptive statistics for demographic data were first conducted. The main observations were: Most respondents are microbusinesses in all economic sectors except for the education and the Courier, Express and Parcel Market, the Retail and the Food services sectors. When classified into the three large economic sectors (primary, secondary and tertiary), 38 businesses correspond to the tertiary sector, out of which 24 are micro businesses. Microbusinesses are organizations with less than ten employees, with an annual revenue set by the Ministry of Economy to up to 4 million mxp and with startup costs (Secretaría de Economía, 2009). It is important to recall that micro, medium and small businesses employed 27 million people in 2019. The three categories are more vulnerable than large companies and as such they struggled the most to survive and to adapt to the COVID-19 pandemic. The overall opening of new micro, small and medium businesses between May 2019 and July 2021 in the country increased 12% but the closing of these businesses in the same period increased in 12% as well (INEGI, 2022). Surprisingly, most respondents have run their businesses for ten or more years and in less extent, for the micro businesses between two and five years.

As for the type of ownership and type of administration, almost half of the respondents reported to be constituted through sole ownership relying on its corporate management on a sole director (mainly micro and small). The other half of the respondents was divided in two groups. Those companies are constituted as a society and managed by a board of directors (mainly medium and large) and those companies with a combination of sole ownership with the board of directors and vice versa (Figure 14.1).

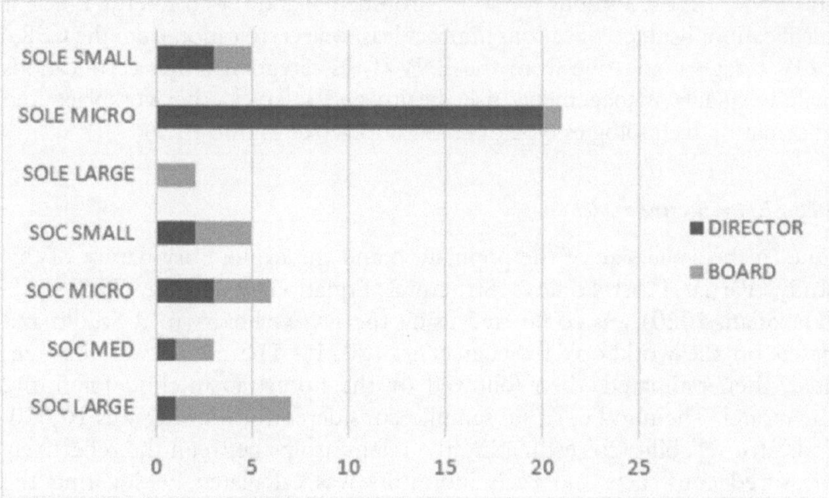

Figure 14.1 Respondents by size, type of ownership and corporate management.

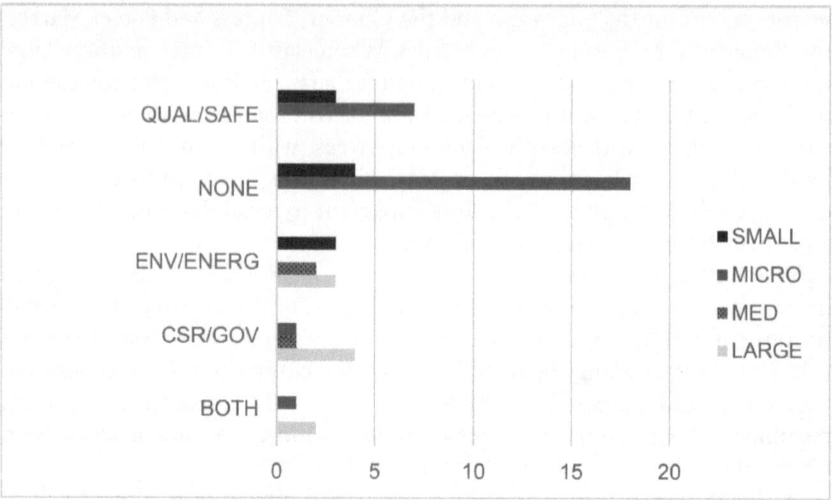

Figure 14.2 Respondents by size and type of certifications.

Finally, more than half of respondents do not report to have any type of certification. This contrasts with the available public certifications for all business sizes at zero cost. From the respondents who do report to have some time of certifications, CSR/GOV stands for an Equity, Diversity and Social Responsibility and/or a Corporate Compliance and Governance certification, and ENV/ENERG stands for an Environmental and/or an Energy-Efficient certification. Both certifications imply at least one certification from the CSR/GOV category and one from the ENV/EFE category. Other certifications include quality management, risk, health and safety in the workplace and information technologies type of certifications (see Figure 14.2).

PLS-SEM reflective model

Due to the small size of the population and the exploratory nature of this study, Partial Least Squares Structural Equation Modeling (PLS-SEM) (Hanafiah, 2020) was conducted using the *seminr* library in R-Studio and based on the workbook by Hair et al. (2021). The model was first created, then estimated, then followed by the bootstrap method for fitting the model. The number of subsamples considered for drawing was 10,000. Indicator reliability for estimating the relationships between the reflectively measured constructs and their indicators was calculated by squaring the loadings. Loadings above 0.68 were only considered. Table 14.1 shows the final items that were considered in the model.

Table 14.1 Items reflected by each construct

Construct	*Items*	*Loadings*
REGULATE	Government environmental regulations	0.911
	Government incentives for green practices	0.778
AWARENESS	Organizational environmental policies and practices	0.702
	Environment-friendly lifestyle of upper and middle management	0.736
	Program to reduce or eliminate food waste.	0.681
	Ability to sponsor food banks.	0.746
SUPPLY	KS with suppliers on green product design	0.803
	KS with suppliers on green process design	0.850
	KS with suppliers on green purchases	0.724
BUY	KS with buyers on green-market tendencies	0.754
	KS with buyers on green marketing	0.873
	KS with buyers on green distribution	0.887
CAPACITY	Capacity to effectively apply new green knowledge to commercial purposes	1.000

Internal consistence reliability indices of alpha, rhoC, rhoA were acceptable within the recommended values >0.70. Convergent validity through the average variance extracted (AVE) was also acceptable within the recommended value >0.5. The Fornell-Larcker criterion of the square root of AVE versus the construct correlations below this number was also met and the heterotrait-monotrait ratio (HTMT) for assessing the discriminal validity of values under 0.85 was also met. These values were confirmed with the bootstrapped HTMT value to test that they are significantly different from 1.00.

Evaluation of the model

Once the measurement of constructs has been confirmed valid and reliable, the model itself will be assessed. First, collinearity issues between the constructs REGULATE and AWARENESS with SUPPLY, BUY and CAPACITY showed values of 1.106 using the variance inflation factor (VIF). VIF values below 3 imply no issue with multicollinearity.

However, when assessing the significance and relevance of the path coefficients and assuming a 5% significance level (alpha = 0.05) where the value zero does not fall into the 95% confidence interval, paths between REGULATE—CAPACITY and AWARENESS—BUY have *t*-values below 1.96 and therefore are not significant.

Next, in order to assess the explanatory power of the model, R^2 and f^2 values were calculated. R^2 for the power of the variance explained in each of the endogenous constructs and f^2 for the effect size of the path coefficients of the predictor constructs. Assuming large effect sizes for values above 0.35

and low effect sizes below 0.15, R^2 values for the three constructs range between <0.25 and >0.15 and therefore are considered sufficient based on the criteria of the small number of predictor constructs and the correction factor introduced to account for the data and model size. As for the f^2 values of the path coefficients, a medium effect was observed between REGULATE—SUPPLY and AWARENESS—CAPACITY while almost no effect is reported between REGULATE—CAPACITY and AWARENESS—BUY.

Finally, to assess the predictive power of the model, the Mean Absolute Error (MAE) measure was preferred over the Root-Mean-Square-Error (RMSE), although, in most instances, RMSE would be used to examine the predictive power of the model, nonsymmetric distribution of prediction errors were observed in some of the indicators. Due to this skewness, the MAE is a more appropriate prediction statistic (Hair et al., 2021, p. 129). MEA values were compared to the naïve Linear Regression Model (LM) benchmark. If all indicators in the model have a lower RMSE or MAE vs. the LM benchmark, the model is considered to have a high predictive power (Hair Jr., et al., 2021:121). In our case, all indicators of our PLS-SEM model had lower MEA values compared to LM values. Therefore, a high predictive power of the model is validated (see Figure 14.3).

Correlation between demographic variables

Correlations between the demographic variables were estimated through non-parametric tests. The relationships analyzed were the size of the company, the type of ownership the type of administration, the economic sector, the number

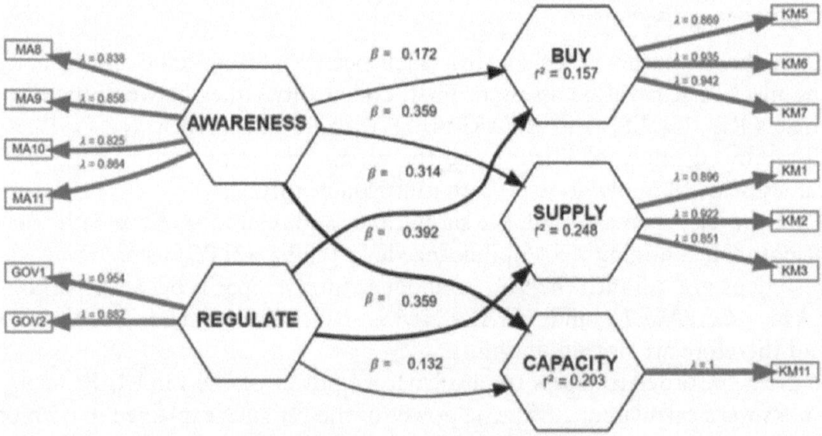

Figure 14.3 PLS-SEM validated model.

of years in operation and the type of certifications reported by the firm. Also, correlations between these demographics and the ecocentric awareness construct were estimated. Each variable comprises the following subcategories:

1. Type of certifications (CERT): None, Environmental or Energy efficient, Social Responsibility or Corporate Governance, Both (Environmental and socially responsible) and Other.
2. The size of the company (SIZE): Micro, small, medium and large companies.
3. The type of ownership (OWN): Society or Sole owner.
4. The type of administration (ADM): Board of directors or Sole director.
5. The economic sector of the firm (SECT): Primary (natural resources), Secondary (industry) or Tertiary (commerce and services) sectors.
6. The number of years of activities of the firm (YEARS): >10 years, 5–10 years, 2–5 years and <2 years.

Chi-square and Cramer's *V* tests for independence were applied. The following sets of variables proved to be dependent and to have a strong association: (1) ADMIN—CERT, (2) SIZE—CERT, (3) CERT—ORG P&P, (4) OWN—ADMIN, (5) OWN—SIZE and (6) ADMIN—SIZE.

The economic sector and number of years of the company are independent from all variables.

In-depth interview

In order to have a qualitative insight to the relationships found in the model, an additional in-depth interview was conducted with a local specialist in business standards and certifications. The interview consisted on four questions: (1) What are your perceived benefits for a company when having a certification and why? (2) To which extent do you think green certifications contribute to the sustainability and/or growth of the company? (3) What effects or impacts do you perceive between regulations and public incentives regarding the adoption of organizational policies and practices that are sustainable, socially responsible and promote transparency and an ecocentric paradigm? (4) Do you perceive any differences between the size of the company and the years of operations of the company regarding their interest and willingness to have a green certificate?

Responses were recorded and transcribed. The main ideas were the following:

Question 1

When you have a certificate, you have already demonstrated that you are competent to perform . . . . The intention of certifications is to ensure that the company is healthy, has good practices and is in a process of continuous improvement . . . . They (companies) should give more importance to get a certification . . . . Usually, companies who release new products will want to get certified to be able to sell . . . . In a globalized world you need to know what to certify . . . but certifications have more value when it comes to something very specialized and very important . . . . Managers must be very clear about their most risky positions to certify them and to ensure that the person will do their job well . . . . I also think that all strategic positions should be certified and specialized because they are the ones who will give vision to senior management.

Question 2

A company must follow national standards in order to operate . . . the rest is optional . . ., unless the company is interested in adopting a given process . . . it is like a triangle, on top you have the national standards, on one corner you have your product or service certifications and on the other corner the staff certifications . . . . It is only through balancing this that a company can be sustainable, because even if it goes bankrupt, it will have the tools to finish the business cycle properly.

Question 3

They (companies) give a lot of importance to what government indicates . . . . Nowadays the state government has launched green programs and are reviewing ecological practices inside companies. There is already a certain culture to improve ecology for the benefit of all. There are also more inclusive programs such as training staff in learning sign language in order to be able to give information to a larger audience . . . and the methodology is simple and worthwhile. . . . New and more green practices exist now. There is even one that is so simple that even a housewife can adopt it . . . in such cases a certification is often not needed. By getting the right training and applying those practices . . . there is already an impact. However, initiatives come from top management . . . and the people who are in strategic positions with the competence to do their job.

Question 4

Certifications are for all, large and small, old and new companies. It is a question of the top management to want to adopt a green certification. . . . I think medium-sized companies are the most open when adopting green practices. Large companies take longer time because of its size, unless they have a 100% economic incentive. New companies are also more excited and open to adopt new practices while for older companies it is harder because there is a culture that is already settled . . . there is more resistance to change.

Results

Based on the quantitative and qualitative data results, ecocentric awareness relies heavily on corporate management, which in turn is highly correlated to its type of ownership, suggesting an alignment with the company's KG and CG. The most important aspect of management is the development of policies and practices that influence the knowledge shared at the level of the supply chain and the company's capacity to effectively adopt new green knowledge for its commercial purposes. Government participation has also proved to be an important agent in raising awareness, by both, regulations and incentives, and has an effect on the knowledge shared through the company's supply and buy chains. So, H_1 can partially be confirmed, specifying that it is through the organizational policies and practices that permeate in the KS dimension.

At the level of correlations between variables, a significant relationship was found between the ownership of the company with its administration and its size. The same is true for the type of administration, the size of the company and its certifications. At the level of correlations between the variables and the items that respond to the awareness construct, a significant correlation was found between certifications and the organizational policies and practices. By combining the above, it is at the CG level that decisions are made regarding who and how its corporate management will be constituted. In its turn, corporate management will determine the company's KG. It is also relevant the finding that adoption of certifications permeates in the organizational policies and practices, suggesting that when certification standards are met, it is highly probable that policies and practices will align to the objectives of the given certification. Size plays an important role as well. On the contrary, the economic sector or the number of years of operations are independent. Such findings coincide with the opinion of the specialist on the perceived benefits of certifications from corporate management and its efforts in developing the policies and practices that reflect standards. Findings also align with the opinion that the size of the company influences the company's level of openness for transitioning to an ecocentric mindset suggesting that smaller companies tend to be more enthusiastic toward this transition than large companies, unless an extrinsic motivation such as incentives, especially economic ones, exist. The above is partially true to H_2 and H_3. In both hypotheses, years of activity and the economic sector are not related, as for H_2, only organizational policies and practices are strictly related to certifications.

The chapter identifies that the participant companies in the State of Guanajuato are particularly micro and small companies, that have been operating for more than ten years and that survived the COVID-19 economic shutdown. The chapter also identifies that, in general, companies that have a sole ownership tend to be managed by one director and those companies who are constituted as a society tend to be managed by a board of directors. Size, corporate management and ownership are strongly related which facilitates the embedment of KG, CG and CSR. This in turn is reflected in the organizational green policies and practices and the ecocentric attitudes within its KS system. The chapter also identifies that regulatory bodies should not only focus on regulation itself but in incentive mechanisms that encourage the adoption of an ecocentric paradigm. This aspect of government intervention highlights the importance of institutional strength and its goal to achieve sustainable, green companies. This chapter emphasized how ecocentrism awareness is being raised inside the organizational culture and how it relates to the ecocentric attitudes within the KM and KG systems through the KS dimension and the structure of the company. Both as a means for sustainability. Regulatory bodies, shareholders and senior management were found to be at the core of this relationship. So, this chapter has several practical contributions toward transitioning to an ecocentric approach: First, regulatory bodies should continue to encourage companies to adopt green certifications beyond the compulsory operational standards. Second, top management is directly accountable for developing and applying organizational policies and adopting certifications supported by shareholders. Third, this alignment contributes to build an ecocentric culture through ecocentric practices that permeate in the KS dimension of its KM strategy. Fourth, in order to remain sustainable, shareholders and top management need to identify strategic employees with the expertise and the capacity to contribute to the transition and adoption of an ecocentric paradigm.

Limitations and future research

As for the limitations of this chapter, a second exploratory study with a larger sample of medium and large companies is recommended to be able to make comparisons between shareholders and corporate management and if the effect of the company size remains significant in relation to the green policies and practices established by the senior administration found in this study. Furthermore, a descriptive study on the actual green behaviors and attitudes within the organizational culture should then be analyzed to assess the quality of the shift to the ecocentric mindset. Certainly, with the willingness and disposition of companies to participate in such studies.

References

Abbas, J., & Sağsan, M. (2019). Impact of knowledge management practices on green innovation and corporate sustainable development: A structural analysis. *Journal of Cleaner Production*, *229*, 611–620. https://doi.org/10.1016/J.JCLEPRO.2019.05.024

Albus, H., & Ro, H. (2017). Corporate social responsibility. *Journal of Hospitality & Tourism Research, 41*(1), 41–65. https://doi.org/10.1177/1096348013515915

Allen, S., Cunliffe, A.L., & Easterby-Smith, M. (2019). Understanding sustainability through the lens of ecocentric radical-reflexivity: Implications for management education. *Journal of Business Ethics, 154*, 781–795. https://doi.org/10.1007/s10551-016-3420-3

Alvarez-Aros, E.L., Bernal-Torres, C.A., & Tovar, Y.S. (2022). Colaboración externa de la innovación abierta y desempeño financiero de las PYMES en Tamaulipas, México. *Revista de Administração de Empresas, 62*(3), 1–21. https://doi.org/10.1590/s0034-759020220301

Becerril-Elías, J.C., & Merritt, H. (2021). Alianzas para la innovación en organizaciones intensivas en conocimiento: El caso de México. *Revista CEA, 7*(14), 1–23. https://doi.org/10.22430/24223182.1780

Bernal Jiménez, M.C., & Rodriguez Ibarra, D.L. (2019). Las tecnologías de la información y comunicación como factor de innovación y competitividad empresarial. *Scientia et technica, 24*(1), 85. https://doi.org/10.22517/23447214.20401

Cajiga Calderón, J.F. (n.d.). *El Concepto de Responsabilidad Social Empresarial.* Empresa Socialmente Responsable. Centro Mexicano para la Filantropía. www.cemefi.org/esr/images/stories/pdf/esr/concepto_esr.pdf.

Cao, Y., & Xiang, Y. (2012). The impact of knowledge governance on knowledge sharing. *Management Decision, 50*(4), 591–610. http://doi.org/10.1108/00251741211220147

CEC. (2021). *Strategic plan 2021–2025. Renewing our trilateral commitment and implementing the new free trade agreement and its supporting environmental cooperation agreement. Canada, Mexico, and the United States.* Commission for Environmental Cooperation.

CEC. (2023). *The SEM process in North America and relevant agreements: Agreement on environmental cooperation.* Commission for Environmental Cooperation.

CONABIO. (2015). *Estrategia para la conservación y el uso sustentable de la biodiversidad del estado de Guanajuato.* Comisión Nacional para el Conocimiento y Uso de la Biodiversidad. Instituto de Ecología del Estado.

CONAPRED. (n.d.). *Norma Mexicana NMX-R-025-SCFI-2015 en Igualdad Laboral y No Discriminación.* Consejo Nacional para prevenir la discriminación. https://nmx.conapred.org.mx/

De Jong, M., Huluba, G., & Beldad, A.D. (2019). Different shades of greenwashing: Consumers' reactions to environmental lies, half-lies, and organizations taking credit for following legal obligations. *Journal of Business and Technical Communication, 34*(1), 38–76, https://doi.org/10.1177/1050651919874105

EEA. (n.d.). *Topics.* European Environment Agency. www.eea.europa.eu/en

EMAS. (2018). *Case study "Involving Employees in Implementing EMAS" (SSCS). [Green Business].* European Commission. https://green-business.ec.europa.eu/publications/case-study-involving-employees-implementing-emas_en

Fios, F. (2019). Building awareness of eco-centrism to protect the environment. *Journal of Physics, Conference Series, 1402*(2), 1–5. https://doi.org/10.1088/1742-6596/1402/2/022095

Freitas Netto, S.V., Sobral, M.F.F., Ribeiro, A.R.B., & Soares, G.R.D.L. (2020). Concepts and forms of greenwashing: A systematic review. *Environmental Sciences Europe, 32*(19), 1–12. https://doi.org/10.1186/s12302-020-0300-3

FSC. (n.d.). *The future of forests is in our hands.* Forest Stewardship Council. [Website] https://fsc.org/en

Gagnon Thompson, S., & Barton, M.A. (1994). Ecocentric and anthropocentric attitudes toward the environment. *Journal of Environmental Psychology*, *14*(2), 149–157. https://doi.org/10.1016/S0272-4944(05)80168-9

Gelino, B.W., Erath, T.G., & Reed, D.D. (2021). Going green: A systematic review of proenvironmental empirical research in behavior analysis. *Behavior and Social Issues*, *30*, 587–611. https://doi.org/10.1007/s42822-020-00043-x

Gochuico, M.T.D. (2021). Development of a tool for measuring ecocentrism as an outcome of environmental communication. *Philippine Social Science Journal*, *4*(4), 155–165. https://doi.org/10.52006/main.v4i4.408

Guerrero, M., Herrera, F., & Urbano, D. (2019). Strategic knowledge management within subsidised entrepreneurial university-industry partnerships. *Management Decision*, *57*(12), 3280–3300. https://doi.org/10.1108/MD-10-2018-1126

Hair Jr., J.F., Hult, G.T.M., Ringle, C.M., Sarstedt, M., Danks, N.p., & Ray, S., (2021). *Partial least squares structural equation modeling (PLS-SEM) using R. A workbook*. Springer.

Hanafiah, M.H. (2020). Formative vs. reflective measurement model: Guidelines for structural equation modeling research. *International Journal of Analysis and Applications*, *18*(5), 876–889. https://doi.org/10.28924/2291-8639

Haro, D.M., & Peña, G.C. (2020). El conocimiento y uso de las tecnologías de la información y comunicación, en las micro, pequeñas y medianas empresas familiares en el estado de Nayarit. *Universo de la tecnológica*, *37*(1), 24–30.

Heras-Saizarbitoria, I. (2020). Environmental management certification and environmental performance: Greening or greenwashing? *Business Strategy and the Environment*, *29*(6), 2829–2841. https://doi.org/10.1002/bse.2546

Huysman, M., & Wit, D. (2002). *Knowledge sharing in practice*. Springer.

INEGI. (June 23, 2022). *Demografía de los establecimientos Mipyme en el contexto de la pandemia por COVID-19*. Comunicado de Prensa num. 335/2. https://www.inegi.org.mx/contenidos/saladeprensa/aproposito/2022/EAP_Demog_MIPYME22.pdf

ISO. (n.d.). ISO 14001:2015(en). *Environmental management systems—Requirements with guidance for use*. www.iso.org/obp/ui#iso:std:iso:14001:ed-3:v1:en

Kaur, V. (2022). Knowledge-based dynamic capabilities: A scientometric analysis of marriage between knowledge management and dynamic capabilities. *Journal of Knowledge Management*, *27*(4), 919–952. https://doi.org/10.1108/JKM-02-2022-0112

Krafft, J., & Ravix, J.-L. (2008). Corporate governance and the governance of knowledge: Rethinking the relationship in terms of corporate coherence. *Economics of Innovation and New Technology*, *17*(1–2), 79–95. https://doi.org/10.1080/10438590701279359

Lara Manjarrez, I.A. (2021). Responsabilidad social empresarial para la competitividad de las organizaciones en México. *Mercados y Negocios*, *43*, 97–118. https://doi.org/10.32870/myn.v0i43.7546

Lee, C.S., & Wong, K.Y. (2015). Development and validation of knowledge management performance measurement constructs for small and medium enterprises. *Journal of Knowledge Management*, *19*(4), 711–734. https://doi.org/10.1108/JKM-10-2014-0398

Martinez, J.E.V., Serna, M.D.C.M., Sanchez, M.D.C.B., & Aguilar, J.T.M. (2023). The impact of ICT and knowledge management on open innovation: Empirical evidence from Mexico. *International Journal of Innovative Research and Scientific Studies*, *6*(1), 193–204. https://doi.org/10.53894/ijirss.v6i1.1201

Mendis, M.V.S., & Welmilla, I. (2021). Green consciousness of employees. *Human Resource Management in Challenging Environments*, *11*, 88–106.

Mendoza-Arvizo, U., & Solís-Rodríguez, F.T. (2022). Calidad, conocimiento e innovación de procesos de manufactura en Ciudad Juárez, México. *Retos*, *12*(23), 83–109. https://doi.org/10.17163/ret.n23.2022.05

Millán, G., Javier, J., & Castañón, Á. (n.d.). Gestión de Conocimiento e Innovación Abierta: Hacia la conformación de un modelo teórico relacional. *Revista Venezolana de Gerencia*, *24*(88), 1199–1222.

Neuenfeldt, E. (2023). *Methods, Techniques and Tools for Knowledge Management.* [Conference Paper]. Comenius University.

Nickerson, D., Lowe, M., Pattabhiramaiah, A., & Sorescu, A. (2022). The impact of corporate social responsibility on brand sales: An accountability perspective. *Journal of Marketing*, *86*(2), 5–28. https://doi.org/10.1177/00222429211044155

Nuñez-Ramírez, M.A., Banegas-Rivero, R.A., Ozuna-Beltrán, A.G., & Atila-Lijerón, J.D. (2020). Gestión del conocimiento y capacidades de innovación incremental en empresas de México y Bolivia. *Información tecnológica*, *31*(5), 101–108. https://doi.org/10.4067/S0718-07642020000500101

PI100CN. (n.d.). *Certificaciones Internacionales. Programa Internacional 100% Carbono Neutral.* www.100carbonneutral.com/quienes_somos.html

Pinzón Castro, S.Y., Maldonado Guzmán, G., & Marín Aguilar, J.T. (2019). Orientación de la gestión del conocimiento y rendimiento en las pequeñas y medianas empresas mexicanas. *Revista de Ciencias Sociales*, *25*(1), 21–34. https://doi.org/10.31876/rcs.v25i1.27284

PROFEPA. (n.d.). *Programa Nacional de Auditoría Ambiental. Procuraduría Federal de Protección al Medio Ambiente. Gobierno de México.* www.gob.mx/profepa/acciones-y-programas/programa-nacional-de-auditoria-ambiental-56432

PROFEPA. (2023). *Convocatoria al "Distintivo de Calidad Ambiental México".* Procuraduría Federal de Protección al Medio Ambiente. Gobierno de México. www.gob.mx/profepa/documentos/convocatoria-distintivo-de-calidad-ambiental-mexico-336256

RainforestAlliance. (n.d.). *[We're all in].* Rainforest Alliance. [Website]. www.rainforest-alliance.org/

Rodríguez, I.S.R., & López, S.R.R. (2021). Gestión del conocimiento y responsabilidad social empresarial en Agronegocios. Caso: Hermosillo, Sonora. *Revista Mexicana de Agronegocios*, *48*(25), 642–655.

Rodríguez-Zúñiga, J., González-Guillén, M.D.J., & Valtierra-Pacheco, E. (2019). Las empresas forestales comunitarias en la región de la Mariposa Monarca, México: Un enfoque empresarial. *Bosque (Valdivia)*, *40*(1), 57–69. https://doi.org/10.4067/S0717-92002019000100057

Ruiz-Corrales, M., Lopez, I.P., Galvan-Vela, E., & Ravina-Ripoll, R. (2022). Knowledge transfers and absorptive capacities as determinants of competitive advantages: The Mexican case. *IEEE Engineering Management Review*, *50*(2), 54–65. https://doi.org/10.1109/EMR.2022.3171981

Sá Freire, P. de, Hawamdeh, S., Dandolini, G.A., & Bresolin, G.G. (2021). Why knowledge governance and learning. In P. de Sá Freire, S. Hawamdeh, & G. A. Dandolini (Eds.), *Series on innovation and knowledge management* (Vol. 15, pp. 1–12). World Scientific. https://doi.org/10.1142/9789811224119_0001

Sahut, J.M., Peris-Ortiz, M., & Teulon, F. (2019). Corporate social responsibility and governance. *Journal of Management and Governance*, *23*, 901–912. https://doi.org/10.1007/s10997-019-09472-2

Sánchez-Medina, P.S. (2022). Entrepreneurial orientation and environmental behavior: An explanation from the values of ecocentrism and conformity of Mexican artisans. *Journal of Developmental Entrepreneurship*, *27*(3). https://doi.org/10.1142/S1084946722500182

Secretaría de Economía. (June 30, 2009). *ACUERDO por el que se establece la estratificación de las micro, pequeñas y medianas empresas*. Diario Oficial. https://www.gob.mx/cms/uploads/attachment/file/550589/DOF.Estratificacio_n_PYMES.pdf

Secretaría de Economía. (2021). I*nforme Nacional Voluntario 2021. Agenda 2030 en México*. Gobierno de México.

SEMARNAT. (n.d.). *Programa Transporte Limpio. Secretaría de Medio Ambiente y Recursos Naturales*. Gobierno de México. www.gob.mx/semarnat/acciones-y-programas/programa-transporte-limpio-190236

Shahzad, M., Qu, Y., Zafar, A.U., & Appolloni, A. (2021). Does the interaction between the knowledge management process and sustainable development practices boost corporate green innovation? *Business Strategy and the Environment*, *30*(8), 4206–4222. https://doi.org/10.1002/bse.2865

Si Xue, C.T. (2017). A literature review on knowledge management in organizations. *Research in Business and Management*, *4*(1), 30. https://doi.org/10.5296/rbm.v4i1.10786

SMAOT. (n.d.a). *Calendario Ambiental. Secretaría de Medio Ambiente y Ordenamiento Territorial*. Gobierno del Estado. GTO. https://smaot.guanajuato.gob.mx/sitio/calendario-ambiental

SMAOT. (n.d.b). *Política Ambiental. Secretaría de Medio Ambiente y Ordenamiento Territorial*. Gobierno del Estado. GTO. https://smaot.guanajuato.gob.mx/sitio/politica-ambiental

SMAOT. (n.d.c). *Normatividad Ambiental. Secretaría de Medio Ambiente y Ordenamiento Territorial*. Gobierno del Estado. GTO. https://smaot.guanajuato.gob.mx/sitio/normatividad-ambiental

Song, M., Yang, M.X., Zeng, K.J., & Feng, W. (2020). Green knowledge sharing, stakeholder pressure, absorptive capacity, and green innovation: Evidence from Chinese manufacturing firms. *Business Strategy and the Environment*, *29*(3), 1517–1531. https://doi.org/10.1002/bse.2450

Straccia, L., Pollo-Cattaneo, M.F., & Maulini, A. (2023). Knowledge management model: A process view. In *Computational science and its applications—ICCSA 2023* (pp. 599–616). Springer.

STPS. (n.d.). *Modelo de reconocimiento "Empresa Familiarmente Responsable". Manual para su aplicación*. Secretaría del Tabajo y Previsión Social. Gobierno de México. www.stps.gob.mx/EMPRESA_FR/002%20%20Manual%20de%20Aplicacion%20EFR%20%28PDF%29.pdf

Thanh Tiep Le. (2022). How do corporate social responsibility and green innovation transform corporate green strategy into sustainable firm performance? *Journal of Cleaner Production*, *362*, 132228. https://doi.org/10.1016/j.jclepro.2022.132228

UNFCCC. (2022). *Decision -/CP.27. Sharm el-Sheikh implementation plan*. Sessional Proceedings. Sharm el-Sheikh Climate Change Conference. Non-official session documents. https://unfccc.int/documents/624444

United Nations. (2022). *The sustainable development goals report*.

USGBC. (n.d.). *Guide to LEED certification. U.S. Green Building Council*. www.usgbc.org/guide-LEED-certification

Vásquez Sánchez, J.R., & Larios-Gómez, E. (2021). Correlación de los factores de competitividad empresarial con la gestión del conocimiento en Marketing en las MiPyMEs mexicanas y colombianas. *CPMark-Caderno Profissional de Marketing*, *9*(2), 170.

Wang, S., Abbas, J., Sial, M.S., Alvarez-Otero, S., & Cioca, L.-I. (2022). Achieving green innovation and sustainable development goals through green knowledge management: Moderating role of organizational green culture. *Journal of Innovation & Knowledge*, *7*(100272), 1–9. https://doi.org/10.1016/j.jik.2022.100272

Yang, Z., Nguyen, T.T.H., Nguyen, H.N., Nguyen, T.T.N., & Cao, T.T. (2020). Greenwashing behaviours: Causes, taxonomy and consequences based on a systematic literature review. *Journal of Business Economics and Management*, *21*(5), 1486–1507. https://doi.org/10.3846/jbem.2020.13225

15 Environmental responsibility and knowledge management in post-industrial organizations of the 21st century

Julia Pérez Bravo and Martha Salvador Ledesma

Introduction

The 21st-century post-industrial organizations base their economy on the lending of services, focusing mostly in the intangible or immaterial (Castro 2019). Nowadays, they are breaking paradigms in regard to the forms that working takes, using new guides of organizational practices, inside of them, the knowledge management, the sustainability and the responsibility in their many edges. Within this 21st-century post-industrial organizations, the hospitality services of the state of Queretaro can be found, which are facing plenty of problems or situations that don't allow them to align with the sustainability goals even though businessmen try, given the fact that being sustainable is one of the new trends needed to align to the Sustainable Development Goals (SDGs), further worsening if it turns out to be the restaurant industry which is 99.87% composed by small- and middle-sized companies. According to the Directorio Estadístico Nacional de Unidades Económicas (DENUE) (Inegi, n.d.), there are 12,713 establishments, which face typical problems of the industry, among those, outdated administrative systems, limited financial structure, lack of quality, lack of working capital, incipient use of marketing, poorly trained human capital, few innovative ideas and difficult access to financing. In addition to the already mentioned problems, it is also worth mentioning the lack of attention that was given to the tourism field development, both at an state and municipal level, this, despite the importance that it meant for the economical and social growth.

Nonetheless, for the purpose of this research, it is worth mentioning that there is a lack of insight into the ways to achieve sustainable organizations. Nonaka and Takeuchi (1999) claimed that knowledge is the most important resource for organizations and those that use it will have the key to attain prosperity. Therefore, knowledge management has become a necessary strategy for organizations to improve results. This strategy can be used to establish green practices or environmental responsibility programs in companies, consistent with the efficient use of non-renewable resources (water, electricity, waste reduction, etc.), which will influence sustainability (economic, social, and environmental development) both in organizations and in the communities involved.

DOI: 10.4324/9781003465058-15

It is worth mentioning that, currently, the restaurant industry represents an asset to the local government, in the matter of projects and strategies that the San Juan del Río, Qro., municipality proposes as a political administrative organism, especially in the secretary of economy, where they are seen as important edges for the sustainable development that establish plans and programs of federal and municipal development.

The goal of the following research was to understand the current situation of companies in the aforementioned industry concerning post-industrial organizations' green practices, specifically those offering hospitality services in the state of Querétaro. This is intended to manage knowledge and generate environmental responsibility strategies that will impact the sustainability of these organizations and society as a whole.

The main research question proposed is as follows:

> What strategies will enable 21st-century post-industrial organizations, specifically those in the restaurant industry in the state of Querétaro, to be environmentally responsible and sustainable to influence both their development and that of the society they belong to?

Sustainability

A background for the sustainability discussed by Martins (2022), in the year 1962, the biologist Rachel Carson mentioned that the environmental destruction generated in those years, mostly due to the use of the DDT pesticide, created great amount of havoc in the United states, mainly to the populations of bald eagles, and gave rise to the first environmental movement. It had such a success that it achieved the creation of the Environmental Protection Agency (EPA) in 1970 with the goal of exclusive care of the environment.

By 1983, the United Nations (UN) created the World Commission of Environment and Development (WCED) led by the then first minister of Norway, Brundtland. Being the most important contribution of this organism, the evaluation of any action or initiative from three distinct approaches: economic, environmental and social.

It was that same Prime Minister Brundtland who, in 1983, claimed that sustainability means 'being able to fulfill current needs without jeopardizing the ability of future generations to fulfill their own.' This aligns with Leal (2016), who additionally claimed that sustainability aims to improve the quality of life, biological diversity, gender equality, and respect for race and beliefs, implying many changes in all social groups concerning attitude, ethics, education, consciousness, and commitment.

Sustainability is of such importance to the development of humanity that SDGs focus on their search through the fulfillment of the 17 objectives that were established by the United Nations back in 2015 and were adopted by 193 countries, addressing plenty of global issues with the goal of improving life conditions for the people all around the world (UN, n/d).

The present research highlights the development SDG 17, same that addresses the "alliances for the fulfillment of goals" and accentuates the importance of world collaboration for the addressing of challenges faced by humanity. In other words, it seeks to strengthen the cooperation between governments, private sector and civil society in order to implement both effective and sustainable strategies that promote the development.

Post-industrial organizations

Post-industrial organizations, as mentioned by Castro (2019), citing Heydebrand (1989) and Sennett (2000), emerged when the international commerce between countries, among them Mexico, opened itself to new markets around the years 1970 and 1990, respectively, which would create a new challenge to the organizations, having to face a whole restructuration by taking the already-existing production models as base as well as the environment in which they develop; as a result capitalism starts to prevail in the global stage, now being necessary to finish off plenty of paradigms such as the industrial structures, with syndicate discomfort, high costs of machinery and labor along the way, consequently it was necessary to make the transition toward a flexible capitalism that would allow organizations to mold themselves in order to fulfill their goals.

This concept of society was, according to Forero de Moreno (2009) proposed by Bell et al. (1976), when he established the term "information society," in which he recognizes that the main axis of that society will be knowledge with it being the axis of both the new economy and of a new society based on information, which implies the he already acknowledged the transition from an industrial and agricultural production based economy toward one whose main asset would be services.

Guerrero (2005) mentions the five dimensions of the post-industrial society.

1. Economic sector: The transition from an economy based on industrial production toward one that produces services.
2. Occupational distribution: It is preferred to hire professionals and technicians
3. Axial principle: Use of knowledge for innovation

4. Future orientation: Use and control of technology and its products.
5. Decision making: Decision making aided by technology.

On the other hand, Castro (2019) mentions the main categories of post-industrial society, highlighting knowledge, information and advanced technology, which had a great impact on both the economy and society. He additionally mentions that post-industrial society bases itself, fundamentally, on services.

A post-industrial society possesses specific characteristics according to its purpose as mentioned by Corvo (2021):

Professional workers: Technical and professional training are the main assets in the labor sector.
Technological progress: The types of work and the process of information technology.
Reproductive revolution: Demographics, where greater reproductive efficiency is found.
Rise of knowledge elites: Use of knowledge for the social changes, information that is born from elites formed in universities, government organizations and companies.
Growth of multiple networks: The combination of technology, communication, management systems and production technologies; are links between organizations and markets.

The networks allow the organizations to develop products or services in the market, being an economic strategy for the establishment of big international companies.

Likewise, he mentions that there are different types of post-industrial societies, such as:

Service society: The largest workforce carries out activities in the tertiary sector, which includes transportation, health, education, commerce, government, entertainment and hospitality services, this according to Coll-Hurtado and Córdoba y Ordoñez (2006).
Knowledge society: This society's importance relies in theoretical knowledge as the source of innovation and political formulation in society.
Technological society: Relies on technological contributions and their control, taking into account the development of new technology as a means of ordering society in masses.
Intellectual society: A new intellectual and rational technology is created, which allows the replacement of intuitions for algorithms.
Sustainable society: It is both an ecology and human satisfaction-orientated society, through science, technology, culture, environmental education, etc.

Added to the displacement of gender roles in professions as well as the globalization of information and knowledge which Corvo (2021) writes allowed the interaction to occur in time and space. One of the most important consequences of post-industrial society is the expansion of the welfare state coupled with the possibility for humankind to have access to more services, such as hospitality services, this thanks to technological progress and the use of knowledge.

Hospitality

In colloquial terms, "hospitality" is a highly used term, which refers to the services offered to people such as accommodation, food and drinks, therefore the experience given must be of welcoming, friendliness, enjoyment, tranquility, satisfaction and so forth, all of this lies on the fact that service offering has gained relevance as a result of the fact that globalization has set the tone for a better relation between countries and in turn has allowed to sparkle in people a new interest in getting to know other nations along with their language, culture, cuisine, history traditions and so forth. Consequently, this has made hospitality a feature in both national and international tourism.

Vázquez Gómez and Osorio García (2016) mention that hospitality has been practiced since antiquity, with it taking importance due to the social and migratory movements. Brotherton (2003) defines it as a combination of tangible and intangible elements. On the other hand, authors (Hepple et al., 1990; King, 1995), cited by Moreno et al. (2020), define hospitality around four basic characteristics: (1) accommodation of a guest, (2) interaction between who offers and who receives the service: (3) combination of tangible and intangible elements; and lastly, (4) the service provider looks for customer guarantee through general comfort.

Vázquez Gómez and Osorio García (2016) mention that in the tourism sector, the concept of hospitality refers to the relation between host and guest, with the need for satisfaction as the main goal, with an economic base, but in a material, psychological and cultural environment.

ABASTUR (2023) in the digital communication platform Entorno Turístico emphasizes that hospitality industries grow due to the requirements of national and international tourism, as well as a result of the requirements and demands of consumers.

In regard to the restaurant industry, as it was already mentioned in the kinds of post-industrial societies, the biggest workforce carries out its activities in the tertiary sector, which includes services such as transport, health, education, commerce, government, entertainment and hospitality, according to Coll-Hurtado and Córdoba y Ordoñez (2006); and the Instituto Nacional de Estadística y Geografía (INEGI), which includes in this industry the food and drinks preparation services. Highlighting leisure, recreation or entertainment to frame this research, Bell et al. (1976) mentions recreation as one of the features accounting for the measurement of quality of life, which in turn also includes health, education and personal development. From there, it can be implied that hospitality services, which include the restaurant industry, are part of a recreational component that has an effect in the change in both level and quality of life in post-industrial societies, about which the author himself stated, are measured in terms of experiences and services rather than in accumulation of material goods. This means that in the restaurant industry, food service gets converted into a social and cultural experience that contributes to the wellness and the quality of life, where the search for culinary experiences and the enjoyment of food become staples for the improvement of life quality in the given society.

Pérez Bravo et al. (2023), citing Sallés (2018), stated that the restaurant sector has its origins in current day Egypt around 512 BC. where archaeological evidence implies that there used to exist a public dining room where dishes within a limited menu were offered, but the restaurant as a concept was used, as Garduño Rivas (n.d.) shares, for the first time in Paris, France, where a local was opened in 1765, where dishes were offered alongside wine, it being considered the first restaurant to exist. Throughout time a continuous growth in this industry can be seen as the number of businesses rises, represented by 515,059 establishments that are dedicated exclusively to the preparation of food and beverages (Zárraga Cano et al., 2018).

This restaurant industry is a mixture of economic organisms that produce food and beverages at the moment and they represent an interaction between distinct economic areas, such as that of agriculture, meat industry, fishing and rural development, among others, affirms the representative of the tourist department in 2009, on the other hand, Barrios Moreno, F. and Loubet Orozco, R. (2021) claimed that the restaurant industry is an engine for the economy and a job generator, accounting for 428 thousand establishments, of which 96% are small and medium sized companies, representing a path toward the Mexican entrepreneurship. In Torruco Marqués (2019) words, by 2015, the restaurant industry is essential to the country touristic development, granting Mexico a privileged situation in the global stage, thanks to its varied cuisine and its quality service.

The food services are carried out by those organizations that prepare and serve food to consumers or diners. On the other hand Solis Morales. A. I. et al. (2021) defines it as the preparation of food for a number of diners bigger than that of a family (collective feeding), having to meet the quality standars for a healthy diet as is it is established by the NOM-043-SSA2–2012.

As it has been mentioned, food services are spaces where food and drinks are offered to a group of persons, which are required to meet certain criteria, such as quality, hygiene, health, nutrition and so forth as well as having certain features for the diners such as health, new dishes degustation, new experiences and celebration of a special dates, among others.

Classification of food services

Food services according to the population they are aimed at can be split into two, commercial and noncommercial (Tejada de Lopez, B. D., 2006). Additionally, noncommercial food services can be further split into self-managed or own and concessionaire.

Additional current data of the Mexican restaurant industry is provided by the digital communication platform denominated Entorno turístico, which mentions that in 2022 the sales were worth 64.9 billion, whereas sales worth 70.9 billion were generated in 2023. On the other hand, CANIRAC estimated sales in 2024 worth 300 billion. The fast food field stands out in México, given that it accounts for more than 40% of all the sales, followed by casual food accounting for more than 30%, with just a 10% accounting for gourmet cuisine.

The use of the concept of knowledge management is born in Europe around the 1990s, Mexico getting involved up until the current century, with the trend of it being a factor for sustainability of even more recent appearance. Although, giving the appropriate importance to Kochan and Osterman (1994) claims in regard to the relevance of making a profit in a workplace, by using employees' knowledge and skills. This same use of knowledge management is intended to be achieved in local restaurants as a strategy for (sustainable) economic, cultural and social growth.

Environment responsibility

Being socially responsible means being aware of the impacts generated on stake holders through the actions that are undertaken in the pursuit in then

Table 15.1 Food service classification

Classification of food services		
Tejada de López	Commercial	They have the purpose of obtaining a payment, offering a varied menu at a certain time, to diverse dinners.
	Non-commercial	They are not meant to make a profit, they offer food according to the kind of dinner, with a subsidy granted by the government or another institution
	Payment of fee	The service provided is not meant to make a profit, seeking only to recover the investment.
Pérez Fierro	Institutional	They can be lucrative or non-profit and focus on nutritional and economic aspects, for instance: Schools and hospitals.
	Industrial	They are usually extra benefits provided by companies for workers.

of various objectives, This social responsibility is defined by Pérez Bravo, J. (2022) as: the combination of obligations, legal and ethical commitments, on both national and international levels in an organization for stakeholders, them being voluntaries and, according the organization's objectives, in full compatibility with social, economic and environmental impacts.

For this research's purpose, a focus on the environmental part was made and as a result the subject in discussion turns out to be environmental responsibility, which in Oxfamintermon (2023) words indicates the commitment level we as people or organizations have toward the environment that surrounds us, with Sierra Raza et al. (2019), claiming that this responsibility lies its foundations on the ethics of commitment in the ways of managing, producing, consuming and relating between organizations and their environment.

Knowledge management

In broad terms, knowledge management is a necessary strategy in organizations for the improvements both in their results and in the impacts on interested parties, having the necessity to manage the insight on human resources in organizations, taking advantage of the economic, social and environmental (sustainable) development of people, organizations and communities in general. In a similar manner, it can play a crucial role in the generation of sustainability strategies in the restaurant industry, that being, using the distinct phases of knowledge management: collecting, sharing, using and updating knowledge within an organization will allow to address specific challenges related to sustainability, such as:

Spreading of awareness and education,
Identification of nest practices,
Continuous innovation,
Adaptation to changes in legislation and regulations,
Integration of sustainable technologies,
Collaboration and networks,
Continuous improvement in operational efficiency.

There is no background to the application of knowledge management and social responsibility as sustainability factors in post-industrial organizations, more specifically in the restaurant industry in San Juan del Río, Qro. On the other hand, considering the current and real needs of humanity, it can be highlighted the premise of the necessity of organizations to be sustainable, that is, guarantee the proper balance between the environmental, economic and sociocultural dimensions. Same approach is displayed by the World Tourism Organization (WTO, 2023) where the spread of a development that supports the conservation of biodiversity, social welfare and economical security in communities is encouraged.

Due to the previously mentioned, it was considered important to carry out research actions through knowledge management and social responsibility in organizations in the restaurant industry that are part of post-industrial organizations, same actions that seek to influence one of the aspects of sustainability, that of environment, with the goal of benefiting in first instance the restaurant industry part of the tourism sector of San Juan del Río, Qro.

Methodology

This research focused on the study of restaurants in the municipality of San Juan del Río, Qro. Using the mixed research method, the documentation was included for the making of needed theory and to create an introduction to the research itself. In regard to field research, research tools were applied, such as an interview to the representative of restaurant entrepreneurs and a survey conducted on a Likert scale for entrepreneurs in the restaurant industry, this with the purpose of identifying the use of resources and tools as indicators of application and existence of the factors of environmental responsibility and sustainability, emphasizing these in the environmental axis. The method used was the analytical-synthetic one, since the issues regarding sustainability and environmental responsibility faced by restaurants in the hospitality industry of San Juan del Río Querétaro were analyzed. In other words, the deficiencies found in the use of factors mentioned to influence sustainability; The research approach was quantitative since instruments that provide quantitative data were used. After reviewing the information from various companies, various proposals for actions on green practices or environmental responsibility were obtained, these for post-industrial organizations in the hospitality industry, more specifically in the restaurant industry of the state of Querétaro that will have an impact on their own sustainability.

Results

Through interviews with different representatives of the sector, it was found that, currently, the restaurant industry of the state of Querétaro is experiencing a significant shift toward a more sustainable and environmentally responsible post-industrial model, this is an adaptation to new economic, social and economic trends and technologies that shape the contemporary business landscape. Following is highlighted among the key changes that are shaping this sector:

Digitalization and technology: Out of the total number of respondents, 66.7% stated that the use of technology has allowed them to contribute to environmental responsibility, since they have implemented the use of mobile applications for online orders, reservations and home delivery services, which has improved operational efficiency as well as allowed to better respond to the preferences and expectations of modern consumers.

Flexibility in business models: A total of 66.7% of restaurants have opted for shared spaces, collaborations with other businesses as well as with the local community and to a lesser extent (11.1%) the creation of pop-up events in order to diversify their offers and reach different shards of the market.

And regarding sustainability and environmental responsibility, the adoption of sustainable practices has become a priority in the face of growing environmental awareness and consumer demand for greener options. The restaurant industry has implemented various strategies to reduce its environmental footprint and contribute to the sustainable development, seeking to generate a positive impact on the environment and reflect the growing importance of environmental responsibility.

The main sustainable strategies adopted being those described next:

Waste management: 88.9% of establishments have implemented recycling increase and waste reduction programs to minimize their environmental impact and 22.2% have adopted composting programs. The separation of organic and inorganic waste has become common in kitchens and dining rooms, as well as the promotion of reuse and recycling and it is found that 44.4% out of the community surveyed applies it constantly.

Responsible sourcing: An increase of 66.7% in the preference for local and sustainable suppliers among the surveyed can be seen, as well as 77.8% in the use of seasonal products. Restaurants not only support the local economy but also reduce the carbon footprint associated with transportation of food.

Energy efficiency: Some measures have been implemented in order to reduce energy consumption, such as the installation of more efficient equipment, thus we have found that 88.9% of the surveyed have optimized lighting and 33.3% have achieved intelligent air conditioning, likewise 33.3% now use sources of renewable energy, such as solar panels, to reduce their dependence on non-renewable sources.

Sustainable menus: 55.6% of those surveyed have stated that they have menus that prioritize sustainable ingredients and 77.8% have vegetarian or vegan options, which is a growing trend in the industry that seeks to satisfy the demands of consumers aware of their environmental impact.

Education and awareness: 33.3% of businesses have incorporated educational programs to raise awareness among their employees about the importance of sustainable practices such as awareness campaigns and 44.4% train their staff on environmental subjects and 33.3% promote habits of responsible consumption to their clients.

With all of this taken into account, the most important strategy now is to seek the creation of strategic alliances with both the federal and local governments in order to achieve sustainability and environmental responsibility and, by extension, align with global trends as well as the SDGs, mainly SDG 17, of which it has been found that awareness about sustainability and environmental care, as well as the addressment of the challenges in this regard, has been growing and is a commitment to all interested parties, who recognize the importance of a joint approach and actions. This situation has given rise to the creation of a series of strategic alliances between the government and the restaurant industry, seeking to promote sustainable practices and environmental responsibility in the sector.

Amongst the most notable initiatives and alliances that have emerged in order to promote sustainability in the Mexican restaurant industry, there can be found:

Environmental Certification and Labeling Programs: In collaboration with the government, several organizations and associations of the restaurant industry in Mexico have implemented environmental certification and labeling programs, programs that seek to recognize and promote those restaurants that have adopted sustainable practices, from waste management to the use of local ingredients and energy efficiency.

Incentives and Subsidies for Sustainable Practices: The Mexican government has introduced various incentives and subsidies aimed at encouraging the adoption of sustainable practices in the restaurant industry, which include tax benefits for those establishments that implement measures to reduce their environmental footprint, such as the installation of renewable energy systems or participation in recycling programs; however, only 22.2% of the surveyed say they possess any of these.

Environmental Awareness and Education Campaigns: Alliances have also been made between the government and the restaurant industry focusing on environmental awareness and education campaigns seeking not only to sensitize consumers about the importance of choosing more sustainable options but also to train owners and employees of restaurants in environmentally responsible practices, similarly to the Incentives and Subsidies for Sustainable Practices, only 22.2% claimed to have participated in these campaigns.

Environmental Regulation and Regulatory Compliance: When asked if they have participated in the formulation of environmental regulations and sustainable and environmental standards, they stated that they have not been taken into account.

Regarding other sustainable practices, it has been found that 44.4% use sustainable packaging, 62.5% use biodegradable cleaning products 22.2% have a backyard garden near the business and 22.2% reuse cooking oil. They also have stated that 37.5% of them donate leftover food, 62.5% make use of homemade products and 88.9% manage perishable products in a way to prevent them from spoiling and it is worth mentioning that out of all those surveyed, none uses meat from farms with humane practices.

Conclusion

This research addressed the relevant topic of knowledge management and environmental responsibility in post-industrial organizations, focusing specifically on the restaurant industry of the state of Querétaro. Through an exhaustive analysis, the challenges and problems faced by this industry were identified, which, despite their economic and social importance, finding solutions for is being prevented by various obstacles, ranging from the obsolescence of past administration systems up to the lack of initiative toward innovation.

The current context of post-industrial organizations, characterized by their focus on services, intangible resources, and knowledge management, highlights the need for the restaurant industry to evolve to align with the principles of sustainability and environmental responsibility. The adoption of green practices and the development of strategies that encourage global collaboration, in line with SDG 17, are positioned as crucial elements for the sustainable growth of these organizations.

In this scenario, knowledge management emerges as a strategic tool. The skills of collecting, sharing, using and updating knowledge within restaurant organizations would not only address specific problems already identified, such as obsolescence in management systems and the lack of trained human resources but also be essential for the establishment of internship programs—green and environmental responsibility. This approach, supported by knowledge management, can directly contribute to sustainability in terms of economic, social and environmental development, both for organizations and for the communities in which they operate.

Furthermore, this research highlights the importance of environmental responsibility in this process. Social responsibility, understood as a set of legal and ethical obligations as well as commitments, must be expanded to include the environmental dimension. Restaurant organizations, by assuming environmental responsibility, would not only comply with an ethical and legal criterion, but also improve their innovation and ecological efficiency, thus contributing to more sustainable development.

Even though there is no previous precedent for the implementation of knowledge management and environmental responsibility as sustainability factors in post-industrial organizations in the restaurant industry in San Juan del Río, Qro. The need for adopting these practices is now imperative. This research, by addressing this void, provides a solid foundation for future actions and strategies that seek sustainable development in this crucial sector.

In summary, knowledge management and environmental responsibility are postulated as key elements to guide restaurant organizations toward a more sustainable future, in line with the current demands of society and the global environment.

A detailed analysis of the results reveals that the restaurant industry of the state of Querétaro is undergoing a significant shift toward a sustainable and environmentally responsible post-industrial model. Key changes include widespread adoption of digital technologies, flexibility in business models and a strong focus on sustainability and environmental responsibility.

In terms of technology, 66.7% of respondents have integrated mobile applications for online ordering, reservations, and delivery services into their tool repertoire, improving operational efficiency and meeting the expectations of modern consumers.

The flexibility in business models stands out, with 66.7% of restaurants opting for shared spaces and local collaborations, highlighting the sector's adaptability to new economic and social trends.

Sustainability and environmental responsibility have become priorities, with strategies such as waste management (carried out by 88.9%), responsible sourcing (66.7% from local suppliers), energy efficiency (33.3% using renewable sources), sustainable menus (55.6% with sustainable ingredients) and education and awareness (33.3% having educational programs).

Creating strategic alliances with the government (as suggested in SDG 17) is highlighted as the most important strategy to achieve sustainability and environmental responsibility. These partnerships include environmental certification programs, government incentives and awareness campaigns.

However, areas of opportunity are identified, such as low participation in the formulation of environmental regulations and sustainable standards and the need for greater participation in government incentives, where only 22.2% claim to have tax benefits.

In summary, the restaurant industry in Querétaro is actively responding to the current trends, adopting innovative practices and committing to both sustainability and environmental responsibility. And although significant progress has been made, there are still challenges and opportunities to be faced in order to strengthen collaboration between the private sector and government, in order to achieve more ambitious sustainability goals.

References

ABASTUR (2023). *Industrias de la hospitalidad y restaurantes en México, un motor económico sostenible: ABASTUR*. Entorno Turístico. Retrieved January 20, 2024, from www.entornoturistico.com/industrias-de-la-hospitalidad-y-restaurantes-en-mexico-un-motor-economico-sostenible-abastur/

Barrios Moreno, F., & Loubet Orozco, R. (2021). Precariedad y perspectivas de los actores del sector restaurantero turístico de Mazatlán, un destino en el Pacífico mexicano. *Trabajo y Sociedad*, *22*(37), 439–457.

Bell, D. (1994). *El advenimiento de la sociedad postindustrial* (R. García & E. Gallego, Trans.). Alianza Editorial. (Trabajo original publicado en 1976)

Bell, D., García, R., & Gallego, E. (1976). *El advenimiento de la sociedad post-industrial: Un intento de prognosis social.* Alianza. https://biblioteca.multiversidadreal.com/BB/Biblio/Daniel%20Bell/El%20advenimiento%20de%20la%20sociedad%20post%20%281252%29/El%20advenimiento%20de%20la%20sociedad%20-%20Daniel%20Bell.pdf

Brotherton, B. (Ed.). (2003). *The international hospitality industry: Structure, characteristics and issues.* Routledge. https://books.google.com.mx/books?id=K9mGcZ99_sC&printsec=frontcover&hl=es&source=gbs_ge_summary_r&cad=0#v=onepage&q&f=false

Castro, R. (2019). Subjetividades y uso de las TIC: una visión crítica al capitalismo contemporáneo. *Revista Gestión y Estrategia*, *54*, 23–38. https://doi.org/10.24275/uam/azc/dcsh/gye/2018n54/Castro

Coll-Hurtado, A., & Córdoba y Ordóñez, J. (2006). La globalización y el sector servicios en México. *Investigaciones geográficas*, *61*, 114–115. www.scielo.org.mx/scielo.php?script=sci_arttext&pid=S0188-46112006000300009&lng=es&tlng=es

Corvo, H.S. (May 30, 2021). *Sociedad postindustrial: concepto, características, tipos, ejemplos.* Lifeder. Retrieved January 20, 2024, from www.lifeder.com/sociedad-posindustrial/

Forero de Moreno, I. (July 2009). La Sociedad del conocimiento. *Revista Científica General José María Córdova*, *5*(7), 40–44. www.redalyc.org/pdf/4762/476248849007.pdf

Garduño Rivas, A. (n.d.). El primer restaurante. *UAEMex.* Retrieved November 20, 2023, from http://web.uaemex.mx/Culinaria/primer_numero/elprimer.html

Guerrero, O. (2005). La gerencia pública en la sociedad post-industrial. *Revista Venezolana de Gerencia*, *10*(31), 463–477. https://ve.scielo.org/scielo.php?script=sci_arttext&pid=S1315-99842005000300007

Hepple, J., Kipps, M., & Thomson, J. (1990). The concept of hospitality and an evaluation of its applicability to the experience of hospital patients. *International Journal of Hospitality Management*, *9*(4), 305–318. https://doi.org/10.1016/0278-4319(90)90038-y

Heydebrand, W. (1989). New organizational forms. *Work and Occupations*, *16*(3), 323–357.

Inegi. (n.d.). Directorio Estadístico Nacional de Unidades Económicas. *DENUE.* Inegi. Retrieved April 20, 2023, from www.inegi.org.mx/app/mapa/denue/default.aspx

King, C. A. (1995). What is hospitality? *International Journal of Hospitality Management*, *14*(3–4), 219–234.

Kochan, T.A., & Osterman, P. (1994). *The mutual gains enterprise: Forging a winning partnership among labor, management, and government.* Harvard Business School Press.

Leal, G.E. (2016). Debate sobre la sostenibilidad. Desarrollo conceptual y metodológico de una propuesta de desarrollo urbano para la ciudad-región Bogotá en clave de ciudad Latinoamericana. www.buyteknet.info/. www.buyteknet.info/fileshare/data/ambides_lect/Naredo.pdf

Martins, A. (October 13, 2022). *BBC NEWS MUNDO.* Retrieved May 15, 2023, from www.bbc.com/mundo/noticias-63161108

Moreno, S., Korstanje, M., & Picaso, P. (2020). El turismo como objeto de investigación. *Rosa dos ventos*, *12*(1), 80–95. www.redalyc.org/journal/4735/473563286007/473563286007.pdf

Nonaka, I., & Takeuchi, H. (1999). *La organización creadora del conocimiento: cómo las compañías japonesas crean la dinámica de la innovación* (M. Hernández Kocka, Trans., 1st ed., Vol. 1). Oxford University Press.

Oxfamintermon. (2023). ¿En qué consiste la responsabilidad medioambiental? Ingredientes que Suman. Retrieved November 6, 2023, from https://blog.oxfamintermon.org/en-que-consiste-la-responsabilidad-medioambiental/

Pérez Bravo, J. (2022). *Responsabilidad Social Gubernamental y Prácticas Laborales* (1st ed.). Ecorfan.

Pérez Bravo, J., Salvador Ledesma, M., & Díaz Nieto, E.S. (December 31, 2023). COVID-19 en el sector restaurantero de San Juan del Río, afectaciones y perspectivas. *Journal of Business and SMEs*, *9*(24), 31–37.

Pérez Fierro, A.M. (2002). Servicios de alimentos: a la búsqueda de profesiones. Universidad Panamericana, 02(Hospitalidad ESDAI), 105–118. https://hdl.handle.net/20.500.12552/6787

Portal CANIRAC – Camara Nacional de la Industria Restaurantera. (s/f). Org.mx. https://portal.canirac.org.mx/

Sallés, D.V. (6 septiembre, 2018). Así es como nació el primer restaurante de la historia. *La Vanguardia*. https://www.lavanguardia.com/comer/sitios/20180906/451384675191/primer-restaurantehistoria-origen.html#foto-1

Sennett, R. (2000). *La corrosión del carácter: las consecuencias personales en el nuevo capitalismo*. Editorial Anagrama.

Sierra Raza, L.A., Paz Marcano, A.I., & López Juvinao, D.D. (2019). Creando valor sustentable. *Business & Sustainability Letter. Económicas CUC*. https://doi.org/10.17981/econcuc.40.1.2019.03

Solis Morales, A.I., Pavón Varela, C. de la L., & Blasco López, G. (2021). Evaluación nutrimental de menús diarios para un comedor industrial de la región de Veracruz—Boca del Río. *UVserva*, *11*, 112–123. https://doi.org/10.25009/uvs.v0i11.2759

Tejada de Lopez, B.D. (2006). *Administración de servicios de alimentación. Calidad, nutrición, productividad y beneficios* (2nd ed.). Universidad de Antioquia. www.academia.edu/41935700/Administraci%C3%B3n_de_servicios_de_alimentaci%C3%B3n_Calidad_nutrici%C3%B3n_productividad_y_beneficios

Torruco Marqués, M. (December 6, 2019). El sector restaurantero representa el 15.3 por ciento del PIB Turístico en México. *Gobierno de México*. Retrieved January 20, 2023, from www.gob.mx/sectur/prensa/el-sector-restaurantero-representa-el-15-3-por-ciento-del-pib-turistico-en-mexico

United Nations. (n/d). *Naciones Unidas | Paz, dignidad e igualdaden un planeta sano*. https://www.un.org/es/

Vázquez Gómez, R.A., & Osorio García, M. (December 20, 2016). La hospitalidad en la prestación del servicio turístico. Una revisión sobre sus planteamientos teóricos en la revista International Journal of Hospitality Management, 2004–2013. *Revista de Investigación de la Ciencia Turística*, *10*, 39–72. https://dialnet.unirioja.es/servlet/articulo?codigo=6088847

World Tourism Organization. (2023). *Desarrollo sostenible | OMT*. UNWTO. Retrieved noviembre 22, 2023, from www.unwto.org/es/desarrollo-sostenible

Zárraga Cano, L., Molina Morejón, V.M., & Corona Sandoval, E. (2018). La satisfacción del cliente basada en la calidad del servicio a través de la eficiencia del personal y eficiencia del servicio: un estudio empírico de la industria restaurantera. *RECAI Revista de Estudios en Contaduría, Administración e Informática*, *7*(18). Retrieved September 12, 2023, from www.redalyc.org/journal/6379/637968306002/html/

16 Challenges and alternatives of ecocentrism, knowledge management and sustainability in post-industrial organizations in the 21st century

Sergio Ernesto Medina-Cuéllar, Elia Socorro Díaz Nieto, David Israel Contreras-Medina and Noé Aguilar-Rivera

Introduction

As part of the evolution of 21st-century post-industrial organizations, challenges set out as *actions that show that someone (or something) refuses to accept some fact and questions whether it is correct* (Oxford, n.d.) are currently faced with the need to take care of the environment. This has generated a societal and organizational revolution where the options focus on the knowledge to create, share and manage green practices.

The knowledge contained in the human being and amplified by organizations is to discern, understand, modify and adapt the issues and situations within the context. This sense has given him a place in the world, although on many occasions, with the false belief of being the highest authority, abusing nature above all.

The above is based on the concepts of ecocentrism, represented by the idea that everything in the natural world has intrinsic value and deserves moral consideration (ten Have & Patrão Neves, 2021; Darnthamrongkul & Mozingo, 2020); knowledge management theory, which locates public and private organizations of the 21st century with a vital role in articulating and amplifying knowledge (Nonaka, 1994), creating it, sharing it and managing green practices to achieve goals. Linking with Sustainable Development Goals (SDGs), this section will conclude with challenges and options for ecocentrism, knowledge management and sustainability in post-industrial organizations in the 21st century, presented in the studies of the book.

- Concerning "Ecocentrism Paradigms as a Way of Knowledge Management for Sustainability in the Post-industrial Organizations in the 21st Century," the challenges focus on adopting an ethical perspective for providing the responsible use of natural resources in decision-making and

DOI: 10.4324/9781003465058-16

investing in clean technologies. The option is to promote environmental education in public and private organizations of the 21st century.

- The challenges relate to "Knowledge Management for a Posture of Ecocentrism and Organizational Sustainability," to take advantage of natural resources to produce goods and provide sustainable services, increase quality and obtain certifications. At the same time, the options are updating new regulations and controls to promote and get an ecocentric mindset.
- Regarding "Theoretical Concepts and Generic Tools to Incorporate Sustainability via Knowledge Management into Post-industrial Organizations in the 21st Century," the challenges focus on incorporating sustainability, its concepts and tools via knowledge management in the primary sector. About the options, focus on organic food production and the link with the productive ecosystem as a fundamental element to ensure the survival of human beings in the future.

Relating to SDGs:

- Zero hunger and clean water sanitation and the study "The Importance of the Aeroponic Cultivation Technique in Sustainable Agriculture: A Study Carried Out with the Cultivation of *Phaseolus vulgaris L.* Var Opus," the challenges lie in being able to access remote and difficult-to-access urban and rural areas (communities), in addition to being able to transfer the knowledge and management for the growth of the bean plant in an adequate manner; while the options are potentially enormous when being able to share this technique to other grains such as corn, sorghum and rice.
- Affordable and clean energy: According to the research "Historical Development of Sustainable Energy Technologies," the challenges are the introduction of infrastructure, capabilities, implementation and maintenance for using technologies such as photovoltaic, wind, hydroelectric and geothermal. As options, the design of policies and programs make evident the benefit of sustainable energy production.
- Decent work and economic growth, with the investigation "Decent Work, knowledge Management and Sustainability in the Technology-Based Company: A Case of Study," the challenges, the contribution to the creation of decent work as equity in access and promotion, compensation and benefits, work-life balance, participation in decision-making, continuous professional development, organizational culture and work environment, job security and working conditions, ethical use of technology, social and environmental impact, collective bargaining and social dialogue, besides environmental impact, social responsibility, research and development, adoption of sustainable technologies, ethical practices and regulatory

compliance. The options are knowledge management through technological innovation, collaboration, knowledge networks, tacit knowledge management, continuous learning, innovative organizational culture, information technologies (IT) and collaboration platforms.

- Regarding industry, innovation and infrastructure, with the study "Management Strategies for Transitioning from Conventional Industries to Green and Low-Carbon Production Systems," in coffee production, the challenge is the creation of knowledge as management practices, processes and equipment to produce environmentally friendly products with economic benefits, taking into account the fall prices in the internationally market. At the same time, the most profitable option is the production of organic coffee.
- Concerning sustainable cities and communities, with the "Relationship of Innovative Sustainable Business Strategies with Dynamic Capabilities in the Apple Production Chain in Southern Brazil," the challenge is to bring innovation to different communities, while among the options is the development of new studies that add to the dimensions of absorption and dynamic capabilities.
- In the topic of responsible production and consumption, with "Sustainable and Ecocentric Change for Knowledge Management in the Telecommunications Subsector," the challenge is to encourage telecommunications companies to adopt sustainable and ecocentric practices in order not to generate socio-environmental damage, taking care of the resource consumption, electromagnetic and waste pollution, besides promote reuse and recycling. As options, the generation and transfer of applications and technologies according to the needs of the people involve the government and other service organizations for the management of effective policies, plans, programs, sectoral projects and public resources after the COVID-19 pandemic.
- Regarding climate action, with "University Social Responsibility, Evaluation and Impact on Student Satisfaction as an Opportunity for Knowledge Management and Sustainability," the challenge is to achieve the participation of the entire community, training and involving institutions and a majority of students. The options include seeking individual initiatives and bringing them to the community, which other educational institutions can use.
- About submarine life, with "Sensors and Signal Processing Used to Increase Knowledge Management of Algae Production," the challenges focus on the development of research and exploitation for the CO_2 capture and in the generation of biofuel, food and metabolic compounds using sensors as optical method (Fluorescence, terahertz), spectroscopy, neural network, machine learning or artificial intelligence for monitoring

its growth process. The options are creating and transferring this knowledge for implementing technological tools.

- About life and the terrestrial ecosystem, with "Wine Tourism as a Driver of Knowledge Management Practices and the Sustainability of the New Rurality," the challenge is to unite human being with nature, combining economic and social development while conserving the environment through work of entities, companies and governments with a real will to transform regions into more biosustainable territory around the wine tourism. As an option, move a similar ecosystem toward the sustainability of other foods in different parts of the world, especially in less developed countries.
- Concerning peace, justice and strong institutions, with "Assessing Environmental Awareness in the Organizational Culture and Its Mediating Role in Integrating an Ecocentric Paradigm into Mexican Companies' Knowledge Management and Governance Systems in Guanajuato," the challenge is the introduction of ecocentric awareness in trading sector located in Guanajuato, Mexico; and as the options the spread of the term, involving government participation toward transitioning to an ecocentric mindset.
- Regarding alliances to achieve objectives, with "Environmental Responsibility and Knowledge Management in Post-industrial Organizations of the 21st Century," the challenges are the creating strategic coalitions between the government and the restaurant industry in Queretaro, Mexico, and private organizations. At the same time, the options are framed within the regulation of certifications, incentives, adhering to awareness campaigns, continuing with sustainable activities such as waste management, compost creation programs and separation of organic and inorganic trash.

The integration of knowledge management and sustainability within post-industrial organizations in the 21st century

Chapters 2 to 4 focus on utilizing ecocentrism paradigms, adopting an ecocentric position and incorporating sustainability principles through knowledge management practices to promote organizational sustainability in the contemporary industrial landscape.

The integration of ecocentrism paradigms and knowledge management is crucial for fostering sustainability in post-industrial organizations in the 21st century. Ecocentrism, which prioritizes nature's intrinsic value and emphasizes the interconnectedness between humans and the environment, offers an ethical framework for promoting sustainable practices (Naess, 1989; Klostermann & Cramer, 2006). In contrast to anthropocentrism, ecocentrism advocates for the protection and respect of nature independent of its utility to humans (Klostermann & Cramer, 2006). This philosophical perspective is particularly relevant in the context of post-industrial organizations, where the integration of environmental considerations into decision-making processes is essential for achieving bioeconomic sustainability (Senge et al., 2008).

The ecological economy, emerging in response to unsustainable consumerism and resource depletion, emphasizes the need to value resources and consider environmental impacts in economic activities (Martinez-Alier, 1987). Scholars like Kenneth Boulding and Nicholas Georgescu-Roegen contribute to this discourse by highlighting the finite nature of resources and the constraints of economic growth (Boulding, 1966; Georgescu-Roegen, 1971).

Knowledge management plays a crucial role in incorporating ecocentrism into organizational practices. By fostering collaboration, knowledge sharing and environmental education, organizations can align their operations with the principles of sustainability (Gray, 2002; Sterling, 2001). Moreover, in the era of the Fourth Industrial Revolution, knowledge management has become increasingly vital for integrating sustainability into organizational strategies.

The convergence of ecocentrism and knowledge management offers practical solutions for addressing environmental challenges and promoting sustainability across sectors. In industries such as energy management and the bioeconomy, ecocentrism encourages the adoption of renewable energy sources and responsible resource management practices (Contreras-Medina et al., 2021; Sun et al., 2022). Furthermore, knowledge management facilitates innovation and differentiation within organizations, enhancing their competitiveness while contributing to environmental conservation.

In this sense, integrating ecocentrism paradigms and knowledge management is essential for promoting sustainability in post-industrial organizations. By embracing ecocentric approaches and leveraging knowledge management practices, organizations can contribute to ecosystem preservation, resilience and long-term success in the 21st century.

The intersection of knowledge management and sustainability across various sectors and industries

Each title from Chapters 5 to 15 explores different aspects of how knowledge management practices contribute to sustainability efforts or how sustainability considerations impact knowledge management strategies within specific contexts. These contexts include agriculture (aeroponic cultivation systems, apple production chain), energy technologies, technology-based companies, conventional industries transitioning to green production systems, telecommunications, universities, sensors and signal processing, wine tourism, organizational culture and post-industrial organizations. Overall, the titles reflect a multidisciplinary approach to understanding the role of knowledge management in promoting sustainability and addressing environmental challenges across diverse domains.

The authors discuss various challenges and alternatives related to ecocentrism, focusing on sustainable agriculture, renewable energy technologies, sustainable business practices and knowledge management in different sectors. Key themes include the importance of interdisciplinary collaboration, innovation and the application of the United Nations' SDGs to address global environmental challenges. Several case studies, including aeroponic cultivation, renewable energy technologies, apple production and telecommunications, illustrate the implementation of sustainable practices across different industries.

The importance of aeroponic cultivation techniques, such as aeroponics and hydroponics, in sustainable agriculture is highlighted as a solution to water scarcity and soil erosion challenges. These techniques conserve water and nutrients while maximizing food production, aligning with the SDGs related to zero hunger and clean water (IRENA, 2023; Ruiz-García et al., 2021). Moreover, the implementation of aeroponic systems has shown promising results in terms of crop yield, water and energy consumption (IRENA, 2023).

In the context of renewable energy technologies, such as photovoltaic solar energy, wind power, hydroelectric power and geothermal energy, the text emphasizes their crucial role in meeting global electricity needs sustainably (IRENA, 2023; Khan & Abonyi, 2022). However, challenges such as high initial investments and environmental impacts need to be addressed for widespread adoption (IRENA, 2023; Osorio-Londono, 2017).

The discussion extends to sustainable business practices, including decent work, knowledge management and circular economy principles, emphasizing their importance for organizational success and adaptation in dynamic environments (Chen, 2011; Farida & Setiawan, 2022; Pandey, 2020). Case studies in the apple production chain and the telecommunications sector demonstrate the positive impact of sustainable innovation strategies on dynamic capabilities and organizational resilience (Shahzad et al., 2022).

Finally, the text explores the transition to ecocentrism in various sectors, advocating for strategic actions and collaborations to drive socio-technical change toward a more sustainable future (Chuang et al., 2020). Embracing an ecocentric perspective and prioritizing sustainable practices are identified essential for industries to contribute positively to global environmental challenges (Leal-Filho et al., 2022).

Overall, the text provides a comprehensive overview of the challenges and alternatives of ecocentrism across different industries, highlighting the importance of sustainable practices and innovation in addressing environmental concerns and promoting global sustainability.

The concept of ecocentrism, which emphasizes the intrinsic value of nature and advocates for a balanced relationship between humans and the environment, presents both challenges and alternatives within various contexts, including education, technology, tourism and organizational culture (Gochuico, 2021; Nonaka & Takeuchi, 1999). In higher education, institutions like the National Technology of Mexico Celaya campus exemplify a commitment to social responsibility and sustainability through institutional policies, student engagement initiatives and the integration of green technologies (Gochuico, 2021). However, there is a need for greater dissemination of these efforts and improvement in student participation to foster a culture of responsibility and sustainability (Gochuico, 2021).

In industries such as algae production and wine tourism, integrating sensors, signal processing techniques and knowledge management practices offers promising opportunities to optimize production processes, reduce environmental impact and enhance sustainability (Lee & Wong, 2015). For example, in algae production, sensors and signal processing are crucial for monitoring growth variables and identifying species, thereby minimizing contamination risks and increasing biomass production efficiency (Lee & Wong, 2015). Similarly, in wine tourism, sustainable practices and knowledge management contribute to regional development, economic growth and cultural preservation while fostering environmental conservation and social inclusion (Mendis & Welmilla, 2021).

The shift toward an ecocentric paradigm within organizational cultures, particularly in post-industrial organizations, necessitates the integration of ecocentric principles into knowledge management and governance systems (Nonaka & Takeuchi, 1999). Research conducted in Mexican companies in Guanajuato highlights the influence of top management, company size and institutional strength on ecocentric awareness and the adoption of green certifications and initiatives (Nonaka & Takeuchi, 1999). Moreover, collaborations between stakeholders, including businesses, universities and government agencies, are essential for promoting awareness and supporting the implementation of sustainable practices (Nonaka & Takeuchi, 1999).

In the context of post-industrial organizations in the hospitality sector, knowledge management emerges as a strategic enabler for addressing sustainability challenges and fostering environmental responsibility (Nonaka & Takeuchi, 1999). By leveraging knowledge sharing, organizations can identify best practices, promote innovation and integrate sustainable technologies to advance economic, social and environmental sustainability (Nonaka & Takeuchi, 1999). However, the transition toward a sustainable post-industrial model requires concerted efforts, strategic alliances with the government and enhanced collaboration between stakeholders to achieve ambitious sustainability goals (Nonaka & Takeuchi, 1999).

The challenges and alternatives of ecocentrism encompass various domains, including education, technology, tourism and organizational culture. While institutions and industries are making strides toward sustainability and environmental responsibility, there is still a need for greater awareness, participation and collaboration to realize the full potential of an ecocentric paradigm in promoting a harmonious relationship between humans and the environment.

Conclusion

Based on the idea of ecocentrism, which states that everything in the natural world has intrinsic value and deserves moral consideration, every living being has the right and obligation to live in balance with nature; unfortunately, this is still not the case. However, the integration of ecocentrism paradigms and knowledge management practices presents a transformative opportunity for post-industrial organizations in the 21st century to address environmental challenges and promote sustainability across diverse sectors. As highlighted throughout the chapters, the adoption of an ecocentric perspective, which recognizes the intrinsic value of nature and emphasizes the interconnectedness between humans and the environment, is essential for fostering responsible stewardship of resources and mitigating the adverse impacts of industrial activities.

As the dominant species, efforts to conserve nature fall to humans. This sense has currently led to the creation of studies, paradigms, programs and activities that seek to care for water in the production such as beans; the exploration of clean energies, the construction of decent and equal jobs; the industry, innovation and infrastructure for coffee production; the development of sustainable communities for the apple chain; responsible production and consumption in telecommunications; actions against climate action in educational institutions; the technology for algae production; the care of life and terrestrial ecosystem in the context of wine; environmental strengthening in companies in the commercial sector; in addition to the alliance between government organizations and restaurants, in which all of these involves the interaction of human beings with nature.

Acording to Villasana et al. (2021) knowledge management refers to the activities carried out by the organization in order to obtain maximum value from available knowledge. Knowledge management includes all activities that use knowledge to achieve organizational goals to address environmental challenges and maintain competitiveness in the market. As organizations currently shift their strategies and priorities toward more green-oriented agendas, human resource management (HRM) professionals need to rethink the mission and expand the scope of their green management practices to improve the how carry manage resources (Aboramadan, 2022).

Villasana et al. (2021): In general, employee behaviours that promote environmental management practices in the workplace refer to green behaviours. Employee green behaviors are considered key to the effective implementation of green practices in the workplace. Additionally, studies have shown that engaging employees in green practices is crucial for environmental management initiatives as this would contribute to better environmental performance and complete advantage. To motivate employees' green behaviours, green human resource management (GHRM) practices are considered a fundamental human resource management strategy to increase employees' environmental awareness in the workplace. GHRM processes aimed at promoting environmental management incorporate several functions such as green hiring, green training, green reward and green performance evaluation.

Jirakraisiri et al. (2021): Research suggests that the ability of companies to implement strategies and innovate is closely linked to their intellectual capital, that is, the ability to use knowledge resources (Subramaniam & Youndt, 2005). Companies adopt different approaches to accumulate and use their knowledge and these approaches manifest themselves as the different aspects of intellectual capital, that is, human capital (p. 44). Environmental management is an issue linked to knowledge management, and to the issue of ecocentrism in this sense, companies must recognize the need for innovating green processes and formalizing the behavior of their workers in environmental management practices.

Research on GHRM has flourished in recent years with studies conducted in various industries such as tourism and hospitality, information and technology and the automotive industry. However, research on GHRM in higher education is limited. Sustainable competitive advantage, strengthening your core competency, improving your green image, taking advantage of new market opportunities and improving your financial performance, can improve your customers' satisfaction, value perceptions and purchase intentions. Therefore, the successful implementation of green strategies has become an important goal for many companies.

First, a considerable amount of research has been conducted on the drivers and consequences. In the case of green strategies, little attention has been paid to the strategy implementation phase. While the limited existing studies suggest that firms develop, or otherwise acquire, the tangible and intangible resources necessary to implement their stated strategy, it is unclear how firms can develop and use intangible resources, such as intellectual capital, to implement a green strategy, state that only a few studies have focused on the implementation of green strategies, which limits our understanding of its mechanism.

Second, most of the literature focuses on green product innovation, rather than green process innovation, despite the significant impact of the latter on the environmental and economic performance of a particular company. It is worth mentioning that green process innovation helps a company reduce waste, consume less energy and produce less pollution. Therefore, this can significantly improve a company's ecological performance. However, knowledge about green product innovation cannot simply be extrapolated to cover green process innovation, because these two different types of innovation require different skills, resources and organizational characteristics that involve different areas and activities within a company and trigger different performance outcomes.

The challenges outlined in the various studies underscore the complexities and multifaceted nature of transitioning toward an ecocentric paradigm. From the adoption of ethical perspectives in decision-making to the implementation of sustainable business practices and technologies, organizations face significant hurdles in aligning their operations with principles of sustainability. However, the options presented offer viable pathways forward, ranging from environmental education and regulatory updates to strategic collaborations and innovative solutions.

Across industries such as agriculture, energy, tourism and telecommunications, the intersection of knowledge management and sustainability emerges as a key driver of positive change. By leveraging knowledge sharing, innovation and strategic alliances, organizations can enhance their resilience, competitiveness and environmental performance while contributing to broader societal goals, as outlined in the SDGs.

Ultimately, the journey toward ecocentrism requires collective action and commitment from stakeholders at all levels, including governments, businesses, academia and civil society. By embracing ecocentric principles and integrating them into organizational cultures, practices and policies, post-industrial organizations can play a pivotal role in shaping a more sustainable and equitable future for generations tö come.

In this sense, the first strategy of action must be considered from epistemological theory, considering the human being as the creator of knowledge and how it has been generated about the importance of nature in the world introducing capabilities, experience, practices and skills it toward an ecocentric approach.

The second strategy is the ontological approach, which interrelates the human being with the organization and nature, creating programs, certifications, activities and green technologies, giving their place to water, climate, underwater life, food and ecosystems and the human beings within their diverse personal and professional activities to achieve post-industrial sustainability of the 21st century.

This book expresses the various theoretical-practical studies of the interrelationship of ecocentrism, knowledge management and sustainability in post-industrial organizations of the 21st century. The book's limitations are recognized, such as considering all the SDGs or particularizing about a way of life and topic of knowledge management; however, it is aware of the efforts being made to care for the environment.

References

Aboramadan, M. (2022). The effect of green HRM on employee green behaviors in higher education: The mediating mechanism of green work engagement. *International Journal of Organizational Analysis, 30*(1), 7–23. https://doi.org/10.1108/IJOA-05-2020-2190

Boulding, K.E. (1966). The economics of the coming spaceship earth. In *Environmental quality in a growing economy, resources for the future* (pp. 1–14). Johns Hopkins University Press.

Chen, Y.S. (2011). Green organizational identity: Sources and consequence. *Management Decision, 49*(3), 384–404.

Chuang, F., Manley, E., & Petersen, A. (2020). The role of worldviews in the governance of sustainable mobility. *Proceedings of the National Academy of Sciences, 117*(8), 4034–4042.

Contreras-Medina, L.M., Medina-Mejía, A.B., & Cruz-Domínguez, L.P. (2021). Sustainable agriculture: Knowledge management and technology adoption in Mexico. *Journal of Agricultural Studies, 9*(12), 23–35.

Darnthamrongkul, W., & Mozingo, L.A. (2020). Challenging anthropocentric stormwater management: Advancing legislation for environmental sustainability in the United States. *Water Security, 10*, 100064.

Farida, I., & Setiawan, D. (2022). Business strategies and competitive advantage: The role of performance and innovation. *Journal of Open Innovation: Technology, Market, and Complexity, 8*(3), 163.

Georgescu-Roegen, N. (1971). *The entropy law and the economic process.* Harvard University Press.

Gochuico, M.T.D. (2021). Development of a tool for measuring ecocentrism as an outcome of environmental communication. *Philippine Social Science Journal, 4*(4), 155–165.

Gray, B. (2002). *Collaborating: Finding common ground for multiparty problems.* Jossey-Bass.

IRENA. (2023). *Renewable Power Generation Costs in 2022.* International Renewable Energy Agency, Abu Dhabi. www.irena.org/Data/View-data-by-topic/Capacity-and-Generation/Country-Rankings

Jirakraisiri, J., Badir, Y., & Frank, B. (2021). Translating green strategic intent into green process innovation performance: The role of green intellectual capital. *Journal Intellectual Capital, 22*(15), 43–67. https://doi.org/10.1108/JIC-08-2020-0277

Khan, A.A., & Abonyi, J. (2022). Simulation of sustainable manufacturing solutions: Tools for enabling circular economy. *Sustainability, 14*(15), 9796.

Klostermann, J.E.M., & Cramer, J. (2006). The contextual meaning of sustainable development: The case of the Dutch drinking water sector. *Sustainable Development, 14*(4), 268–276.

Leal-Filho, W., Vidal, D.G., Chen, C., Petrova, M., Dinis, M.A.P., Yang, P., & Neiva, S. (2022). An assessment of requirements in investments, new technologies, and infrastructures to achieve the SDGs. *Environmental Sciences Europe, 34*(1), 1–17.

Lee, C.S., & Wong, K.Y. (2015). Development and validation of knowledge management performance measurement constructs for small and medium enterprises. *Journal of Knowledge Management, 19*(4), 711–734.

Martinez-Alier, J. (1987). *Ecological economics.* Basil Blackwell.

Mendis, M.V.S., & Welmilla, I. (2021). Green consciousness of employees. *Human Resource Management in Challenging Environments, 11*, 88–106.

Naess, A. (1989). *Ecology, community, and lifestyle: Outline of an ecosophy*. Cambridge University Press.
Nonaka, I. (1994). A dynamic theory of organizational knowledge creation. *Organization Science*, *5*(1), 14–37.
Nonaka, I., & Takeuchi, H. (1999). *La organizacion creadora de conocimiento*. Oxford University Press.
Osorio-Londono, I. (2017). *Environmental, Social and Economic Impacts of Small Hydroelectric Plants (SHP) in Antioquia* (Doctoral dissertation, EAFIT University, Colombia).
Oxford. (n.d.). *Challenge*. Retrieved December 21, 2023, from www.oxfordlearnersdictionaries.com/definition/american_english/challenge_1#:~:text=noun-,noun,most%20serious%20challenges%20we%20face
Pandey, V. (2020). Energy infrastructure for sustainable development. In: W. Leal Filho, A. Azul, L. Brandli, A. Lange Salvia, & T. Wall (Eds.), *Affordable and clean energy. Encyclopedia of the UN sustainable development goals*. Springer.
Ruiz-García, P., Conde-Álvarez, C., Gómez-Díaz, J.D., & Monterroso-Rivas, A.I. (2021). Projections of local knowledge-based adaptation strategies of Mexican coffee farmers. *Climate*, *9*(4), 60.
Senge, P.M., Smith, B., Kruschwitz, N., Laur, J., & Schley, S. (2008). *The necessary revolution: How individuals and organizations are working together to create a sustainable world*. Broadway Business.
Shahzad, M., Qu, Y., Rehman, S.U., & Zafar, A.U. (2022). Adoption of green innovation technology to accelerate sustainable development among manufacturing industry. *Journal of Innovation & Knowledge*, *7*(4), 100231.
Sterling, S. (2001). *Sustainable education: Re-visioning learning and change*. Green Books.
Subramaniam, M., & Youndt, M.A. (2005). The influence of intellectual capital on the types of innovative capabilities. *Academy of Management Journal*, *48*(3), 450–463. http://dx.doi.org/10.5465/AMJ.2005.17407911
Sun, Y., Shahzad, M., & Razzaq, A. (2022). Sustainable organizational performance through blockchain technology adoption and knowledge management in China. *Journal of Innovation & Knowledge*, *7*(4), 1–11.
ten Have, H., & Patrão Neves, M. (2021). Ecocentrism (*See* anthropocentrism; biocentrism; environmental ethics; zoocentrism). In *Dictionary of global bioethics*. Springer. https://doi.org/10.1007/978-3-030-54161-3_220
Villasana, L., Hernandez-Garcia, P., & Ramírez, E.R.F. (2021). La gestión del conocimiento, pasado, presente y futuro. Una revisión de la literatura. *Trascender, Contabilidad y Gestión*, *6*(18), 53–78. https://doi.org/10.36791/tcg.v0i18.128

Index

Note: Page numbers in *italics* indicate a figure and page numbers in **bold** indicate a table on the corresponding page.